EDITORI/

When it comes to gangsters,
This is a captivating and different kind of true-crime story.
Nicholas Pileggi, Author
Wise Guy
Casino

What a story this is—a vivid picture of a real gangster
with a code of honor. It makes me glad I've been
lucky enough to stay on Michael's good side.
Nick Taylor, Author
Sins of the Father
A Necessary End
American Made

The Last Jewish Gangster is a fascinating character study
of an unapologetic gangster. David Larson masterfully
weaves this tale in Michael Hardy's own words, resulting
in a powerful, detailed story of a mobster's life.
Cathy Scott, *Los Angeles Times*
bestselling True Crime author
The Killing of Tupac Shakir
The Murder of Biggie Smalls
Murder of a Mafia Daughter
Death in the Dessert
The Millionaire's Wife

I met Michael J. Hardy (Hardin) on the day he threatened
to kill my client in 1978. A lot of bad guys threaten to kill
people, but rarely mean it. This book is hauntingly real
and engrossing as David Larson channels Michael Hardy.
Logan Clarke, Private Investigator

THE LAST JEWISH GANGSTER

THE MIDDLE YEARS

BOOK TWO OF THREE

DAVID LARSON

WILD BLUE
PRESS

WildBluePress.com

THE LAST JEWISH GANGSTER Volume Two published by:
WILDBLUE PRESS
P.O. Box 102440
Denver, Colorado 80250

WILDBLUE PRESS is registered at the U.S. Patent and Trademark Offices.

ISBN 978-1-957288-09-3 Hardcover
ISBN 978-1-952225-07-9 Trade Paperback
ISBN 978-1-952225-08-6 eBook

Cover design © 2022 WildBlue Press. All rights reserved.
Cover photo: Courtesy Nancy and Ira Kutner
Interior Formatting/Cover Design by Elijah Toten
www.totencreative.com

THE LAST JEWISH GANGSTER

BOOK TWO OF THREE

TABLE OF CONTENTS

ACKNOWLEDGMENTS

To Nick Pileggi, for bumping into Michael Hardy in 1980 and for your continued encouragement and inspiration.

To Jimmy Blatt for saving Michael's ass in 1991, again in 1998, and for taking our call in 2014.

To Theresa. Always there, always patient, always present. This could not have been done without you.

To Shirley, Michael's mother. Without your neglect, your son would have never become a fearless gangster.

To Nancy Kutner, Michael's sister, for your encouragement and rare photos.

To Beta Writers MeetUp.

Your dogged tenacity in challenging my storytelling, forced me to become a better writer.

And, to Michael J. Hardy, who by all accounts should have died decades before, or rotted away in a prison cell. That until the end, you possessed such extraordinary wit and recall is amazing. That you allowed this author into your life to capture your voice on paper is a wonder.

You passed away January 2, 2016, but you will not be forgotten, this book, a testament to that.

And, how can I ever forget Lord Chancellor of the Manor, your companion until the end?

AUTHOR'S NOTE

In the first volume of Michael J. Hardy's autobiography, *The Last Jewish Gangster, The Early Years*, Michael recounts the first twenty-four years of his life to his Jewish lawyer, Jimmy Blatt, while he awaits trial in Los Angeles in 1991 for murdering his wife.

He tells of his birth in 1944 to two first cousins, his mixed heritage of Southern Baptists and Ukrainian Jews which informs his life, and being raised by his maternal grandparents in Brownsville, a Jewish stronghold in Brooklyn.

But it's his mother, Shirley, who rejects him after his birth, that sets Hardy on a path to a life of crime. Shirley only cares to run with the top gangsters and mobsters in Brooklyn (Bugsy Siegel is Michael's godfather). She denies Michael her love and that's what drives him all his life— the need to prove that he's tougher than any gangster she's known, then she'll love him. His world turns hard after his grandfather dies when Michael is twelve.

The first volume captures his struggles growing up, living on couches, his troubles in school, the gang he rumbled with, his short time in the Army, bullets he took during a gun battle with the Gottis, his first crimes and stints in jails and prisons, and then the birth of his four children. It ends with Michael, at nearly twenty-four, entering the world's most dangerous prison in Mexico, La Mesa del Diablo (the Devil's table). He agrees to take his mother's counterfeiting rap in hopes she would love or admire him.

Never safe, but never afraid, is an apt way to describe Michael's life as he struggles to control his hatred toward his mother which he rages against the world.

*Be careful who you call your friends. I'd rather
have four quarters than a hundred pennies.*
— Al Capone

1

La Mesa Prisión, México 1968

While I'm in the Tijuana jail for sixteen days, I hear lots about La Mesa Del Diablo Prisión, *The Devil's Table*. You can basically buy your way out of anything in this prison, if you don't die first. And I don't plan on dying. So, I need money. Lots of money. That's never been a problem for me any other time in my life. All I had to do was rob someone.

But how am I gonna do that here?

Here I am, a twenty-four-year-old gangster who's done hundreds of armed robberies and know how to impose my will to take what I want. Now I'm in a country where I don't know their rules, don't have connections, and don't speak their language.

Fuck.

The van thumps to a stop and the back doors fly open. Afternoon sunlight floods in as Mother and I try to adjust to the scorching sun. I help her out into the sally port, the area between the first and second gates of La Mesa Prison.

A guard immediately grabs her arm and escorts her toward a door to the right. She looks at me over her shoulder, her bright red hair framing frightened eyes. Something passes between us at that moment, an understanding that this will be the last time she'll use me like this, if I manage to live long enough to have a next time.

I take it all in, shielding my eyes. Above and all around me are fifteen-foot-high, double-thick concrete walls. On top of those walls are guards in wrinkled green khakis carrying M-1 carbines, wearing green hats and cheap sunglasses. As I move forward, a growing throng of dirty prisoners comes to watch the new tenants arrive. They shove their fingers through the small squares in the thick chain-link fence.

"¡Dame un dime, gringo. ¡Dame un dime, gringo! Por favor, un dime, gringo."

What kind of fucking place is this?

I learn later that all they were asking for was a dime. *A lousy fucking dime*. I'll soon find out exactly what a dime can buy in La Mesa. The collection of faces belonging to those fingers looks like every Mexican bandit I've ever seen in movies. That's when it hits me. I'm here. I'm really here in a Mexican prison. For how long, I have no idea.

The prisoners go quiet, and we all turn toward a short man with a full moustache approaching. He's dressed in a starched tan khaki suit with gold epaulets and military hat and accompanied by two armed guards. Spreading sweat stains darken his suit's armpits. He moves toward me, his hand out, a toothy grin. "I am your comandante, Paco," he says in fair English.

I nod cautiously. We shake hands, mine firm, his somewhat limp. "Nice to meet you, Paco. I'm Richard Mandell."

"So, Ree-shard, it is very nice of you to come sit at the devil's table. My table. Come with me to my office, gringo."

I'm surprised no guards escort us, almost like, in a twisted way, I'm his honored guest. We walk into the headquarters building past his assistant who jumps up and salutes as we approach Paco's office. The comandante moves to the center of his room and stops. I take in my surroundings, plush I'm sure, by Mexican standards. Large mahogany desk, tall oak bookcases, dark red wool carpet, brass lamps, and a velvet painting of Elvis on the wall behind his desk.

You gotta be shitting me.

"So, Ree-shard, now you give me your dinero. All you dinero." He holds out his hand and smiles, his huge teeth too big for his mouth, like they belong to a shark.

What kind of shake-down is this?

I bend down, take off my right boot, pull out two twenties and a ten, and hand them over.

He fans them out and holds a twenty up to the light. "This give you three nights in tanky-A, in carraca. Now, you no clothes. Put here." He points to a nearby chair.

"That's all I have Paco."

"I believe you, Ree-shard. But no believe Americans who no tell Paco truth."

I look around me, wondering if any guards are nearby. I comply and remove my white T-shirt, white Levis and socks, now standing only in my gray boxers.

Paco points to my underwear. "En total, Ree-shard."

I drop my drawers and toss them on the chair. Paco methodically examines each item, turning everything inside-out, especially focusing on the seams, feeling for anything hidden.

Thorough son of a bitch.

When he finishes, he points for me to first lift my ball sack, then bend over and spread my ass cheeks. I know the drill. I've been through it enough times before in the US jails and prisons.

At least that's the same.

Satisfied, he states, "You dress now." He goes to his large mahogany desk and gestures for me to take a chair across from him after I finish putting on my clothes.

He takes his time to light a cigar, then flips open a file and fires off his first question, "So Ree-shard, how much dinero you can get?"

You want more?

After my previous sixteen days in the Tijuana jail, I'm ready for this question. I heard I'd have to cough up mordidas, "little bites," soon. I need to lean on my family until I can figure out a way to make money in here.

Be patient, my little friend.

"I can have some sent soon."

"Good. This is good. I love dinero. My favorite is American money, but no the kind you bring to my country. That was your big mistake. Muy grande. My favorite gringos are the ones who have *real* dinero. For them I make good deals. You get dinero soon, then we see. Tonight, you sleep in tanky-A. I no send you to the corrale with the animals. I send you to tanky-A and you speak to Cabo Baron." He pushes four crumpled dollar bills at me. "You take now." He waves his arm toward the door. "Esteban!" he yells, and his assistant comes in. "Get Pablo to take gringo to tanky-A. Have Baron to fix him up."

Chief guard Pablo Moran, a fifty-something Yaqui Indian gives a sloppy salute, and escorts me out of Paco's office. I can tell he's been at La Mesa forever by his worn and unpolished boots and holster, his 9mm pistol, and the old M-1 he carries. We walk out and pass by the second gate into a large open field with the outlines of a baseball diamond.

A few hundred prisoners mill about. A dozen notice us and come running toward us. Now I have to wade through their out-stretched hands as they beg for dimes again. Pablo turns to me. "Venga gringo. I take to new home."

Okay, Mike, check it out. You're in the shit now. You're gonna need to figure out how to live long enough to see your kids again or die trying. So play dumb and just watch and listen. Just become a dumb white man. Nothing more, nothing less. Watch and listen.

I take it in. Everything. Unlike the US prisons I'd been in, this one has armed guards who walk within reach of prisoners.

Are your guns loaded?

The prison's security are the concrete walls a hundred yards long that form a huge square block with eight manned guard towers equally spaced on top of the walls. After we leave the open field, we pass into a courtyard. Pablo continues in broken English to point out areas in La Concha, the small plaza we're in.

To the left is a small restaurant, Maricone, owned by Pere. "Good food," he points. Past it is a grocery store called Ciprion's. "Buy food." I find out later it's owned by Ciprion who used to be the bodyguard for the Governor of Baja California until he got caught in some kind of political shit storm. A jewelry store, barber shop, and other small businesses are built into the walls of the plaza.

What kind of fucking place is this?

We enter the corrale where the animals live, the lowest of the low of prisoners. These are the ones who have no money, not even enough for a shower. I find out later that all they subsist on is rice and beans, unless they can beg or steal some dinero, maybe a dime.

Pablo points to the right of us and grunts "La Bartola," a small building that's the short-term hole. It's about five by eight feet, made of red brick and has a lone thick iron door with a small slit in it. It looks like it might be able to house four prisoners with a bucket for the toilet. "You bad, you go," he states.

We finally stop in front of tanky-A. Pablo barks as he stands in the opening, "Abri la pinche porta, collaro! Baron, Venga!"

I peer inside. The smell almost knocks me over, like opening the trunk of a car that's been sitting in the summer heat for a few days with a dead body inside. About a hundred wall-to-wall bodies are stuffed into a building that should maybe house twenty men. Then there's the color. Everything's a shade of cold brown concrete, all coated with a layer of dirt.

Walking toward us from the back of the room comes a fat, sloppy guard with a massive moustache. Pablo yells, "Baron. Paco say you fix up this gringo." With that, Pablo Moran turns and is gone.

Baron waves at me, "Venga, gringo! Ju come to my casa, no?"

I step inside. He looks me over.

"So, gringo, how much dinero you got?"

Jesus. You got you hand out too?

"I'll have some soon."

"Bueno! I love gringos' dinero."

My eyes adjust to the muted light, and I notice the prisoners. Some are curled up, maybe dead. Eyes turn to look at me. Some lifeless. Some for begging. Others for taking.

Play dumb. Don't give them any reason to think you're anything more than just a stupid gringo.

Pablo continues to explain that on each side are little rooms called carracas stacked on top of each other. I notice the malformed concrete steps leading to upper rooms. It looks like the warehouse where all the banditos from the movie *The Treasure of the Sierra Madre* might have been stored.

"Mira! You got to pay me talacha, thirty dollars a month. I give you a week to get. If you no get in a week, I send you to el corrale."

"Don't worry, I'll get you your precious dinero."

"Bueno! Now I take you to el otro gringo."

"What?"

"No muchos gringos here. You live him. He got buena carraca. Venga."

We walk toward the back and stop in a doorway of what must have been the hole for tanky-A at one time, but now houses a young American. He looks at me in a way I can only describe as despair. The room is only big enough to house a dwarf in minimum comfort.

This is what thirty bucks a month gets me?

"Gringo, un más compañero for you. I leave you gringos. You talk. Gringos always like for to talk. Oh, gringo how you call you?"

"Richard. Richard Mandell."

"Ree-shard. You gringos got funny names. Me go now."

I size up my roommate. About twenty, scared, a little beat down, average height and weight, brown hair.

No threat.

He sticks out his hand, "My name's Pete, Pete Day. I'm from the Bronx." We shake.

After we both get over the shock that we're going to have to share a broom closet, he tells me he's in the Navy. He completed basic training in San Diego, came down to Tijuana to score some drugs, and got ratted out by the people who sold him the drugs.

"I've been here six months already." He looks around and sighs, almost apologetically. "Well, since you're going to be sharing my pad, I guess you can take the floor."

I look down at the dirty wood. "Thanks, man. I really appreciate it."

"Listen, Richard—"

"Rick, call me Rick."

"Okay, Rick. I gotta to tell you some important shit. This is shit I had to learn the hard way and it cost me big time, especially money. This place is like nothing you know. You're going to see things in here that will blow your mind, man. I mean stuff you never believed could happen. Sit down and relax. We got some time before Wilkenson comes."

"Who?"

"We call him that after the Wilkinson Sword Company. Don't worry for now, just listen." This Bronx boy goes on to give me the lesson of my life, telling me how this prison works and how to get what you need. "It all starts and ends with money. Then it's up to your balls and maybe some luck to stay alive from day to day. But on the other hand, they allow visitors for overnight stays, for a price. Tuesdays are for wives. Thursdays for girlfriends. And Sundays for families where they even bring in carts with tacos, ice cream, and stuff."

"No shit?"

"Yeah?"

"How many prisoners?"

"About eight hundred. And of those, maybe twenty-five Americans. Oh, and about twenty women. And you can even start or run a business in here. Of course, you have to pay taxes to the comandante and others to keep the wheels turning." A shadow blocks the doorway, and we look over. "Ah! Wilkenson. Que pasa, hombre?" Pete stands.

"Nada," Wilkenson says.

In the doorway is a skinny Mexican in his late forties, long black hair and wearing a black overcoat, and in the heat. He looms like a large raven and grins to expose a few missing teeth.

"Show him, man!" Pete says.

Wilkenson flares open his coat. I realize why they call him Wilkenson. Hanging on the inside flaps of his coat is the best collection of knives I've ever seen, let alone in any jail or prison I'd been in. Hawkbills for gutting. Serrated spear points to inflict a different kind of damage. Needle points and Wharncliffes. Tantos, clip points, and switchblades. All different lengths, different handles. All with fine edges. All for one purpose.

Jesus.

I ask, "How much for that?" I point to a traditional needle point bayonet over a foot long. A blade that can go through leather.

He takes it out and lays it across his forearm, like he's a wine steward in a fancy restaurant. "Esta? Sí! I can tell you are a man with a good eye for fine steel."

"Cut the bullshit, Wilky," Pete says. "This is Rick, my friend from New York. Give him a good price, man."

"Sí! For you, one dollar, amigo."

I hand him one of my four crumpled dollars and he hands me the bayonet. He snaps the bill and holds it up to the weak light coming through the doorway.

"I love all the pictures of your great presidents." He smiles, stuffing the bill in a pocket. "Magnifico." With that, he hands me my knife and he's gone.

I look down at the bayonet in my hand and run my fingers over the hilt and edges. It looks like what I had in boot camp when I signed up to be a paratrooper at seventeen. A strange new sensation comes over me. Patriotism. An appreciation for anything and everything that's American. The great presidents.

God Bless them all, alive or dead. And the money with their pictures.

Pete breaks my concentration, "Hey, you smoke shit?"

"What?"

"Reefer."

"I did once, but it didn't do anything to me."

"Here, take a few hits. This is really good shit."

I take a few deep drags and hold my breath. It feels like a soft pillow flutters down onto my eyes. "Cool."

2

First Days

"Wake up! Wake up, man!" Pete shakes me. "We got to go out for La Lista."

"For what?"

"The count, man. It's almost seven-thirty. Time for the count."

I can't believe I slept through the night and am still half-asleep when we stumble into the plaza with all the prisoners from tanky-A, mostly Mexicans with a few Americans milling about. Pete nudges me and whispers, "Hey Rick, you got fifty cents?"

"Sure. What for?"

"You got to pay them half a buck a day to keep from working."

When the guard comes by, I give him a buck and nod toward Pete. The guard checks his sheet and moves on.

"So, Pete. Where do you get your money?"

"Usually the first of the month, from my family."

"If you're gonna need more from me, maybe we should start a tab."

"I'll pay you back, man. I just got to get something going in here."

My stomach grumbles. "Okay. So, when do we eat?"

"I don't know. When do you want to eat?"

"Now."

"Well, eat then."

What the fuck?

I look at him like he's speaking a foreign language.

"Oh, you want to know when they're going to feed you, right?" After I nod, he continues, "Well, they ain't going to feed you. You're a federal prisoner and this is a Mexican state prison. They only feed state prisoners here. The federal prisoners get what they call a chivo every two weeks. That's about fifty pesos."

"How much is that?"

"About two-fifty."

"How the fuck am I supposed to eat for two weeks on that?"

He points. "Well, you can go over to the bean line and give it to the line chief. He's a very good Mexican."

"Yeah, aren't they all?"

"He killed over a hundred and fifty men as a bandit in the mountains of Guerrero to fight in the resistance."

After I check out the bean line, I decide I'll eat another way. It only has five menu items—oatmeal, beans, fried beans, refried beans, and rice. We walk across the plaza to a restaurant called El Griego's. I sense the prisoners watching me, the new gringo, to see what I'll do. I keep my head down and shuffle my feet, trying to walk and act like there's no threat, but it's hard to hide my six-one, 250-pound size.

Nothing you need to know about ... yet.

Pete tells me how El Griego's is owned by a Greek named George. He was a fisherman who got caught poaching lobster inside the national waters of Mexico and is doing five years. His restaurant is the best place in the joint to get a burger. Breakfast costs us a dollar-fifty, which I paid. Now I have only fifty cents left.

Over breakfast, Pete continues my education. "There are three prices for everything in here. This is how it works. If you're Mexican and want to buy a pint of tequila, it's only one dollar. If you're Mexican-American, it's two-fifty.

And if you're American, you get the privilege of paying five bucks."

A man walks by with a monkey on his shoulder. "What the—!" I say.

"Oh, him. He's a former drug lord. He had a parrot and a dog in here. In fact, you can have anything you want in here as long as you pay for the privilege. I heard the dog population got so big at one time, they ran in packs. And without prisoners feeding them, they attacked everyone."

"Nice touch."

"And we've got some very interesting wildlife in here as well."

I arch my eyebrows.

"Nasty critters. All deadly. If you get bit, they won't let you die. Well, not as long as you have money. If you're going to die in here, it's going to be from another prisoner. I've been here six months and seen eleven killings."

Jesus.

"Good to know. So, where can I take a shower?"

Pete grins and rubs his thumb and index finger together.

"What's this gonna cost me?"

"Ten cents for three buckets of water. And bring your own bar of soap and towel."

"You've got to be fucking kidding me."

"Out back they've got a cauldron of hot water and a kid who brings you the buckets. One bucket to get you wet and lather up, the other two to rinse. Oh, and don't forget to bring your knife and watch out for rattlesnakes, scorpions, Gila monsters, even tarantulas. Or in case someone might want to make a play against you."

"Sounds like the Ritz."

Pete laughs. "Or you can just pay twenty-five cents and have a real shower in the privalista area near the infirmary. Still gotta bring your own soap and towel."

So, that's the Ritz.

We split up so I can wander around the plaza to check things out for myself. Also, since I only have fifty cents left, I need it to stretch for me, not Pete. As I walk by the only carraca in the plaza, a large well-dressed American leaning back in a chair says, "Nice boots."

"Thanks."

What's your deal?

He stands and holds out his hand. "I'm Val Caldwell." We shake, his paw huge. Val stands about six-foot two, maybe two hundred forty pounds, late forties and balding. He carries a best friend smile. Rounding out his appearance are pleated dress pants with cuffs, loafers with no socks, and a white short-sleeve shirt. "You're new," he states.

Jesus, you look like you're at a resort.

"Arrived yesterday."

"Saw you roll in. We've been expecting you."

I raise my eyebrows.

"Been following your case in the papers. Seems you and your mother were running an international counterfeiting ring."

I shrug. "It's not what it seems."

"It never is. Hey, I kind of thought maybe it was you when I heard your mother would be going home today."

How the fuck do you know?

"You sure?"

A mondalero, usually a ten-year-old kid who lives in the corrale looking to get tips, runs up to tell me that I'm wanted at the front gate. He just stands there looking at me.

Val smiles. "I think he wants some change."

I give him a quarter and he runs off.

"If I were you, I'd be a lot cheaper with these people. You'll get a lot more out of these bastards if you give them less."

"I'll remember that. Say, could you excuse me while I go see what's up?"

"Sure, kid. Come back and we'll talk more."

As I walk toward the front gate, I look back at Val. I just can't get it out of my mind I've seen this guy somewhere before.

"Gringo, gringo!"

I look down to see Paco. He reaches up to put a hand on my shoulder. "I think Ree-shard, you mind is someplace else, no? I have good counsel para ti. While you here at my table, you keep you mind here." He taps his head with an index finger. "No everyone like you gringos like Comandante Paco. I am amigo of all gringos, even the pinche gringos, like ones in the corrale who have no damn dinero. But maybe they will get someday. Quien sabe? Oh mira gringo, you got visit."

"I do?"

"Sí, venga into mi oficina."

Paco leads me into his office where my mother and Uncle Morty stand beside attorney Gilbert Herrera. "Michael, uh, Richard," Gilbert says. "Say what you need to your mother. I'll be back when you're finished."

He walks out of the office with Paco. I look to Morty, and he just shakes his head. "It'll be okay, kid. We'll get you out."

"Morty, what I need is a good lawyer and money. Everything in here has a price tag, every meal, even the showers. They don't give you shit."

I look to my mother. Aside from being scared, she gives me nothing. For once in her life, she has nothing to say. Between being grateful and shame, I guess she chose shame.

Awkward moments pass. "I guess you better get going," I say. Morty and I hug, and he slips me a few dollars. My mother doesn't move, not knowing what to do. She wants me to forgive her, but I don't know how, and don't want to. Finally, I say, "I'll be okay."

What a lie.

As they walk into the outer office, Gilbert pokes his head in. "I'll be in touch soon. Very soon. We'll get you out of here." Then he's gone and Paco comes back in.

Paco gives me a shark-tooth smile when he fans some bills, "We get you a good carraca now gringo. A muy buena carraca."

I'm let out back into the yard. With every step I take across the field, the more alone I feel, like I'm on a desert island and I just watched the last boat with the last person sail away. But with each step I also become more determined to get the fuck out of here.

Keep your head in here, Mike. Don't you go thinking about anything on the outside. It only fucks up your mind. Stay present. Stay here. You'll be back with your kids. You'll find a way. Just play dumb.

Val waves me over. "Well, your mother's gone."

"How'd you know?

"There isn't much that happens in La Mesa I don't know about, Rick. I've been here almost eight years." He stands and puts his hand on my shoulder. "Come on in. I'm cooking lima beans with ham hocks."

I follow him. He introduces me to his white schnauzer, Savage. We hang out, eat, drink sodas, throw some scraps to Savage, and talk for a long time, well into the night. I don't tell him much about me except that I'm from Brooklyn and work construction.

Well, that's half right.

Val tells me how he played pro football for the New York Giants. And that before he got busted in 1962, he ran the largest car dealership on the west coast.

How much of your shit is real?

"I came to Tijuana to meet a couple of agents from the Cuban government. The meeting was in a whorehouse. Before the night ended, I put together a deal to sell three cargo planes full of arms to Fidel Castro. Gonna net me half a million. I left the whorehouse to buy some tequila at the nearest liquor store to celebrate. When I went paid with a twenty-dollar bill, I was arrested by the Mexican secret service for counterfeiting. Fuckers switched the money on me."

He was given seven years in La Mesa, four for the arms deal that never happened and three for counterfeiting.

Does that mean I'll get three years?

After five years, he got busted again for running a hot car ring inside La Mesa. At that time, he lived in a trailer behind the comandante's office where he and a small team would tear cars down to the frame, change all the numbers, build them back up, and send them back to San Diego.

Eventually someone across the border got busted and gave up Val. When that happened, the Mexican police, and Major Gonzales from the Federales, arrested him. The Major, who oversaw La Mesa, was Val's silent business partner in the car ring and was making lots of money on the deal. He acted shocked, shaking his head and sneery in disgust. "How could such an operation take place right under my nose?"

For that, Val got another six years which brought his total to thirteen. During his first seven years in La Mesa, Val used to go into Tijuana to go drinking with Major Gonzales. When the Major got too drunk to drive back to the prison, Val would drive. Val thought his party would last forever.

I don't know it at the time, but in many ways, I'm a light at the end of the tunnel for Val. Something tells me to dig myself in and let this guy continue to think I'm a harmless dumb white boy.

Don't give him anything to hold against me. Be cool.

Val and I toast with bottles of Coca-Cola to end my second day in La Mesa del Diablo. "Welcome to my world, Rick."

After morning roll call, I'm back in Paco's office. Seems my mother's future husband, Rogelio Gutierrez, the federal policeman who lit her cigarette while we were locked up in the Tijuana jail, has something for me. Money. One hundred dollars to be exact. Now I have enough for meals and to get a decent mattress. I also received a package from Aunt Florence with some clothes.

After breakfast with Pete, I head over to Val's and am shooting the bull inside his carraca when someone knocks.

"Venga entro," Val says.

In walks a young Latin guy, about twenty, slicked back hair, clean cut with a thick gold chain around his neck, and three gold rings on his fingers.

"Rick, I'd like you to meet my pistolero, Carlos Cohen. He's from New York too."

"How ya doing?" I ask in a thickened Brooklyn accent. No reaction. We shake hands.

"Okay."

I feel this pulse in my gut, the one that tells me the kid in front of me is one hard case and I shouldn't relax around him. Carlos looks me up and down like a Doberman eyes another dog who might think about taking a bite out of his bone but doesn't want to growl too soon. It's getting too cramped inside Val's house.

"Well, I guess I'll split, Val."

"Don't go. Let's sit out front and drink a few cokes."

I nod cautiously. "Okay."

I help Val bring out folding chairs and a small cooler. He reaches in and pulls out two Cokes. He and I sit in the shade with our drinks and yak while Carlos stands off to the right of us watching the field, his eyes hidden behind sunglasses, scanning from side to side, being a good pistolero.

Out of the corner of my eye, I catch Carlos muttering under his breath while he stares at a skinny Mexican passing by. "Piece of shit," he mumbles.

"What's the matter with him?" I ask Val.

"Oh, he just wants to kill that Mexican."

"Why?"

"It's a long story," Val answers and takes a long pull on his Coke. "Taki Vasquez is one of the most notorious killers in this prison. He's been in La Mesa fifteen years and during that time he's killed six men in stand-up knife fights, and I can't tell you how many he's sent to the hospital. He also killed a Mexican police officer with a gun. Taki and two other guys, Chino and Alvaro, had a lucrative business going in La Mesa robbing prisoners every time they got money." Val reached in his cooler for another Coke.

"When Carlos came to La Mesa with that thick gold chain around his neck, the three vultures made a move on him out back while he was taking a shower and relieved him of his wealth. That was too much for Carlos. He waited until his chance came a few days later. He took one of my paring knives and stabbed Chino about twenty times until Chino begged him, "En nombre de Dios, alto."" *In the name of God, stop.*

"Chino was sent to a Tijuana hospital where he spent the next eight months recovering. Alvaro was smarter. He confessed to a killing so he would get taken out of La Mesa and go to the Tijuana jail. Now Taki, he's a different story. He's an old vulture. Notice how he even looks that way with his large nose and scrawny neck? He's not leaving, not as long as there's some meat to peck at."

Carlos makes strange sounds, like a caged animal who missed a meal. We stop talking to watch Taki pass by. Carlos begins to move, but Val stands and puts his hand on his shoulder. While Taki passes, our eyes meet for a second, just long enough to set off my little alarm again. This one tells me I'm going to see more of the vulture. There is no doubt he's one of the Mexicans Paco told me about who doesn't like gringos.

Stay fucking awake, Mike.

Carlos wanders away to cool off and Val plops back down. "About a year ago, Carlos killed a New York cop with a gun. He thought it might be good to disappear for a while, south of the border. He wasn't in Tijuana but a couple of hours when three banditos tried to rob him on Rosarito Beach. Bad move on their part. Carlos stabbed all three of them and was arrested by the Mexican state police."

When Taki and his gang heard that Carlos was a robbery victim, they targeted to take him down. As it turned out, Carlos wasn't liked by anyone but Val, and that was for obvious reasons. Hell, if I was planning a prison break from La Mesa, I'd want a lunatic like Carlos Cohen out front with me. I sensed Carlos was a dangerous killer who had yet to reach his potential. But Taki, in an illogical kind of way, represented a more immediate threat to Carlos because of Carlos' relationship with Val.

I could almost read Carlos' mind when he rounded the corner of Val's carraca and saw me lounging there, trying to act like the dumb white boy I wasn't. I could tell he caught a glint in my eyes that told him I wasn't going to back down from him or anyone else. I knew if Carlos was going to snap, it was going to be with the speed of a sidewinder, but not without a rattle first.

What I had going for me was that I did fit the stereotype Mexicans had of gringos. Blond, big, slow. As long as I could maintain that I was okay. But in a place like La Mesa where a man's life is worth less than what he has on his body, you had to stay on edge to survive.

I knew I had a confrontation coming, and it was going to be with either Carlos or Taki. The way I saw it, Taki was the more dangerous of the two. First off, he'd already killed six men in knife fights. That meant he had very good skills with a knife as well as the balls to stand his ground. When he passed Carlos, I saw contempt, not fear in his eyes.

Mexicans have a saying, "un hombre viva en los ojos," *A man lives in his eyes.* Whatever you need to see in a man, you can see it in his eyes. I just hoped that when I looked into Taki's eyes, he didn't see too much in mine.

Carlos, on the other hand, was dangerous but driven on a much different kind of fuel. While Taki moved on ice, Carlos moved on rage. That was easier to spot.

Val went on to tell me how Comandante Paco and his guards have an interesting outlook on escape. "As long as a prisoner doesn't hurt anyone or destroy anything, he's entitled to give it a shot. They believe it's the nature of man to want to be free. They also have a law that states if you escape, your remaining prison time keeps running. If you can outlast your sentence while you're free, your prison time runs out. They also have another policy, if they catch you escaping, they'll kill you on the spot."

That kind of makes sense.

My third night in La Mesa was in the broom closet with Pete, only I managed to wrangle a bed. Well worth the two weeks' talacha money, but not the bed bugs. Before I fall asleep itching myself, one question swirls in my head.

How can I get more money?

3

First Killings

A week passes and I've settled into a routine. More importantly, I developed a keen sense of where danger lurks, what money can buy, and some of the unstated rules. Most of that changed today.

I lunch at El Griego's by myself and stroll into the plaza after I finish my burger. I pass Baron, the chubby cabo of tanky-A. I say hello to him, but he ignores me.

That's strange.

He seems preoccupied watching a guy riding a bicycle who everyone calls El Bicicleto. Baron drills his eyes harder into this rider each time he circles. I go to ask Baron what's going on when he pulls out a .38 from under his shirt and yells, "Pinche rata."

He strides directly toward the rider and empties his thirty-eight with uncanny accuracy. The rider's face immediately turns into a huge hole, and at least two shots catch him under his chin, causing him to fly back. That blows another big hole right through the top of his head. The rider is dead before he hits the ground, his bike ambling across the yard until it bumps into a wall and falls over. Two inmates scramble for it.

Val grabs me and pulls me toward his carraca. I can't look away from Baron who stands over the dead rider cursing and spitting, even as El Bicicleto lays there with no face.

"Rick, come in. You don't want to be out here."

As I step into Val's carraca, I watch guards run into the plaza from all directions, rifles pointed at Baron.

"What the hell was that about?" I ask.

"Bad business. It's been brewing for a while. Seems El Bicicleto ratted out Baron a few weeks ago over some steak he stole, and he'd been waiting for a chance to kill."

"Waiting for his chance? It seems he could have done it twenty times since I showed up. Especially since this guy's been peddling around the plaza every day like he's practicing for the Tour de France."

"I know. I know. He wanted to wait until Comandante Paco came back from down south. This way he won't be locked up for more than one night."

What the fuck?

"You mean to tell me Baron will be back working in tanky-A by this time tomorrow?"

"Of course. You don't think Paco's going to lock up someone who makes him so much money, do you?"

That was the first man I saw die in La Mesa. The full force of just how quickly a man's life can end in here, and how no one cares—that hit me hard.

A week later, Pete and I wrap up breakfast at El Griego's, what we'd call ultimate breakfast burritos in the States. We walk outside and I'm surprised to notice a Mexican laying on a mattress in the middle of the field, really a shadow of what a man should look like.

I nod toward the man. "Who's that guy?"

"Oh, that dude? I think his name's Alfonso. He's got TB so bad they carried him out of tanky-B into the field last night."

"Why's he laying out there?"

"Because he's dying, and he's been coughing up chunks of lung and they don't want him to infect anyone in the infirmary since he's going to die soon anyways. The guys in the corrale threatened to kill him and burn his body if they didn't take him out of tanky-B."

"You mean he's just going to lie out there in the sun until he's dead, with no food or water?"

Pete shrugs. "Guess so."

"Call that mondalero over here for me, will ya?"

Pete yells, "Oye venga!" He turns back to me. "What do you want me to tell him, Rick?"

"Tell him I want Alfonso fed and watered three times a day—until he's dead. Tell him I'll pay for the food, and I'll give him a dollar a day to do it."

After some haggling with the skinny runner, Pete tells me he'll do it. As the mondalero walks away, he looks back at me and scratches his head mumbling something about "loco gringo." I stare at Alfonso in the middle of field, no one within thirty yards of him.

You don't deserve to die without someone caring.

I watch Alfonso for two days as he slowly coughs up his life. On the third morning when I walk by before breakfast, I find him lying on his back, stiff, staring up at the sky with his eyes open, like one last plea for the heavens to take him. I guess the heavens did.

It takes a few more weeks, but now a steady flow of money comes from my aunts, Uncle Morty, and grandmother, usually delivered to me every Sunday in person by a relative. Nothing from my mother. I was finally able to upgrade my carraca with Pete, getting us out of the broom closet and leaving the bed bugs behind.

I continue my habit of having breakfast at El Griego's, sometimes with Val, today being one of those days. We can see the action in the plaza from our table. I crane my neck toward the front gate as a buzz ripples through the compound, a throng of animales rushing out to beg for dollars, not dimes. A man enters with a throng of people in his wake. Medium height, late forties, with a little paunch, and gray mustache. He's bald with gray hair on the sides, khaki pants, short sleeve shirt, and loafers. Impeccable.

"Who the hell's that guy?" I ask Val.

Val shakes his head. "Oh man. Rick, meet Patricio Baccera Ortiz, el grande trafficante. He's the biggest drug dealer in northern Mexico. The papers said he got into an argument with a Cuban who works for Los Hermanos, that's the Hernandez brothers, Juan and Beto, Patricio's primary competition. Seems the Cuban told Patricio he was going to kill him and Patricio's not the kind of guy who you tell you're going to kill. If you want to kill him, you kill him first, then tell him after."

Ha. Even I know that.

"Patricio went to his car, got his Thompson machine gun, and went after the Cuban in the middle of the day on a Tijuana side street. The Cuban was cut in half after Patricio emptied his Thompson into him. I'm surprised you didn't hear about it."

"I don't read Mexican."

"Too bad. You're going to miss a lot."

As Patricio and his entourage pass, I notice two deep indentions in Patricio's skull. "What happened to his head?"

"Some kid shot him in the head twice while he was in Las Isles de Maria. Patricio was in there because he got caught with two hundred thousand dollars of bad money, money I gave him. And he was carrying a machine gun. Obviously, Patricio lived to kill the kid who shot him."

As we watch the Patricio parade, Val turns to me. "Why don't you want to learn to read and write Mexican?"

"Why? Because I'm not going to be here long, that's why."

Val laughs. "That's what you think."

What the fuck?

I don't like it when Val talks shit to me, but I have to remain cool and act stupid. I watch Patricio's parade continue, suitable for a king. He leads an entourage of no less than twenty Mexicans. Each one carries a piece of furniture, from a large color TV set, to lamps, steamer trunks, and even a stove. He looks like some kind of East Indian sultan, or a potentate from the time of Marco Polo. The only thing missing is camels and slaves waving large palm leaves.

"What's the story with the parade?" I ask.

Val shoots me a look of resignation. "Things are going to be a lot different now with Patricio back."

"What do you mean?"

"Last time he was here, he ran the whole place. Every guard, every peon, every Comandante, even the director was on the take."

"You mean he had more juice than you?"

Val winces. "A lot more. First of all, he's Mexican. You wait. You'll see it happen." Val lets out a long sigh. "I stayed in touch with him after he got out last time. Had my girlfriend meet him to deliver his cut so I could keep my hot car operation going."

"You mean you trusted him not to rape your woman?"

"Rape my woman? That's a joke. Patricio's queer!"

My mouth drops open.

"Yes, he likes to fuck young vatos. Some of the worst killers in this place have slept in Patricio's bed."

No fucking way. A fag drug lord in New York would be dead sixty seconds after someone found out.

"He's a goddamn fag?"

Val leans in. "Hey, watch what you say about him, Rick. He might like to fuck boys, but he's the most powerful man in La Mesa now, and that makes him the most dangerous. You know Pedro Moreno?"

I nod.

"He was one of Patricio's boys and he's killed twelve men for him, so far. A month before you got here, Pedro took a contract on this drug dealer inside the corrale. He gets this guy drunk in his own carraca on strong mescal and Tizwin, this crap the Apaches brew. When the guy falls over, Pedro sticks him in the chest. The guy's so drunk he doesn't feel it and doesn't die right away, but his heart keeps pumping out blood that leaks down through the floorboards to the carraca underneath. The guy below feels something warm dripping on his face. He turns on the light, looks at his hand, sees the blood, and screams. He thought it was his own blood until he looked up and saw his ceiling leaking."

Val takes a few deep gulps on his Coke and belches. "Well, the guards came in and found this guy with a huge hole in his chest, but he was dead by then. I think he was number twelve for Pedro Moreno, unless he killed someone else I never heard about. He also did a lot of hits for Patricio when he was on the outside. I've seen him kill five times since I've been here, not counting the one in tanky-A. Sometimes I think he likes to put on a show."

Val shakes his head and swigs his remaining Coke.

"Pedro was seeing Leticia when he was free his last time out. She's Patricio's niece. She was here before. She and the rest of the family will be showing up soon."

I chuckle. "What the fuck?"

"When they bust Patricio, they bust his whole clan. Plus, the Comandante of the Federal Police, Jesus Aguile, he's leaving office after six years, so he'll bust everyone. All the drug traffickers who were paying him off are going down. We'll see a procession of drug kings walking into this place, and they all love cocaine."

"No shit."

"That's not all. Patricio thinks he's the Mexican version of Al Capone. That's why he likes to keep a Thompson machine gun around. He even had one in the last time that he was in here."

A homo Mexican drug lord who thinks he's Al Capone and carries machine guns. Just what I need.

Ten days after Patricio's arrival, Val's prediction comes true. A convoy of family members, drug dealers, and lieutenants in Patricio's organization pour into the prison. A new kind of order settles into La Mesa. And new construction begins. Trucks dump cement day and night. New carracas spring up everywhere off the plaza, a large one just completed on the second story above Ciprion's grocery store to house Patricio in style.

It's mid-afternoon when I walk into the plaza, taking in everything going on. I spot Taki Vasquez speaking to El Engenero who runs a general store where he lives with his family. By his glance, I sense they're talking about me. As I approach, Taki moves on. "What's up, El Engenero?"

"Que paso, gringo?"

"Good. Good. How are you and your family?"

"Fine, amigo."

"Nice day, Eh?"

"Sí. Hey, I have to tell you something, Richard. You know the cabrón who was just here?"

"Yes. I've seen him around."

"This is good. Then you know he killed muchos hombres and is a bandito. Mira, I must warn you, he asks many questions after you."

"Like what?"

"He ask me how much dinero you spend. If I were you, I watch myself. This one es muy mal."

"Gracias, El Engenero."

Yeah Mike, watch yourself.

That night, I settle into my bedbug-free mattress situated at the far end of my latest large carraca, still rooming with Pete. I'm reading a magazine and nursing a Miranda orange soda when I look up and spot Taki Vasquez at the door. The twinge in my gut sets off. I look over at my coat hanging on the wall next to him with my knife inside. *Fuck!*

He ignores Pete and looks to me. "So, gringo, you got un dime para me?"

Don't show him who you are yet. Stay dumb. Be cool.

I put my magazine down and sit up. "No man, I got nothing for you. You better find someone else."

"No gringo. I know you got dinero. You give to Taki now."

Pete scoots back on his bed, his knees bent up to his chest. Taki steps into the doorway and leans against a wall, his left hand inside his pants pocket, most likely on his knife, his right hand wrapped around half a bottle of Coke.

I stand casually.

Taki goes on, "Puto, you give me un dime. If no, I kill you."

So that's it. I can give you a dime, but you'll be back by the end of the week for a dollar. And then a short time later, you'll introduce me to your jar of Vaseline. No fucking way.

I never paid off anyone in my life and know there's only one thing to do when a man threatens your life, especially in a place like this. I smile at Taki and take a sip from my Miranda soda. He relaxes ever so slightly, an almost imperceptible grin beginning.

One quick stride across the small room and I drive my right knee into Taki's pocket where his left hand holds a knife. At the same time, my right hand grabs his throat, and my left hand smashes my soda bottle on the door frame. I jab it into his face. I think I take out his eye, an eruption of blood spraying the room. I ram the broken bottle into his throat, tearing at his flesh. He gasps in surprise, air coming out in gurgles, his arms flailing.

I spin him around, put my right arm around his neck in a choke hold while I keep stabbing him in the face. When he starts to go limp, I toss him onto the floor in the doorway, pounce on his back, slam his head into the floor, and strangle him, my hands slippery with all his blood.

You're not leaving this place alive, motherfucker.

I hear a familiar distant voice grow louder, repeating the same phrase, "Alto gringo! Alto gringo!"

I ignore the voice and squeeze harder. A dull thud. A blackness swallows me. I'm out.

When I come to, three faces look down at me. Pablo Moran with his M-1, Pete, and Comandante Paco.

Paco smiles. "Gringo, you meet one of the Mexicans I tell you when you first see me, no?"

I rub the lump on the back of my head.

I guess so.

"Come gringo. We go."

I stand slowly, trying to get my balance. I look down at my white jeans and white tee shirt. They're completely red. I don't see Taki anywhere.

Did it really happen?

I look back at my carraca. It's red with blood and so is Pete. His eyes tell me he's freaking out. I nod to him and mouth, "It's okay."

Pablo Moran and Paco lead me across the field toward the front of the prison, not saying a word. I feel like a man walking to stand in front of a firing squad. Finally, Pablo smiles, "Look at this mess! Chingada, you are a gringo with huevos grandes. I think you want to kill this cabrón many times, no?"

Not really.

I just look at him. We stop in front of the infirmary. Inside the open door, I spot Taki laying on a table, blood dripping onto the floor. An attendant stands next to him, poking at his massive facial and neck wounds, shaking his head. I can't tell if he's breathing, my vision still blurred.

"Gringo, you do this?" I turn to face Patricio Baccera staring at my bloody clothes.

"He tried to rob me."

"What did he want?"

"Said he would kill me if I didn't give him a dime."

"You did this over a dime?"

I shrug. "Well, yes."

Patricio mumbles something under his breath in Spanish, looks at me in disbelief, and shakes his head. "Do you know who I am?"

"Yes. You're Patricio Baccera."

"I am Patricio Baccera Ortiz. I am boss here, here at the devil's table. Maybe I am el diablo tambien, no?"

Paco interrupts, "Ree-shard, you go with Pablo now. He take you to las tumbas."

Patricio barks at Paco, "Mira! Esta vato es un hombre. He no go into las tumbas, you chicken shit punk. You make deal with this gringo."

Paco looks sheepish and doesn't know what to say.

Patricio continues, "If you no make no deal, you go to Las Isles de Maria to be a chicken shit punk comandante there." Patricio turns to me. "You got money gringo?"

I pull out a hundred and two singles. Patricio grabs the hundred and gives it to Paco. Then he motions to Paco.

Paco says, almost like an apology, "Can you get five hundred mas, Ree-shard?"

"I can, if you let me use the phone."

"Mañana, Ree-shard. In the morning then," Paco adds. He looks into the infirmary, shakes his head, and walks away with Pablo.

"So, tell me, gringo, you like killing cabrón es?" Patricio asks, slapping me on the back.

I look into the infirmary. "Is he dead?"

"If not now, soon. You make many holes in his neck and face." He nods his head for me to follow him. We walk across the field toward tanky-A. "You no sleep in tanky-A tonight. You live in los privalistos primeros near me. I own many carracas. When you get money, you pay me. Three hundred. Now, I think you shower. You smell like a vulture at a fiesta."

I walk into my carraca to find Pete trying to clean up the mess. He's still numb from seeing the killing. I hand him a dollar. "Hey. Have someone else clean this up tomorrow, okay?" I grab my stuff and say goodbye to Pete.

"Where you going?"

"I don't really know for sure."

While I shower Taki's blood off, I can't help but wonder what my future holds here at the devil's table. But somehow Patricio Baccera is going to be involved. Here's a man I would normally have nothing to do with, but he saved my ass.

One thing for sure, he's gonna tell me why.

4

Pistolero

Light floods my room on a beautiful June morning. I stretch and for once, don't bump into a footboard or someone else. And I'm not scratching because of the bedbugs. I rub my eyes open, and it takes me a few seconds to realize I'm in new digs. Next, I notice how sore I am everywhere, especially when I touch the lump on the back of my head. Then it all comes back to me. Twisting that broken bottle into Taki's neck and face, blood spraying everywhere. I hold my hands up to the light. No blood. No cuts.

A fourteen-year-old mondalero knocks on my carraca door and pokes his head in to invite me over to Patricio's pad. At least that's what I guess he says. Something about el jefe.

I toss on some clothes and head over. Patricio's standing by his front door decked out in a red silk robe with matching slippers. He's proud to show me around his palacio.

So, this is the life of a drug king.

His place reminds me of a suite at a Holiday Inn. Everything's new. It's got a massive shower, twenty-five-inch Zenith color TV with remote, wall-to-wall orange shag carpet, sofas, tall lava lamps, and a huge velvet painting of a shirtless matador on the wall.

What is it with Mexicans and this velvet crap?

He winks at his mondalero and says something that makes him blush and laugh before he runs off. Patricio leads me to the patio where servants bring us breakfast. Fresh squeezed orange juice, coffee, huevos rancheros, tortillas, and beans, always beans. We take in the morning under a bright orange umbrella overlooking the prison and farther off, the city of Tijuana.

Patricio grins, "You sleep good, gringo?"

I nod, shoveling a warm tortilla in my mouth. "Yes. I mean, sí."

"Killing makes you hungry, no?"

"I guess so."

He picks up his coffee, his pinkie finger daintily pointing out. "You know, I must tell you, I hate gringos. But I never see one in La Mesa with the balls to take down Taki. You do me big favor. Last time I here, Taki take contract on me from otro trafficante. I have many ears and many eyes in here. So, I put knife to his gut but no deep. The reebs..." He opens his robe to expose his belly and taps on his ribs. "They do not let me."

"Ah."

"I try. He is, how you say, one tough son of bitch vulture. But no more. He is muerto." He grins and takes a sip of coffee, a wide smile spreading across his face. "So, Richard, you work for me?"

Uh-oh.

"Doing what?"

"You be my gringo pistolero. Maybe sometime I ask you for some cosas pequeñas."

He studies my reaction and can see I don't understand.

"I may ask a small favor." He puts his thumb and index finger close together. "To give you drugs to sell to the other gringos, mostly the marijuana, sometimes the heroin to gringos with no soul. But you must never deal to Mexicanos. I'm afraid even I cannot help you if you do that."

I gulp down some orange juice. "Why's that?"

"My people have problem with gringos. They are still upset at your government for the land you have taken from them. So, in all truth, I must say that when a gringo shows up with dinero to spend, we let him live. But when a gringo has no dinero and wants to take the bread out of the mouths of my people, he dies. You must admit, you have already taken from some very rich and very powerful Mexicans."

I wrinkle my brow. "Who's that?"

"The Bustamantes, the men who own Caliente Racetrack. I know them. You are lucky to be alive. So that is why you will never deal to anyone but gringos."

I look into Patricio's eyes. Here is a man who likes to screw young men and use cocaine, but also a man who has people killed and he doesn't even have to leave his carraca to do it.

I guess under ordinary circumstances, I'd never sit in the same room as you, but this is not ordinary.

"So, you be mi gringo pistolero?"

"Sure. I can do that."

He beams, clapping his manicured hands together. "Bueno! Bueno!"

I clear my throat and lean in. "But before we go any further, there's one thing I must make clear to you, Patricio. I like women. Only women. And even though I owe you much, maybe my life, I feel I must tell you this so there's no, you know, mix up."

"Well, I must say this is always the problem with my life. One must always accept the good with the bad, no?" He laughs. "But I tell you that I only fall in love with my own people. I respect you for telling me. But I already knew this when I decide to have you work for me."

"You checked up on me?"

"Yes. I know all about the eight hundred men and women in La Mesa, even you."

That first Sunday after I started working for Patricio, Morty came for his monthly visit and brought the $500 to pay off

Paco, pushing an envelope across the table to me. We were at our usual table at Cipriano's. The way he looked at me, with his intense brown eyes, told me he sensed something changed. "What's up, kid?"

"Not much."

His eyes wandered around the restaurant, and he looked out toward the yard. "Can't you see how everyone's taking looks at you and avoiding us?"

I shrugged. "Yeah, well, I had to take care of some business. A guy got in my shit. Threatened to kill me."

"And, what'd you do?"

"I killed him."

"Jesus, Michael. How much time you gotta do for that?"

I let out a big grin. "None. The comandante put it down as self-defense. That's why I needed the five hundred."

"What?"

"To pay off the comandante. Oh, and I'm a pistolero now."

"A pistolero. That some kind of hit man?"

I nod my head.

"I suppose they're going to get you a pistol too?"

"Once they trust me, they'll get me whatever I want. My boss is partial to machine guns." I lean in close and whisper. "Patricio Baccera Ortiz is in here because he gunned down a rival Cuban drug lord. Cut him in half with a machine gun. He's the most powerful drug lord in northern Mexico. Now he's the most powerful man in La Mesa. Oh, and get this, he's a fag."

Morty lowers his head and give me a what-the-fuck-does-that-mean-to-you? look.

I shake my head. "He only likes cute Mexican boys. I'm okay."

After a week pushing drugs for Patricio, I'm already pulling down thirty dollars a day. That's more money than I ever made working a legitimate job on the outside. All I have to do to keep my dinero flowing is deal drugs to the twenty-five Americans in La Mesa, and they need it to handle all the shit that' going down. I'm living like a prince now, with fifteen-year-old Gonzo, my junkie houseboy, cleaning my place and washing my clothes for twenty-five cents a day. At over two thousand dollars a day, my patrón, Patricio, lives like an emperor.

The notoriety of what I did to Taki is good, to a point. As long as I'm working for the most powerful drug lord in La Mesa, I've got some protection. Above everything else, my dumb white boy days are over.

Now everyone knows how far I'll go for a dime.

I'm still on speaking terms with Val, but our friendly relationship evaporated overnight. With Patricio in charge of La Mesa, and Val no longer in any kind of control or authority, the balance of power shifted, and Val had to assume a subservient position, begging for scraps, which he hates. That doesn't keep him from trying little ways to lure and control a continually shrinking population of young vatos he plans to use for an escape.

Since I'm in Patricio's inner circle, and with my Spanish language skills improving, I'm getting an inside view of how everything goes down in La Mesa. Patricio's entire clan joins him in prison, someone new arriving almost daily. Federale Comandante Jesus Aguile lived up to his word. Before leaving office, he busted some of the biggest drug traffickers in Mexico and they're all coming here. That means more competition inside La Mesa, which means more killing.

Patricio's sister, Lupe, opens a restaurant next door to Pele's on La Concha and her authentic Mexican cooking is already known as the best in La Mesa. Right away I get into the habit of eating breakfast and lunch at the El Griego's and dinner at Lupe's.

My wife, Sheila, moves from Brooklyn to San Diego with the kids and stays with Aunt Edwina. We have conjugal visits on Tuesdays, the day reserved for wives, and I get to see her with our kids on Sundays. Even though I'm stuck inside for who knows how long, we decide to work to put all the badness behind us.

About three months into my stay, I make arrangements with Paco, which means fifty bucks, for Sheila to stay with me Tuesday nights, something reserved for favored prisoners. My wife never felt comfortable when she visited me Tuesdays since there weren't many people who came to the prison those days. She liked it when she could blend into the crowd. I understood how she felt being gawked at by hundreds of prisoners whenever she walked across the yard, so I tried to cater to her.

It's about two-thirty in the afternoon when we go to El Griego's to get some lunch. We walk to the back of the room, and I grab my usual table with my back to the wall, my eyes to the door. I order the veal cutlet and Sheila orders a burger.

We've been at the table maybe five minutes, and in the middle of our weekly catching-up chit chat about her and our kids, when I notice a vato from the corrale coming in the front door. His wild eyes alert me that something nasty's about to go down, and he's got a hand in his pocket. I reach under the table and finger the hilt of my knife, getting ready to push Sheila behind me if some shit goes down.

I scan the room. Just a few patrons. A Mexican wearing a red bandana sits two tables to the left of us, but he has his back to the door. The vato walks past us, up to the Mexican and yells, "Puto." When the Mexican turns around to see who's shouting, the vato empties a revolver into the Mexican's face until the gun clicks empty. Blood sprays everywhere. I jump up, grab Sheila and almost knock down the shooter getting out of the restaurant.

I rush Sheila to my carraca and sit her on the edge of my bed. She can't stop trembling as I wipe the blood off her with a towel.

"Oh, my god. Oh, my god," she keeps repeating.

She's in shock.

Her eyes are wide, and she keeps staring at my shirt until I realize there's a big chunk of the Mexican's brains splattered onto the fabric. I change my shirt.

I'm worried about her because she has a weak heart from rheumatic fever when she was a little girl. She'd never seen anyone killed before. When Paco comes to my pad an hour later to tell me all visits for the day are cancelled, I feel relieved. I really didn't know what more to say to her to calm her down.

Sorry, baby. Just another day in La Mesa.

After that, Sheila only comes to see me Sundays with our kids, and there aren't any killings, everyone on their best behavior. I get the kids ice cream cones and they munch on churros, getting the sugar and cinnamon all over the place.

Her last Tuesday with me in La Mesa is so intense, her eyes always looking around, no matter where we were, she can't enjoy our time. I try to remain calm and not get into any arguments about anything.

"I had to throw away that dress."

"You looked pretty in that one, but I understand," I say.

The loudspeakers announce it's time for everyone to leave. As we stroll toward the front gate, Sheila pauses. "Michael, there's something I need to tell you."

What now?

I nod to her.

She lowers her head. "I'm going home. Back to Brooklyn and taking our children. I—I just can't take this place anymore."

I lift her chin so I can look her in the eyes. She looks just like Natalie Wood in the movie *Splendor in the Grass*, frightened and worried, something her heart can't take.

I glance around the prison grounds, and for the first time since the day I arrived, I see what she means. "Sure. I understand. But hey, my mother promised she'd get me out of here soon."

"I hope so."

We hug and I kiss her. I take in her scent. I can't help but wonder when I'll ever do that again or see my kids. Then, she's gone.

The front gates close. I let out a deep sigh and turn to gaze at the prison with fresh eyes. I'm standing in the middle of La Mesa del Diablo with its fifteen-foot-high walls and its eight manned towers. As I walk back to my carraca, I do a quick tally. I've seen five people killed already, one by my hands. I have a lawyer who isn't sure if or when I'll be released, and a mother who has yet to visit or send me anything. I'm the pistolero of a fag drug lord who runs La Mesa. I live in a private carraca. People fear and respect me. I'm making enough money to get by, in style for here. I'm alive but that could end any moment.

I can't think of you or the kids anymore, Sheila. Not in here. It's too dangerous.

5

Letting Go

I get in the habit of spending evenings at Patricio's. He entertains all the chingóns, the other drug dealers in La Mesa with food, drinks, and drugs. If it's a warm night, we sit outside on his patio while he passes around a huge bowl of cocaine. I'd never done coke before, but right off I like the buzz it gives, amping me up, like I'm extra alert and alive. We all hit the spoon with each pass. The only problem is, I'm the only one who doesn't speak fluent Spanish at Patricio's parties.

Patricio can speak English, but not very well when he's high. He did twelve years in San Quentin and hated gringos so much that he refuses to speak our language now, except to me. But he understands everything.

No shit you understand.

One good thing about coke is that it helps me learn Spanish faster. After only a few weeks or Patricio's parties, I realize how my life's getting simpler once I know the Mexican street rap they talk. It cuts through the bullshit.

I also get better deals on everything in the joint. That I'm Patricio's gringo pistolero, and that I killed Taki, that helps with my deal-making more than anything.

I've gotten to know a big-time drug dealer named Cruzito, a rival of Patricio's, an old man who usually sits to my right at Patricio's when we're passing the bowl. Patricio has everyone sit in a certain order as if they're his guests at some fancy banquet. Cruzito's skinny, maybe sixty, with dark wise eyes, and slicked-back black hair. Around his neck, he wears a large chunk of turquoise encased in thick silver.

He tells me he came from Nayarit, not too far from Guadalajara, and that he likes Americans since he lived in Arizona for a while. He still listens to American music, but he likes Nayarit's the best. Patricio makes fun of him, saying it sounds like parade music with a polka beat.

It's just after one in the morning and the night's winding down. We're about to start on a new bowl of coke which was brought into the room by one of Patricio's pretty boys. Patricio hands me the bowl and as I'm about to take a hit, he gives me an urgent look that tells me to stop. He smiles and says, "No, Richard, we must not insult our guest."

I nod and pass the bowl to Cruzito.

The old man takes a couple of good hits and is going to pass the bowl back to me, but the houseboy takes it and makes some excuse to leave the room.

I light up a joint the size of a Cuban cigar and pass it to Cruzito.

He takes a big drag and I watch a lazy smile spread across his face. As he exhales, the old man leans forward, almost in slow-motion, and topples onto the floor. Everyone laughs. They think he's done too much coke/ After a few minutes, several men come over to him. Patricio becomes the most concerned, like a mother hen watching over a sick chick. Patricio checks Cruzito's pulse. He shakes his head. The old man is dead.

Patricio nods to his houseboys and barks that the guests are to be ushered out. As I go to leave, Patricio stops me, and gives me a sly grin. "Richard, go now to wake up the guard Julio and tell him to come quick."

After I get the guard, who I know is heavy on Patricio's payroll, Patricio whispers, "Go now to you carraca."

The next day the yard is buzzing with news of Cruzito's death. The word is he died of a stroke during the night and was found by a guard in his carraca. At that moment, I knew Patricio started his mission to eliminate his competition.

What part you gonna have me play, Patricio?

It's early September 1968 when I get another visit from Gilbert Herrera, my attorney. Every time we meet, there's nothing new to report. If I was in the States, my lawyer would be up the DA's ass to get something going. I just don't get the Mexican justice system, if you can call it that. Stopping at the door on his way out, Gilbert casually asks, "The confession you signed, what exactly did it say?"

"I don't know. It was in Spanish."

Gilbert stops, closes the door, and motions me to sit. "Why didn't you tell me this earlier?"

"You never asked. Look, I told them I brought the money over the border and then they pushed a paper at me to sign."

"Anything else?"

I shake my head. "No, they just wanted to beat on me some more."

What's he getting at?

"This is muy bueno. I will check on some things and get back to you." Like he just unearthed some secret treasure, he leans in to whisper, "Do not say anything about this to anyone. Yes?"

"Okay."

It's been over a month without a call or letter from Sheila. That's not like her. When Morty's leaving after another Sunday visit, I have to ask him, "What's going on with Sheila?"

He gives me a look, a wince that tells me something's up. I think I know what's coming. "Hey kid, what happened to her when she was here..." Morty shakes his head and gulps. "The killing with all that blood, not knowing when you'll get out, her raising your kids by herself. It's bad for her, Michael. Real bad. She's on welfare again."

"That's kinda what I thought. Thanks for being straight up with me, Morty." We slap each other on the back.

"See you in a month, kid."

That night I don't go to Patricio's. No amount of coke can help with where my head's at. Instead, I go back to my room and take out some paper. The last time I wrote a letter was seven years ago when I was locked in the stockade at Fort Dix, and President Kennedy got me out of the brig.

Jesus, that's like a lifetime ago.

This time there's no president to write to. Instead, it's a letter to my wife, and I know what I've got to say.

Dear Sheila,

I know I've fucked up my life, our lives, but I can't seem to help it. I'm stuck in a Mexican prison while you're in Brooklyn with the kids trying to get by. I wish I could say something to make things better, but I can't. And I'm not going to promise you anything I can't deliver. I've done too much of that. I can't get you any money and I can't be there to help. But there is one thing I can do.

You're still a beautiful woman, Sheila. You're young. I have no right to ask you to wait for me, especially when I don't know when I'll ever get out of this shit hole. So, Sheila, my wife, I give you this—your freedom. Your freedom to find another man.

Hopefully, you'll meet someone who will treat you and our children with respect and take care of you like you deserve.

That's all I got to say.

Love, Michael

I try to read over the letter, but I can't, my eyes unable to focus through the tears. I let out a deep sigh, fold the letter, and slip it in an envelope. Sealing and addressing it makes it final. I whisper to the envelope that holds so much of my heart, "You take care." I let go a deep sigh.

That's it now.

6

Party to Forget

A few days later, on Sunday, September 15, Patricio sits down next to me at dinner in his sister Lupe's café. "Listen, Richard, en la mañana, I have on my patio a fiesta grande to honor our Mexican independence."

"I thought that was Cinco de Mayo."

He laughs. "No, that is a party gringos have so they can drink mas tequila. You come. We talk some, no? Es muy importante. Maybe you do a thing for me?"

Finally, the favor.

"Sure. What time?"

"After eleven en la mañana."

The next morning I'm up for 7:30 roll call, pay my fifty cents to get out of work detail, and stroll over to El Griego's for breakfast. As I sit down to eat, Val Caldwell plops down at my table. "Hey, Richard, you going to Patricio's for his big shindig today?"

"Yes, as a matter of fact, I am."

"I'm probably not telling you anything you don't already know, but Patricio and his crew plays for keeps. You gotta watch your back."

What's your game?

"Thanks, Val. I'm watching."

"Just a heads up, Richard."

"Yeah, much appreciated."

I spot Carlos Cohen, Val's pistolero, hanging by the door trying to stare me down. I turn back to Val. "What the fuck is up with Carlos?"

"He's still pissed you killed Taki."

"You gotta be shitting me. That's fucked up."

"Yeah, you know Carlos."

"Actually, no, I don't know him. And don't care to."

I lose my appetite, get up, and walk past Carlos, looking him in the eye the entire time. I'm daring him to make a play, but nothing.

Pussy.

At eleven a.m., I head over to Patricio's for the big fiesta. Since its Independence Day, Comandante Paco lets Patricio invite outside guests to his party. The place is decked out and filling up with people, cooks tending to grills and tables spread with food. I spot him dressed in white linen, a red silk scarf around his neck, snake-skin loafers, no socks.

"Buenos días, mi patrón." I give a little bow.

He grins. "Como estas, Richard?"

I flip my hand side to side. "Así, así."

"Why you look so malo?"

I tell him about Carlos Cohen.

"Sí. That Cuban is chicken shit punk. I hate all Cubans. They talk too loud, too much, and say nothing. They are all with, how you say, sangre de chango! Monkey blood. You must be careful with this one. He is muy pelegroso. I kill one of his relatives. That is why I come here."

"That Cuban was related to Carlos?"

"Sí. They are all of the same mother and father. The whole island is motherfuckers."

I nod my head. "Okay." I knew Patricio hated the guy he machine-gunned in half. I didn't know he hated all Cubans.

"Come now, Richard, we have a little chiva."

"No, no thanks, Patricio. I don't do heroin."

He laughs. "No, No Richard. I got a little, how you call it, goat? We kill and eat for the fiesta."

"Oh, sí, sounds good to me."

He waves for me to follow him over to a group of maybe twenty guests gathered in a circle. The crowd parts for Patricio and me. El Cheflon is in the middle straddling a goat, holding its head in his left hand, his right hand wielding a huge butcher knife against the goat's neck. As he slices across the animal's throat, I look into El Cheflon's eyes and see a glint. I know that look from a few times in my life. It's the look of madness but at the same time, a sane kind of nature. It's the lust to kill, to take life, to have control over it, to be the master of life and death.

The goat struggles briefly, kicking its legs, as its jugular spurts blood all over.

"Trucha! Trucha! ¡Pinche leandro peto!" Patricio yells. "You get the pinche sangre all over the fucking roof."

El Cheflon looks up, shrugs his shoulders, and gives Patricio a sheepish look. If anyone else had said any two of those words to El Cheflon, he would have killed them on the spot.

Patricio pulls me over to a corner table on his patio and waves over one of his boys to bring me a plate of food. "Sit down, Richard. Eat." Patricio pats me on the back as I'm handed a plate of huevos rancheros.

I shovel it in as I missed my breakfast.

Patricio leans in. "I got un problema. Maybe you can help me, no?"

"What is it?"

"I would like for you to kill this Miguel Barragone for me."

There it is.

I almost choke on a piece of tortilla. Mike Barragone, known as Don Miguel, is an old-time gangster in his sixties with thinning gray hair. No threat. He was arrested about the same time as me and my mother. He was the guy with a plane full of bales of marijuana we slept on. "Why me for the job?"

"Because he likes you and lets you in his house. I no have anyone he would let in his house. You are the one."

I'm fucked.

I don't want to kill Mike Barragone because I like him. But I can't say no. If I do, I'll be dead.

"How can I kill him with his pistolero in his house? He's always there, and he keeps his hand on his gun."

"You think of something."

"Patricio, he likes me, but he doesn't trust anyone, even me. Also, how do I shoot Don Miguel? His house is only thirty feet away from the guard tower. The guard will hear and shoot me."

"Come with me, Richard."

I get up and follow Patricio to the back of the patio, the side that faces the rear wall of La Mesa. There's a guard in a tower on top of the wall maybe a hundred feet away. Patricio puts his hand in his pocket and pulls out a .22 Ruger semi-automatic fitted with a silencer. "Mira, Richard."

He aims at the middle part of the wall and fires. There's hardly any noise at all, except the working sound of the slide, and a ping that sounds like a dragonfly buzzing by your ear. I look around. None of the guests turn around and the guard doesn't notice.

"You try now," Patricio says as he hands me the gun.

I pull out a handkerchief and take the pistol. I don't want to leave any of my fingerprints on Patricio's guns. *You never know where they'll end up.* I take aim at the same spot and pull the trigger. The gun makes the same sound as before, but this time the guard on the wall looks around.

He spots Patricio and yells something I can't make out. Patricio yells back, "Buenas días." Patricio turns to me. "That chicken shit punk, he thinks it's some kind of fly. How you like this one? It makes no noise."

"Nice. I've never shot one so quiet."

"You take now and kill the cabrón pinche bastardo for me, no?"

I don't know what to say, so I play it by ear. "I'll go to his house a couple of times this week to see what's happening. Yes, if I get a chance, I'll do it."

"Esta bien! Es good."

Patricio slaps me on the back and heads back to rejoin his guests. I slip the .22 under my shirt, tucked into my pants. I look around La Mesa and take a deep breath. There's something calm and settling about having a piece again.

I stay on the patio, eat goat all day, and do lots of coke through the night. A batch of hookers comes in around ten and the party hits another gear. By midnight, it's going so strong, that Patricio hands Paco $200 and pays the mariachis $500 more to keep playing until five o'clock the next morning.

After the last song, I stumble into my carraca completely exhausted. Before I crash, one thing keeps tugging at my brain—*Is this how I'm going to spend the next twelve years of my life?*

7

The Tunnel & The Fire

Patricio made a deal with El Director of La Mesa, Senor Martinez, Comandante Paco's boss. The deal was simple. Patricio would finance the building of new carracas to be erected out of cement and cinder block, then he'd rent them out to all the prisoners. What this guy could teach about capitalism. The old wood structures would be torn down since they were made mostly from scraps and cardboard. One of them is even made from the body of a forty-seven Chevy. The guy who originally owned the car, was probably buried beneath it.

The entire area behind Ciprion's grocery, which is directly beneath Patricio's carraca, is nothing but shacks. They're packed together. The first time I walked through them it felt like I was in Calcutta, at least that's what they looked like from the pictures in *National Geographic*. Entire families live there. Like Jimmy Kelso with his wife and four kids. That's where the ten-cent shower is as well. Three buckets of warm water, bring your own soap. I hang out there sometimes to pick up gossip and other news about what's really going on inside La Mesa.

You get to know people when you're doing time. I get friendly with a guy named Angelo D'Rienzo, an Italian from Boston, about forty, inside for some drug deal gone wrong. He used to work as Val's pistolero before Carlos Cohen came along, so he got demoted to other duties of lesser prominence. I run into him sitting on a huge boulder in the back of little Calcutta.

"Where you been keeping yourself, Angelo? I haven't seen you lately."

He looks around to make sure no one's listening, then points to a shack. "I've been right over there in Wado's place."

"What's he got that interests you, a new TV?"

He looks me straight in the eyes. He knows he can trust me. "He's got a tunnel going in his house."

"Really?"

"I'm telling you straight. We've been working on it for three weeks. Val's backing the whole thing."

"What the fuck? You got a way out of this fucking zoo?"

"I'm telling you that I've been in that hot tunnel for three weeks with only a fan in there to breath. I think we are about five or six days away from breaking through. I know we're under the stream. It's been leaking while I've been shoring it up for the past few days."

"Who's in it with you?"

"Like I said, Val Caldwell's financing it. Me, Wado, and Carlos have been doing the digging."

I nod to him. "I want in, man!"

"I don't know. Carlos hates you and Val's convinced you're planning to kill him."

"Why does he think that?"

"I don't know. He's been that way since you started working for Patricio and especially since old man Cruizito died. I think that shithead Carlos has been hyping him up."

"That explains the cold spell I get from Val lately. Anyway, I don't really give a shit about either of them. I want out of this place, and I'll do whatever I have to do to get in on that tunnel."

"Listen Rick, I think we might be able to work out something at the last minute. I could let you know when we're twenty-four hours from breaking through. You show up and I bet you can bogart your way into the deal. But you'll need a pistol."

I smile. I don't want him to know I'm already packing. "I can take care of that."

Angelo comes to me four days later. I'm prepped and ready to let Morty know I might be on my way out, got my stuff in order. "Richard, I got some bad news."

What the fuck now?

"Yeah?"

"We got two days of digging left and I just got word they're tearing down the shacks tomorrow for the new construction Patricio's doing."

I look across at the assemblage of twenty-six shacks. "Where they starting?"

"Three or four shacks down from Wado's pad."

I scratch my head. "What the fuck we gonna do?"

"I think we should start a fire to burn down the line of shacks that lead up to Wado's. If they find the tunnel, they won't know which pad the tunnel was in."

"A fire?"

"Yeah, a fire. I'll take care of it."

Just after eight that night as I'm watching *The Mod Squad* in my carraca, Penny looking all hot in her bellbottoms and long blonde hair, a bright beam of light sneaks through a crack in my door. A rumble of low noise grows. I swing open the door. Every wooden structure in Calcutta is on fire, people running everywhere. *Fuck.* Guards shout. The speakers in the compound blare warnings for everyone to go to the middle of the yard. Sirens from approaching fire trucks drown out everything.

I get to the middle of the field and look around for Angelo but can't find him. When my eyes locked on Val's, his face pale, his jaw trembling.

Three fire trucks roar into the yard, hoses immediately yanked off the back, firemen already watering down the mess. One of them drags a hose over to Wado's shack and begins to douse the flames. I'm watching closely because I'm hoping they won't discover the tunnel. I glance away for a second, and when I look back, the fireman's gone. Only his hat is on the ground and it's moving.

What the...?

A few firemen rush over and drag him out. An hour later, the loudspeakers announce we can all return to our carracas, everyone except the poor bastards who were living in the shacks. They've got nowhere to go.

There goes my chance to escape.

The next morning at breakfast, a mondalero tells me that they threw Angelo in the hole. I leave my meal and go into the yard and knock on the thick metal door. "Yo! Angelo, Angelo! Can you hear me?"

"Yeah, I can hear you."

"What you doing in las tumbas?"

"They found a shirt inside the tunnel after they pulled the fireman out. They said it was mine."

"You mean your pizza man shirt?"

"Yeah, that shirt."

"You mean you left your fucking shirt in the tunnel?"

"I know."

"When's Val getting you out?"

"I don't know. I sent word to him, and he says I put myself in here because of the shirt. He refuses to pay off anyone. After all I've done for him. That's bullshit. That's wrong."

"I don't blame you. Don't worry, Angelo, I'll come up with something, just give me time."

I head up to Patricio's pad. "¡Hola, patrón!"

"Buena días, Richard."

"Hey, what happened last night, Patricio?"

"Su amigo, Angelo, El Italiano, he set the shacks on fire. But you know that already, no?"

"Sí, I knew it, but I wanted to know if you knew anything else."

"Well, he has done me a great favor. Now I can build more carracas and I can make mucho dinero. I know this man did not do this for me, but it has done me much good."

"Listen patrón, maybe you can help Angelo. Val won't. And I know Angelo will be very grateful."

"Sí. I hear that chicken shit punk Val has moved away from him. So, I will help this man, but you tell him that he must wait many days until it cools off. The fireman who broke his leg and shit his pantaloons, he cousin of Comandante. So, you tell this Italian I will help him soon."

"Gracias, patrón."

"Now, Richard. You visit my good friend Miguel Baragone for what we discussed?"

Fuck. I was hoping you'd forget.

"Sí, but it's going to be hard to get to him. I'll keep trying."

"Bueno. Es muy importante." He holds out his hand. "But until you have a plan, you need give pistola back to me."

Fuck.

A week later, Patricio finally arranges for Angelo to get out of the hole. After he gets cleaned up, we sit down for breakfast. The first thing I say is, "That dirty son of a bitch, Val. I can't believe he left you in the hole."

"I know man. He treated me just like some kind of punk. I want to burn that bastard."

8

Collecting

A month passes and I'm in a new carraca trying to hang a picture, hammering nails into cinder block walls, when I hear a commotion outside. I step out my door which is located on the second story. Out in the plaza, a circle has formed, and the prisoners are yelling at two men in the middle. I look up at the guards in the towers and they're yelling as well, enjoying the show.

In the middle of the circle is Carlos Cohen with a small sword and he's moving toward El Cheflon who's got a knife and running out of space to back away from him. I know Carlos is about to spring on El Cheflon any second.

I yell, "Mira! ¡El Cheflon, Mira!"

El Cheflon looks up at me and so does Carlos. I throw my hammer down to El Cheflon. At that instant, the confrontation changes. Cheflon grabs the hammer and wades in at Carlos, swinging the hammer from side to side. The crowd really gets into it now. Before either of them can do any damage to each other, guards rush onto the plaza. Both men drop their weapons and are marched off to the tumbas. Carlos glares up at me.

You come after me, I'll be ready.

Four days later, El Cheflon gets released and comes to find me. "Listen gringo, you saved my life. That puto was going to kill me if you didn't send down that hammer. Whatever you need, you tell me, and I do it for you. I cannot be your amigo because I may kill you someday. But I owe you."

Army trucks, with over a hundred soldiers, rumble into the middle of the yard in the middle of the day. Loudspeakers blare in Spanish, "You will cooperate with the Army as they conduct a search. Anyone resisting will be arrested."

With that, the soldiers disperse in two-man teams and comb through each carraca, turning over beds, checking mattresses, backs of drawers. Everywhere someone might hide a gun, knife, or drugs. All us prisoners can do is watch, as over the course of the next few hours, loads of contraband gets piled onto the flatbed of a truck. Hardest hit was Wilkenson, the guy who sells knives to new inmates and anyone else looking for protection.

I head over to Patricio's after the truck leaves. He's on his patio, a young vato giving him a neck massage, his eyes closed. We complete the customary hello-how-are-you and then I get to it. "How hard did they hit you, Patricio?"

He gives off a huge grin. "Me? No me."

"You were tipped off?"

His smile is even wider now. "Paco. He tell me two days ago. I have him take my machine gun, all my other guns and my drugs. So, no problem for me today."

I wonder what that cost you.

I'm grabbing a bite to eat with Angelo at Lupe's restaurant, a bowl of beans and raw onion soup, the best. I make it a point to keep in touch with Angelo because he's still in Val's group, which means he knows what Carlos Cohen is up to. As we're eating, I spot a weird-looking guy outside, sitting on the wall across La Concha, a wall that separates the corrale from the rest of the prison. He's holding a huge cinder block and hovering it above some Mexican prisoner sleeping below him.

I'm so fixated by what's going on, I don't hear a thing Angelo say until he waves his hand in front of my eyes and almost yells. "Hey, Rick, what's the matter?"

"You gotta—" I stop in the middle of my sentence. The cinder block falls onto the face of the unlucky Mexican and I hear a squashing sound. I push my plate aside and stand up, pointing out the window. "Angelo, look at that dude. Look at him."

I walk out onto La Concha toward the wall, Angelo trailing behind me. By now a small crowd forms and a guard meanders toward the commotion. At the bottom of the wall the Mexican lay dead, his head replaced by the large cinder block. I look up to the top of the wall at a completely crazy guy, his eyes wild. Young, maybe twenty, skinny, scorched so dark by the sun I can't tell what nationality he is. He's got heroin needle tracks on both arms. The crowd steps back because of the spreading puddle of blood.

Comandante Paco leads a group of seven guards to the scene. He turns to me. "What happened, Richard?"

"I don't know, Paco. Looks like this guy's dead."

"So, how does he become dead?"

"I think that block killed him." I motion to the crazy guy on top of the wall.

Paco looks up at him and says in Spanish, "Did you do this?"

The crazy man nods, "Sí."

"Why?"

"He was lazy. All he did was sleep all day and he should work."

Paco barks to the guards, "Take him to the hole."

Minutes after he's locked away, as it always does, word spreads through La Mesa that El Ladrillo, Spanish for "block," killed a prisoner. That's what he'll forever be called. Somewhere along the line, this man lost his soul and snapped.

I won't ever let that happen to me.

The next morning I'm standing for la lista next to the hole. Paco comes out and opens the iron door to the hole for the count of the two guys inside, El Ladrillo and another prisoner put inside to sleep off a near drug overdose. No sooner does Paco walk in, than he backs out and begins to puke. Between his retching, he curses El Ladrillo to the beginning of his family tree.

I find out later that sometime during the night, El Ladrillo got hold of the edge of a can and slit the other man's throat and waited until he bled out. Then he cut into the man's belly and was chewing on it when Paco opened the door. After that, El Ladrillo was given single occupant status in the hole until construction could be completed for a cell built just for the young cannibal. After that, I never saw him again.

"A cannibal, Michael? Jesus, you can't be serious," Jimmy Blatt says, shaking his head. "I know you spent a year in there." He holds up the single sheet Interpol report with its lone paragraph. "What else happened? Check that. I'd just like to know how you got out of there."

"I'm getting to that. But I've got to tell you something, Jimmy. It was, without a doubt, the longest and strangest year of my life, and I never felt more alive."

9

Surviving

It's early November 1968. In America, Nixon just got elected and nothing's going right in Vietnam. But in the Devil's Table, none of that matters.

Angelo and I are finishing up lunch at El Griego's when six army trucks roll into the yard. I turn to Angelo, "What now? They just turned this place upside down a couple weeks ago."

"I don't think that's what's going on," he answers and fidgets.

He's right. Soldiers tumble out, one standing beside each truck holding a clipboard. The loudspeakers blare, "The following prisoners are to report to the yard immediately."

A list of names booms across the compound. I gulp. I'm waiting for my name. Angelo his. The list is somewhere around sixty names. I know a few. They repeat the names again. As each man tentatively enters the yard, a soldier pairs up with him and escorts him into the back of one of the trucks where they disappear under the tarp.

I catch Patricio bounding down the stairs, his bodyguard El Cheflon, as always, by his side. "What's going on?" I ask.

"They take to Islas de Marias." He catches the look on my face. "No of your amigos. I know."

"You helped make up the list?"

He nods. "Sí. Some do not like Patricio. It is something I do not understand. What is there not to like about me?" He laughs and pats his belly. "Some judges tambien decide for them. Still others, they take because they no buy drugs from Patricio." He roars again. "They rot now on the island. That is where rats belong."

I better keep pushing your drugs.

I got moved out of my private room and into a large five-man carraca. I did a few things that made Paco have to do something. When they shook down the entire prison, they found my knife and some drugs, and he didn't like the way I treated some of the Mexicans who were always trying to hustle me for dinero. I could have had Patricio fix it, but he's still waiting on me to hit Mike Barragone, and I don't want to give him another excuse to push harder.

Paul Highs, a tall, gangly, curly-haired blond hippy, early twenties, just entered La Mesa and he's sharing the carraca with me. I didn't need to ask, because his glazed eyes already gave me my answer, but I did anyway. "Whatcha in for?"

"Fuck man, they busted me for selling weed." He leaned in and whispered, "Where can I score some shit?"

"You won't be selling anything in here. That's my business. How much money you got?"

Shit, I'm starting to sound like everyone else in here.

'Highs' is perfect name for him. All he wants to do is get high. He tells me he's got people on the outside who'll send him money. That's all I need to know to set up an account, sell him a few joints, and have him owe me.

What a fucking pot head. His brain is so fucked up, that the next day I catch him on his back in the middle of the yard with his eyes closed, headphones on, tapping his feet to the music. Problem is, some thief cut the wires to his headphones and took off with his radio, but Paul's feet kept time to the music that's no more. It takes him a few minutes to figure out his radio's gone. Some mondalero comes up to him later and offers to help get his headphones back, but he needs some rescate, *that's ransom*. He pays, of course.

Just about the same time, I spot another guy coming into La Mesa. Right away I've named him American Bob. He's got big hair, a big personality, and he must lift iron 'cause he's fucking huge. He's young, loud, and funny, but carries a hard edge under the surface. Val latches onto him right away. With Carlos Cohen thrown into the hole because they found a gun when they tossed his place, I'm guessing Val's looking for a new pistolero.

A few days later, I'm visiting Val and he's complaining about all his health problems. Hardening of the arteries, painful feet, the list goes on. I'm tired of hearing people whine all the time, and Val's getting real good at it, but I listen anyway 'cause sometimes I pick up some valuable rumors in between the bullshit.

The horse doctor they have in La Mesa isn't good for shit. He doesn't even use gas or Novocain when he pulls teeth, so you can imagine how he is with real medical problems. "Donna's got some doctors coming over from the States to look me over. I think I might need an operation."

"That's too bad, Val," I say, like I really care. "Hey, what's going on with that new guy who just came in? You know, Bob, the big young gringo."

"He was running drugs across the border and some kid ratted him out here in TJ. So, he killed the kid and left him with some Mexican to dispose of in a tub of acid, but the Mexican fell asleep. A couple days later, two agents kidnap Bob from the front of his house in San Diego. Oh, and get this shit, one agent was a Federale, the other FBI."

"Jesus, that's not right. Kidnapping an American from his own home. Fucking traitors."

Later, American Bob finds me at El Griego's over lunch and right away sticks out his hand. "I'm Bob. Val says we should meet."

We shake. *What a huge paw.* "Everything going okay for you?"

"Yeah. Just getting used to this place."

"It takes a while." I don't offer him a seat. I'm still sizing him up. Here's a guy who killed already and it's written all over his face.

"Maybe we can talk later, you know, after you eat? With all the Mexicans here, it's nice to hang with some Americans."

"Sure."

American Bob is the perfect name for you.

As he walks out, I think about all the killers I've known in my life. For the most part they aren't any different than anyone else, that is, on the surface. In La Mesa, a man's life, who he is, what he is, and what he's capable of doing is written on his face in bold letters. And a man never lets his face make appointments his balls can't keep. Here in La Mesa, that's absolute.

It's nearing Thanksgiving and Paco's planning a little celebration for the twenty-five Americans in La Mesa. I can only guess what his version of a turkey will be for us, most likely vulture. Business is good because the Americans' families send more money for the holidays, and that means more drug sales for me.

It's mid-afternoon, and it's been drizzling all day. A mondalero tracks me down at El Griego's. He tells me Patricio wants to see me.

Fuck! You going to push me to hit Barragone again?

When I arrive at his carraca, El Cheflon is there, and he's anxious, shifting his weight from foot to foot.

Patricio nods and me. "We have some business to discuss."

"What's up?"

"I have this bastardo, Chuy, a chicken shit punk in the corrale, who owes me dinero, for long time now. Today you collect for me."

"Okay." I glance over at El Cheflon.

Why aren't you doing this?

"You both go. And take this, Richard." He reaches into his belt, pulls out the .22 Ruger with a silencer, and hands it to me. "You get three hundred, maybe four hundred. Okay?"

You're trusting me with your gun again.

I nod. Without even looking at El Cheflon, I can tell he's pissed. I slip the .22 behind my jacket, tucked under my belt and we head out. The guard eyes us as he opens the gate to the corrale. Most everyone's inside because of the rain, so it's easy to find Chuy in his carraca. When we walk in, he knows what it's about and he's pissed, but not afraid.

That's not good.

He's bigger than most Mexicans, I'd guess five-nine and 200 pounds. Greasy black hair. Pock-marked face. He's on his bed.

"We're here to collect the four hundred you owe Patricio," El Cheflon says in Spanish.

Right away, Chuy stands up and gets into it with El Cheflon. He's talking so fast, it's hard for me to pick up everything, but I know what he's saying. "I told Patricio to leave me the fuck alone. I'll get him his fucking dinero when I'm ready."

"Today, Chuy. Now," El Cheflon states.

"Fuck you," Chuy says and pulls a knife. "And fuck Patricio."

El Cheflon's eyes light up. He wants a piece of Chuy. I reach behind my back and in one motion, whip out the .22 and smack the side of Chuy's face. He stumbles back onto his bed. El Cheflon is on him in a flash and wrestles the knife away.

"You pull a knife on me, motherfucker?" El Cheflon barks as he waves the knife in front of Chuy's face. I know he wants to cut him up bad.

"I'm not giving you shit," Chuy says. Then he looks at me and rattles off a stream of obscenities.

I can't catch it all and have to ask El Cheflon. "What the fuck did he say?"

"He say he kill you when he sees you in the yard."

"He did?" I stare at Chuy and his eyes tell me everything I need to know. "Stand back."

I raise the .22 and squeeze off one round into Chuy's forehead, another into the middle of his chest. Two little buzzes. Two shells clink on the dirty concrete floor. Chuy slumps back into the wall.

"Stupido," I yell. "You're supposed to say shit like this AFTER you kill someone."

El Cheflon looks to me. I can feel his respect. As I stoop to pick up the two brass shells, I say, "Let's toss this place and take what we can."

It takes only a few minutes to find the money, just over two hundred and some drugs. As we're about to walk out, I glance over at Chuy. His mouth hangs open, like he wants to say something.

"You got something else to say, motherfucker?" He doesn't move. "I thought not."

We step out just as the rain's letting up and move away from Chuy's carraca. Getting into the corrale is one thing, getting out is another. The guard will be sure to search us. As El Cheflon and I stand in a doorway to try to figure out our next move, two voices yell nearby. They emerge from a carraca and continue going at it, something about a Seconal pill. I know these guys. Alvaro and Camao.

It's heating up to the point where they're shoving each other and swearing. Nothing like a good fight to give everyone something to do on a rainy day in La Mesa. When Alvaro reaches under his shirt and pulls out a knife, Camao takes one out of his coat. They begin to circle each other about five feet apart. The whole place erupts with prisoners cheering them on. I like watching knife fights. So does the guard at the gate as he runs over to watch.

That's when El Cheflon and I stroll out of the corrale. Outside the gate, we to turn to watch the fight. Each man holds a hand over their heart to deflect a fatal strike coming at them, the other hand low, swinging its blade, looking for an opening. They both take a few swings but no hits yet. Then Camao slashes a cut into Alvaro's face. Alvaro counters by charging Camao, who loses his balance. In that split second, Camao's left hand moves and Alvaro thrusts his blade into Camao's chest. Camao steps back and looks down at the blood pumping out of the hole.

I'm waiting for him to drop dead, but instead he gathers himself and lunges at Alvaro. When he does, Alvaro tries another thrust at Camao's heart. This time Camao uses his left hand to push Alvaro's blade out of the way, then rams his knife deep into Alvaro's chest and Alvaro collapses, dead. Camao slumps down to the ground and mutters something about "mi madre" then falls on top of Alvaro.

We turn and walk away, El Cheflon heading back to Patricio's. As I cross the field to El Griego's, I stop to look back. I'd never seen two men kill each other at the same time. I remember when I was eight, Daddy Roy telling me about the coliseum in Rome and the gladiator fights. I thought then how I could never watch people kill each other. I look up at the gray sky.

Daddy Roy, I'm in La Mesa now. There's death all around.

As I'm finishing a burger, American Bob plops down. "Rick, what happened in the corrale?"

I tell him about the knife fight. "What brings you here?"

"You seem connected."

I grin.

"So, Rick, how can I get my hands on a gun?"

I study him. "What for?"

"I got a job."

No, there's something else going on. Who you wanna hit? But that's a question I can't ask.

"Doing what?"

"Working for Johnny Camacho dealing."

You don't need a gun for that.

"Really?"

He leans in. "Yeah, and he also wants me to do a hit."

"Guns are hard to get and cost a lot. How much you wanna spend?

"Whatever it takes." He slides me something in a small piece of aluminum.

"What's this?"

"A little down payment. A little blue cheer. Thought you might want to trip."

I take the last bite of my burger and stand. "Okay. Gimme a couple days. I'll see what I can do."

"Thanks." He shakes my hand but something's not right. Something in his eyes tells me there's more going on here, at lot more.

On my way over to Patricio's, Angelo stops me. "Hey, Rick, I've been looking for you."

This Italian from Boston is someone I've learned to trust. "What's up?"

"You know those two dudes who arrived a week ago?" I nod. "Well, they've been hanging out at Val's a lot." He looks around, no one can hear what he's about to tell me. "I overheard Val talking to them and American Bob about taking you out. And after that, going after Patricio."

That's why Bob wants a gun.

"What the fuck's wrong with Val?"

"He's getting all paranoid and talking crazy shit."

"Thanks for the tip, Angelo. I owe you. I gotta go."

I head to Patricio's. As usual, he's got a little party going on, this time just family. When they hear I witnessed the knife fight, sixteen-year-old Trumpas, Patricio's killer nephew, wants a detailed retelling. He can't seem to get enough. Between my Mexican slang, and acting out the fight, he revels in every detail.

Afterward, I pull Patricio aside, hand him back the pistol, and let him know, "I have to come back later to talk to you. Es muy importante."

His eyes glisten like a proud papa whose son, his gringo pistolero, faithfully does his bidding.

I killed for you.

10

Clean Kill

Before I head over to Patricio's, I pop American Bob's blue cheer LSD. I'd done acid a few times before and knew it takes a while to kick in. At Patricio's, after I have a big hit of coke, I lean into him. "Listen, Patricio. I must tell you something."

"What is it, Richard?"

"Well, you know the blanco called American Bob?"

"Sí. What about him?"

"He came to me today and he told me he just got a job working for the Cuban, Johnny Camacho. And he needs a gun."

Patricio's eyes narrow. "Who is this gringo Bob? You know him?"

"Sí, patrón. We've spoken a few times."

"That is good, Richard. Mañana I want for you to sit with this gringo after la lista and talk to him."

"About what?"

"Whatever gringos like to talk about. Maybe you speak to him about getting some gringa chicas, no?"

"Okay." I say I have to leave because the acid is coming on and I want to be in my carraca when it hits full force.

Just as I close the door to my pad, the stuff slams my brain like a freight train. All I can do is lay on my bed and put a radio to my ear to listen to some music, any music, even some scratchy AM rock and roll coming out of San Diego.

After a while, and I have no idea how much later, I roll over and puke up everything and wish I'd never heard of anything called LSD. I think my cellmates come in and out of the room. One of them gets pissed because of all my puke. I don't remember much.

Gradually my mind stabilizes, and I've got an urgent need to read. I grab *Justine* and *Juliette*, two books written by the Marquis de Sade. I'm a slow reader. But jacked up on LSD, I'm able to finish both books as morning light cracks through my door. I look at my watch and stumble out into the yard for the 7:30 daily la lista. My brain hurts. Bad.

"Good morning, Rick," Pete says.

I groan.

"You look like shit, man. You take a bad trip?"

I wave him off, too painful to talk. That's when, through the thick fog in my brain, the night's discussion floods back. Patricio said something about sitting down and talking to American Bob after the count. Bob walks toward me from the baseball field.

"Hey, Rick, how you feel this morning?"

"Like shit, Bob. You ought to know. That acid was bad, man. I don't know what was in it, but it fucked me up real good."

"Hey, you never know about acid. It's different every time. Listen, I know I just asked you last night, but have you been able to get a line on a gun for me yet?"

You want to kill me now?

"No."

We pay our fifty cents to get out of work detail for the day, then move to this little grassy spot near the hole. Paul Highs wanders over and joins us, lighting up a joint. We squat in a small circle and after only a few hits, my head clears, but everything remains in slow motion. As I pass the joint to Bob, I catch a glimpse of Chepe coming our way, the sixteen-year-old cousin of El Cheflon. He's always bad news. I know he killed his math teacher and a cop in Mexicali.

I don't think anything of it when he steps in between me and Bob, bends down slightly like he whispers something to Bob and keeps going. I look over at Bob and he's fallen on his back. Paul and I laugh thinking he's so high, he fell over.

Bob's voice wheezes, "That guy hit me."

"What do you mean, man?" I ask.

Bob's wearing a white tee shirt and a US Army green field jacket. He grabs the lapels and pulls open the front of his jacket. There's blood spreading all over his white tee shirt, pumping out from a hole in his chest. I grab my handkerchief and stick it in the hole.

"Don't bother, Rick. I'm going to die."

"That's bullshit, man. You're gonna make it." I know he'll be dead in less than a minute, but I want to give him a last hope. I look across the yard at Chepe who's watching. He nods at me.

I wave for a guard to come over. He calls for the horse doctor who rolls Bob over. Chepe's blade went all the way through Bob's back, even his jacket. Clean. Nothing could have stopped him from dying. Two guards lug Bob's dead body over to the infirmary.

Paul's mouth is still open when asks, "What—what just happened?"

"This is how it is here in La Mesa. Bob was an animal in this jungle. He fell prey to our food chain. Gazelle eats grass, hyena eats gazelle, lion eats hyena—and nothing eats the lion. Now, unless you want to be the lion's next meal, you tell the policia you saw nothing. Understand?"

Paul eyes widen. He gets it.

Later in the day, I head over to Lupe's where I run into Angelo. Walking in, the spices hit my nose and I realize I haven't eaten all day. I order a double taco plate and two hot bowls of bean and onion soup.

"What happened this morning, Rick?" Angelo asks.

"What happened? Bob's dead. What the fuck do you think happened, Angelo? Listen, I don't want to get into this. I'm not anxious to speak about shit that doesn't concern me, and neither should you. Murder's like a virus—you open your mouth to talk about it, you breathe it in, and bingo, you die."

"I get the point. Subject changed. So, what else is new?"

I push my bowls of soup away and shake my head. "This place is finally getting on my fucking nerves."

"Finally?" He laughs.

"I'm going to call my fucking lawyer and find out exactly when the fuck he's going to get me the hell out of here."

"I could use that too."

11

Going Home

With the holidays coming, everyone's getting in a better mood. Sunday visits with families are turning into real parties, but no one comes to see me. I get an early Christmas present, when right after Thanksgiving, Val goes to the hospital. He's only thirty-nine, and in the six months I've known him, I've watched his health fall apart in front of my eyes.

My second early Christmas gift comes in the form of a collaboration between the Mexican and US governments. A new agreement was signed which allows for the extradition of prisoners, and Carlos Cohen is the first to leave La Mesa. From the Devil's Table to the New York State prison system. Just like I told Patricio, the American government never stops, especially when someone killed an NYPD cop in cold blood.

Things become simpler in La Mesa with Val out of the picture and Carlos gone for good. I relax a little. I make a call to Ricardo Herrera and meet with him a week before Christmas. He says he thought something good might break for me in the new year.

Sure, like I've heard that shit from you before.

My first Christmas in La Mesa. A few presents get sent from my family. Some underwear, socks, boots, and a new jacket. But as usual, nothing from my mother. I don't expect anything, but I always hope.

Morty flies out to be with me New Year's eve. He repeats the same bullshit Ricardo Herrera told me about getting out of here soon. We have a good day together and make each other laugh, something I missed more than I expected. As he's leaving to catch a red-eye back to New York, he gets a serious look on his face.

"Hey, kid. If it were me, I'd want to know this." He pauses and shakes his head slowly, like he's working to shit out a constipated load of words. "I'm sorrry, Michael. I'm just going to tell you."

"Go on."

"Sheila, she met someone."

"Who?"

"Some cop."

"I told her to forget about me. But a fucking cop, Morty?"

"Yeah." He hangs his head.

There's something you're not telling me.

"What else?"

"He's Puerto Rican."

After he leaves, all I want to do is go up to Patricio's and lose myself in a bowl of coke, forget all about Sheila and some spic cop who's fucking her and playing father to my kids. I need to put the months here out of my mind—the knife fights, LSD, pushing dope, having to make a hit on Barragone, Val's shit. All of it.

Patricio's party is a big one. I grab some redheaded hooker and fuck out my anger against Sheila and my mother all night long. No matter what I do, I can't shake the image of Sheila being with another man.

I get up late and feel like a wreck, my head throbbing from a huge hangover and the memory of Morty's words— *Sheila met someone.* There's a singularity of purpose running through my mind.

I've got to get the fuck out of here and get Sheila back.

A mondalero asks me to come to Patricio's when I'm ready. I'm ready.

He comes toward me wearing a red silk robe with matching slippers. "Happy New Year, Richard." He takes hold of my forearms.

"Same to you, mi patrón."

"I have made a new promise, you call this the ree-so-lu-tion, no?"

"Yes. What is it?"

"The doctors say too much coca no good for me. I take a break. And you, any promise to the new year?"

"I plan to get out of here."

Patricio laughs. "So does everyone, Richard. Something else?"

"Get my wife back."

"Sí. She is muy bonita. But you can have any woman." He waves an arm out toward the horizon.

That's not an answer.

"Now, Richard, I have something for you. I wanted to give you en la noche, but you were busy. Venga."

I follow him into his bedroom, and he brings out a large wooden box with highly-polished silver inlays. He puts it on his coffee table and opens the lid. Inside the red velvet-lined box is a collection of pistols, the centerpiece, a beautiful nickel-plated Colt .45 model 1911 with an ivory-carved grip.

He picks up the .25 Star automatic beneath it, and with great ceremony, hands it to me. "Now I give this to you, Richard. You keep it for your protection. You must keep it safe. I do not want it found by the policia. I can depend on you?"

It's not the type of weapon I'd carried with me on the streets of Brooklyn, but who cares, this isn't the streets. "Gracias, mi patrón. Sí, you can depend upon me. Do not worry."

Patricio hands me a box of ammo. "Take bullets for the gun. This is more than you will need."

I heft the pistol in my left hand, my shooting hand. It feels so right.

I'll get out of here this year or die trying.

Rumor has it that Val's scheduled to come back in four weeks. With American Bob dead and Carlos Cohen in prison in New York, it's up to the two dirtbags from San Diego to provide Val protection. They go by the unoriginal names of Smith and Jones, and they plan to smuggle a gun into La Mesa. As it turns out, a very bad plan. Smith's wife bakes a huge birthday cake and puts a gun and ammo inside it. They know the guards are sloppy when it comes to checking food brought in, especially by a woman. But Smith's wife brags about it to her neighbor. The neighbor calls the FBI. They contact the Mexican police. They're waiting.

Smith and Jones are thrown in las tombas and from there, sent to Isla de Maria.

I watch the news on January 20, Richard Nixon's inauguration. I think back about President Kennedy, how I shook his hand, and now he's gone. Then there was his little brother, Bobby, who was killed last June. Then there were all the killings in La Mesa, even the ones I did. They haul their bodies outta here like dirty laundry. Who knows where they end up? There's a finality to life that hits me hard.

I've got to find some way to get the fuck out of here.

Val hobbles back La Mesa in early February and looks weaker than before. He's feeble in other areas too. Most of his followers have disappeared or been swallowed up by the small-time drug dealers. He won't be financing any tunnels or planning any other escapes.

I'm doing my best to stay out of shit, just counting time, working the system, selling drugs to the Americans, and pulling off a few scams here and there. With Patricio staying off the coca, his parties have tapered off, and all the craziness they used to whip up. There's an order to life in La Mesa. I'm keeping the twenty-five Americans in line and Patricio's doing much the same with the 800 Mexicans. Killings are down and that's good for everyone.

On Friday, April 11, I'm called to Paco's office. I sense something's not quite right when I walk in, Paco fidgeting behind his desk, his eyes uncertain, not even a cigar in his mouth.

What the fuck?

He pushes his phone toward me. "You talk now to Ricardo Herrera, you lawyer."

I pick up the receiver and dial. "What's this about?"

He just motions to me with his hand to make my call, like he's shooing a fly. A thousand possibilities swirl in my head, but the one I want, I can't think about.

Ricardo answers. "This is Richard. Richard Mandell. Comandante Paco said I should call you."

"Yes, Richard. I have good news. You are to be released Monday."

I look to Paco for his reaction but speak into the phone. "You mean I'm getting out of here?"

"Yes."

"Wha—what do I gotta do?"

"Nothing. It has been arranged. Your family put up the twenty-five hundred for bail. I will be there on Monday after siesta to finalize everything. Have a good weekend."

"Yeah, you too."

I stare at the phone and realize Monday will mark exactly one year since I was arrested at Caliente Racetrack.

Paco clears his throat and I look to him. "So, Richard. You leave me. Too bad. There is more dinero for us to make together."

I smile. "I'll miss you too, Comandante."

On my way over to Patricio's, I work to control myself.

Hope is the most dangerous drug in here. Until you walk out that gate, keep your head straight, Mike.

Patricio greets me with a huge grin in his usual red silk robe and matching slippers. "Ah, Richard. I no need ask como estas?" He laughs.

I'm no longer surprised by what he knows. "Oh yeah. I'm doing good alright."

"When you out, we keep in touch, yes? Maybe we do some business."

"Sure. Sure."

He gives me a hug. Because I don't know how to embrace a gay man, I stiffen and pat him on the back. Patricio pulls away to look at me. "You will always be my best gringo pistolero."

"You mean your *only* gringo pistolero."

We share a laugh reserved for old friends.

"I must ask you, Patricio. What about the business you asked me to do about Miguel Barragone? I never took care of that."

"No problema, Richard. He hear about the contract and become a good dog."

Jesus, you had me worry about this shit all this time?

The next three nights, I have trouble sleeping. Nothing seems real. I prepared myself to do the full twelve years. Now, I've got a life full of maybes in front of me.

Maybe I can get Sheila back. Maybe I can be the father I should have had. Maybe I can get a real job, go straight—for real this time.

Nothing but days and nights full of maybes.

During the weekend, I clean up a few loose ends and sell Angelo my bed in the carraca and TV. As I'm packing up my clothes Monday morning, I tell him, "Maybe you should consider changing lawyers. Mine doesn't say much, but he got me out of here."

He bobs his head. "Yeah, maybe I should."

I look around my carraca one last time. A sturdy bed with no bugs. My seventeen-inch color TV. A few books on a small beaten-up wooden table. Shag carpet, probably green at one time, but so dirty and worn it almost looks the same gray color as the concrete it rests on.

I turn to Gonzo, my junkie houseboy. He stands by the doorway, lost, the shakes hitting him. I hand him a dollar. "I spoke to Angelo. You work for him now."

He gives me a weak, "Gracias," then he's gone for a fix.

One more late lunch of a burger and Coke at El Griego's, this time by myself. At four o'clock, I wander over to Paco's office with a full duffel bag and a lump in my throat. Ricardo Herrera's there. I hand him my Marquis de Sade books and give him a nod. Paco signals one guard to go through my bags while another one pats me down, even having me take off my boots. Patricio told me they'd put me through this drill, so I'm prepared. Out of the corner of my eyes I spot my lawyer take my gun out of the book and slip it in his pocket.

When the guard finishes, he turns to Ricardo and motions with his hands. "Los libros, tambien."

Ricardo hesitates, then gives them up. Paco's eyeing everything carefully, his shark teeth chewing on a fat unlit cigar. The guard opens *Juliette* and his forehead wrinkles. He fans the book and it has a huge section cut out in the shape of a gun, a .25 Star to be exact. He asks Ricardo, "What happened to this book?"

Ricardo shrugs and looks to me.

"Oh, I already read those parts," I answer.

Paco stifles a laugh, but the guards are still confused. He barks at them, "Enough now. Go."

It's just Ricardo, Paco, and me. There's an excited tension in the air. It tastes like hope, and I swallow hard.

Paco clears his throat. "I will miss you, Richard." His eyes moisten.

Yeah, you'll miss the money I made you.

"It's been, how should I say, an experience of a lifetime, Comandante."

Ricardo interrupts. "Your ride is waiting outside." He hands me my gun.

"I will." I shake Ricardo's hand, grab my books, pick up my bags, and head out the door.

I stand in the sally port, waiting for the gate to open. I look to my left and recall the first time I walked through this gate, the prisoners' fingers poking through the thick chain link, their weak voices begging for dimes.

I know what a fucking dime buys now.

An unmotivated and skinny guard shuffles as he swings the gate open. I step outside the walls of La Mesa del Diablo into the free world. I stare ahead and stop. A late model blue Ford Fairlane idles in the driveway. The driver's door opens and my mother steps out. Her bright red hair is as perfect as always, and she wears a new green suit. I move to the car and toss my bags in the back seat. Then I go to her and kiss her on the cheek. "Hello, Mother."

"Michael," she says and nods. I don't expect anything else, but I'm hoping.

It hits me how fine a line it is, the difference between being inside or outside of those fifteen-foot-high walls. I look around one last time and let out a deep breath. "Let's get the fuck out of here."

We follow our lawyer's advice and wait at his friend's place to make sure there's no news of my leaving, then drive across the border at eight o'clock to catch a red-eye to New York. I try to keep my legs from shaking as we enter Lindberg Field, my burger from lunch teasing indigestion. I glance around, waiting for someone to cuff me. I can't wait to get on the plane.

Mother sits in first class while I'm in economy with a few empty seats next to me. I doze for most of the flight, then wake when we touch down at JFK early the next morning, Tuesday, April 15, 1969. I go through the same thing here, expecting someone to bust me. Richard Mandell may be out of La Mesa, but Michael J. Hardy's got plenty of people wanting him.

Morty's waiting by the curb for us in his cab. When we finally hit the highway, I breathe. We pass familiar dirty cars and cracked sidewalks, fresh graffiti on walls and overpasses. Then there's the noise and the smells of a well-worn city. Home.

But what's waiting for me?

Texas wants me for questioning about my father's involvement in millionaire Ruth Holland's murder. *I don't know him or any shit about that.* The Treasury Department still wants to talk to me about counterfeiting. *That was my mother's money.* Their agents and the FBI, who want me for interstate flight to avoid prosecution, were at La Mesa to grab me, but someone misinformed them when I am getting released.

Thanks, Paco.

There's a detective in LA who needs to question me about using false identification and some other made-up charges for embarrassing him. The State of New Jersey's got a parole violation they'd like to serve. Then there's the State of New York, where I just landed. Last time I checked, they don't like felons faking a mental illness and escaping from a state mental hospital when they have ten-plus years of jail time coming at them.

Morty's in a good mood and genuinely happy to see me. He and I do all the talking on the way back, lots of catching up about the neighborhood, my mother sitting in the back, saying nothing.

When we arrive at my mother's home, my two sisters are waiting for me in the entry, hopping around like excited schoolgirls, which they are. Out of the corner of my eye, I catch my mother watching them greet me. They hug me. There's laughter. Mother walks out of the room.

Yeah, welcome home, Michael.

La Mesa del Diablo Postscript
    The people I met in La Mesa del Diablo still visit my mind from time to time. My year there was by far the most exciting and the most dangerous of my life. Always on the edge, testing every aspect of the human condition, victim or prey, fight or flight, love or hate, greed, lust, or fear. Always life or death.
    I kept in touch with Patricio Baccera Ortiz after I left La Mesa and got caught up on much of what happened to the cast of characters I met there. And off and on from 1969-1971, I did runs into Mexico to pull jobs for Patricio. My involvement with my El Patrón and subsequent trips into Mexico ended abruptly following the hijacking of a large shipment of pot and the killing of the driver along the Ensenada highway. But that's a story to be told later.

This is what happened to some of the inmates I ran with at La Mesa del Diablo.
    Angelo D'Renzo contacted my lawyer and got released later in 1969, returning to Boston.
    Petey Day returned to the Bronx after his release six months later in 1969.
    The aptly named **Paul Highs** got out of La Mesa in 1970 and I'd guess spent the rest of his life getting high.
    Val Caldwell died in 1975 in La Mesa while planning the last one of his endless escapes, not that he would have been able to even walk out, his feet so crippled from sports and diabetes.
    Miguel Barragone was never hit by Patricio and eventually regained his freedom and retired to his hacienda, alive, free, and very rich.

A year after I left, **El Cheflon** made a move on Pedro Moreno, a pistolero for another drug lord. El Cheflon had words with Pedro in the yard and insults were exchanged. At that point, El Cheflon emptied a .25 into Pedro Mareno who threatened him with a knife at the time. With eight well-placed slugs in his body, Pedro lived only a few seconds longer, but long enough to stab El Cheflon so bad it put that psycho killer in the hospital for six months.

When El Cheflon came out of the hospital, he and his cousin Chepe tried to hold up a poker game that was run in tanky-A by Wado Secado, a bank robber. Wado didn't play that day, he just ran the game and took his cut. El Cheflon and Chepe came into the tank at two in the afternoon, drawing their guns, and demanding money from everyone at the table. Wado stepped out of his carraca above them along with four pistoleros and a gunfight erupted. When the smoke cleared, four men were dead, El Cheflon and Chepe among them.

El Cheflon was twenty-one years old and had killed at least that many men in his very short and violent life. Even to this day, he is considered by many in Mexico to be their version of Billy the Kid. The local populace near the border sing songs about him and his name has appeared in books and movies. Like Billy the Kid, he is a lot more famous now than he was when he was alive, but El Cheflon was a lot more dangerous.

My attorney **Ricardo Herrera** ran for political office against the established opposition. He got his car machine-gunned and had to leave the country for a while. He was later made the chief of the Baja California Police.

It is not by accident that I keep this part of my story of La Mesa until the very end. To say that **Patricio Baccera Ortiz** was an amazing man would be a massive understatement. His lifestyle in many respects was completely alien to me. He saved my life and for that I am indebted. But a life pays for a life, and as far as I'm concerned, my debt was paid in full three times over.

Out in the yard in La Mesa in 1972, Patricio got rough with some new kid, holding him by the shirt and slapping him. I can imagine what he wanted. The kid was probably cute, and Patricio was interested in having another boyfriend. In a flash, the kid reached over and grabbed Patricio's Colt .45 from his belt and fired two shots into his chest. A minute later Patricio was no longer alive.

He was the last of his kind to be sure, one of the most powerful trafficantes in northwestern Mexico at that time. A truly dangerous man. Maybe he wasn't the Al Capone of Mexico, but he was more gangster than Tijuana or La Mesa del Diablo ever saw.

12

Jimmy Asks

It's April 1991 and I'm in LA County Jail. Jimmy Blatt, my lawyer, shuts off the tape recorder, flips a page of his yellow legal pad and leans back, his perfectly manicured hands intertwined behind his neck. He studies me, almost to the point of making me uncomfortable.

"Let me see if I got this right. We're at the point in your life's story where you're a month shy of your twenty-fifth birthday, right?"

"Yeah. May twenty-four, nineteen-sixty-nine, I turned twenty-five."

"And you're forty-six now."

I nod. "Yeah. I know what you're gonna ask."

His eyebrows raise. "And, what's that?"

"What'd I do the last twenty-one years of my life, right?"

Jimmy picks up his pen and it hovers over his yellow pad. "And?"

"Well, I started out by trying to go straight and get back with my wife and kids. But some other *opportunities* came my way."

"Like what?"

"You know some of them from my arrest and prison records."

He leans in. "Tell me a few where you didn't get arrested."

I can't help but smile. "How much time you got, Jimmy?"

"How many more tapes am I going to need, Michael?" He chuckles.

"Hey, Jimmy, we haven't talked much about my case lately. Anything going on I should know about?"

"Nothing's changed. And that's good. They're trying to build their case, and they're having some trouble."

"How do you know?"

"Remember, I used to work in the DA's office. I still know people over there."

"So, you *do* have some connections."

Jimmy shakes his head. "Not the kind you want. By the way, who are some of the people you've rubbed elbows with? You know, names I'd recognize?"

My mind whirls through the decades. "First off, I guess is Bugsy Siegel. He was my godfather. And through my mother I met Meyer Lansky, Joey Adonis, and some of the guys they did business with. Then there were the Gottis, Gene, Ritchie, and John. I already told you how they shot me twice in twenty-four hours. And their boss, Sonny Franzese. I had Sammy the Bull Gravano work in my crew for three years. And I met lots of other made men on the inside, you know, in prison."

I take a sip of water and continue. "Notable? Well, there was John *the wad* Holmes, the porno star, and Doc Holliday right here in LA County. And Angelo Buono, you know, the Hillside Strangler. I nearly choked him to death."

Jimmy sits up and shakes his head.

"I shared a cell with E. Howard Hunt. He was by far the coldest motherfucker I ever knew. Solid ice. I also got to know some judges, law enforcement officers, and others in your line of work pretty well, like Rudy Giuliani."

Jimmy tilts his head. "Who?"

"Rudy Giuliani, the guy who cleaned up crime in the city. I cut a deal with him to reduce my prison time when I gave him a dirty cop and even dirtier US Marshals."

"I'd really like to get into that in more detail later."

I give him a weak smile. "I got nowhere else to go."

Jimmy gathers his papers and stands. "Let's pick up on this next week. Wednesday work for you, same time?"

I'm escorted back to my cell, finish off a dinner of meatloaf, mashed potatoes, and something green that's over-boiled and odorless. There's nothing good on TV, so I just lie on my bed, my head swirling with memories from the last twenty-one years. The cons and kidnappings, the hundreds of robberies, the airline ticket scam, dozens of bank jobs, the car theft ring, my ten years in Hollywood and the stars I partied with, the gunfight where I took six bullets and died, and the birth of my daughter Deborah.

Deborah. I named you after my sister who left us too soon. You're only twelve and I have so much hope for you. Learn from me. Make better choices than your daddy.

Maybe I'll even get out of here and have the chance to be the father you and your older brother and sister deserve.

Maybe...

13

Back in Brooklyn

It's late Friday morning, May 9, 1969, less than a month since I got out of La Mesa del Diablo prison in Mexico and two weeks before my twenty-fifth birthday. My mother still hasn't said anything to me about doing her time. Not a thank you. Nothing. I never expected her to, but I hoped. And I'm never gonna to ask.

I got nothing going on. No action. Nothing. I sleep on the couch in my mother's apartment on 4th Avenue and 14th Street and watch TV. It's a real nice place. Too nice. I don't get how she can afford the $1,000-a-month rent. She works at Macy's as a salesclerk and her new husband, Rojullio Gutierrez, the Mexican federal agent who lit her cigarette in La Mesa a year ago, he's washing dishes at a Hojo nearby.

That's all you're good for.

I tried reaching out to my wife, Sheila, but she doesn't want to see me or let me visit my kids. Besides, she's dating a fucking Puerto Rican cop in the 27th precinct, and he's married. That makes it a little too dangerous for me to see her. At least I've got a new identity to help me avoid the six law enforcement agencies who want a piece of my ass. My mother's connections within the police still work, so they give her place a pass.

Before Mother leaves for work, she and I get into it good. It starts when she opens the refrigerator, stomps her feet, and lets out an exaggerated sigh. I know what's coming. I crane my head over the sofa where I'm watching more crap about the Vietnam War on the morning news. I've got a pint of cottage cheese in one hand, a spoon in the other. She catches me looking in her direction.

"Michael, is that my cottage cheese?"

I shovel in the last bite and drop the spoon into the empty pink and blue Knudsen tub. I grin and garble, "It was."

She comes at me glaring, her face matching the color of her hair. "I suppose you think that's funny."

"Hey, I was hungry. I'll pick up some for you later."

"You're always hungry. And what are you going to buy cottage cheese with? You've got no money."

I did a year for you in fucking La Mesa. I'll eat all your fucking cottage cheese that I want.

She snatches the tub out of my hand. "Christ almighty, you stink." She shakes her head. "You're worthless. Why don't you at least take a shower?"

Not another word falls between us as she picks up her purse and slams the door on her way out. All I can do is wince and go back to watching TV. My stomach grumbles. Still hungry, I glance at the door.

I wondered when you'd start jumping in my shit.

It's quiet in the apartment after I turn off the TV. I wander over to the window. Out on the street, a gray drizzle works hard to wash the city clean. A hot dog vendor shuffles his feet with his back to the wind, steam pouring out his boiler. Somebody in a late model red Chevy leans on their horn, waiting for two lazy teenagers to get out of their way. Same old Brooklyn.

I catch my reflection in the window—a three-day beard and the same dirty robe. I head toward the bathroom to get cleaned up, but instead find myself going into the closet and reaching up on the top shelf. In the corner, under a pile of wool scarves and a stained gray cap, there it is. Cold. Uncaring. Good for just one thing.

It's my .25 Star, the semi-automatic Patricio gave me as a going-away present in La Mesa. The one I smuggled out in a book. I grab it along with a box of ammo, head to the living room, and plop on the couch. I load the eight-shot clip and slap it into the grip. I ratchet a bullet into the chamber and pause. One final time to reflect.

Who's gonna miss me?

No one.

Anything going on?

Nothing.

Will I get to see you, Daddy Roy?

Probably not.

I turn my piece around, place my thumb on the trigger, and hold the muzzle an inch away from my heart. I draw in a deep breath and when I expel the air, it feels like I've finally let go of all the shit that's wrong in my life. One last thought crosses my mind.

Hey, kids. I hope you make better choices in your life than your old man.

I keep my eyes open 'cause I want to see it all. I pull the trigger.

Click.

"Piece of shit," I yell. I pop out the clip, inspect it, and slam it back into the grip. This time when I ratchet a bullet into the chamber, I double-check to make sure it's there. I'm pissed. This time there's no ceremony. I turn the gun around and pull the trigger.

Click.

"What the fuck!"

Sweat gathers on my forehead while I break down the gun and inspect it.

The firing pin. The fucking firing pin. It's out of alignment. Fucking Patricio gave me a fucking gun that doesn't fucking work.

Now that I'm directing my anger at someone else, my rational thinking comes around. I look down at the pieces of my gun, then glance around my mother's apartment and nod my head.

Enough with your fucking self-pity. Now go do something.

I shave and shower, find Morty in his cab, and borrow thirty bucks from him. Five of it goes toward a big tub of *fucking* cottage cheese, and twenty-five bucks for the Edwards Employment Agency. They get me a job starting Monday at a construction company called Talludo & Webb. They're working on renovating the Hudson Army & Navy Store around the corner from my mother's apartment. I'll be busting my hump six days a week for twenty-five bucks a day, all under the table. I'm not afraid of a little hard work.

I lay low at my mother's apartment for the next few weeks, not wanting to get into it again with her.

With my first pay, I buy a '58 black Pontiac for $200. It runs, but that's about it. I'm getting on my feet a little, and it feels good. Friday, May 23, the day before my twenty-fifth birthday, Morty calls and asks me to drive over to the Westside to meet Lester Auerbach, a friend of his. I tell Morty I'm tired and just want to crash, but he insists and something in his voice tells me it'll be worth it.

I spot Morty's cab when I pull up and he hops out. He's got a huge smirk on his face. "So, what's happening, kid?"

I answer cautiously, "Nothing other than busting my ass on this job and driving all the way over here. Why'd you have me come out tonight?"

"I wanted you to meet my friend Lester. I've got a little birthday surprise for you."

"Okay. So, what is it?"

He's got this big smile on his face again, all excited. "Come with me up to Lester's and I'll show you."

We walk in to a nothing-special apartment. Lester seems nice. I glance around looking for my surprise. Nothing. Lester offers us beers. It's just after nine o'clock and we're sitting in his living room talking about this and that. Don

Rickles is insulting celebrities on TV in the background. There's a knock on the door. When Lester jumps up to answer it, I catch him and Morty nodding to each other.

What the fuck's going on?

Lester comes back into the living room with a tall, beautiful Asian girl. I'm transfixed.

Lester presents her like he's a game show host. "Michael, meet Tanya."

I jump off the couch, my mouth hanging open. I hardly notice Morty and Lester move toward the door. Morty calls to me on his way out, "Happy birthday, kid."

Tanya walks up to me and takes my hands, staring me in the eyes. Short black bangs almost touch her dark eyes set in the middle of a perfectly round face with the smoothest skin I've ever seen. Her black mini-dress and heels complete her look. I have to ask, "When do you have to go?"

"I stay until you want I go."

That ain't happening for a while.

The next day I'm over at Morty's with family to celebrate my birthday. When I enter, Morty gives me a slap on the back and asks, "Well?"

I give him a big nod. Right behind me, Aunt Florence brushes past from next door wearing oven mitts, holding a pan with a big roast and potatoes. She kisses me on the cheek on her way to the kitchen. My three sisters, my mother, and Rojullio are already there. Drinks are poured and they toast me. It's okay.

During dinner, every time Rojullio opens his mouth to say something stupid in his thick Mexican accent, I remember my time in La Mesa del Diablo, and the year I did there for my mother. There she is at the head of the table. "Queenie." Red hair all perfect, throwing her head back and laughing, strands of pearls around her neck, thick perfume.

You coulda never done the time.

They're all happy I'm working a real job and staying out of trouble. For gifts I get some clothes and a hair trimmer to keep my new Fu Manchu mustache neat. Nothing from my mother though, like the gift of life she gave is all I'll ever need, or ever get. When I take in her with my sisters and her new husband, and then Morty with his family, it hits me hard.

I gotta get something else going. And I need to get the fuck out of my mother's apartment and back with Sheila and my kids.

A week later when I'm going through the wash, I find a purple blouse belonging to my twenty-year-old sister Nancy. It's all tore up. When she gets home from work, I have to ask. It takes a while to get to the truth.

"Michael, nothing happened to me. I mean, he tried. That's how my blouse got torn. But my friend Mary, she got raped."

What the fuck?

"Just tell me where you met them."

She lowers her head. "At the bar across the street."

"What were their names and what did they look like?"

She whispers, "Ali from Canarsie, and Larry, he's the bouncer there. He's black."

My left hand twitches. "You mean you and your girlfriend were hanging out with a Black? Then he raped your friend and the other guy tried to rape you?"

She lowers her head and nods.

I go into a rage, pacing in front of the TV, looking for something to hit. "How fucking stupid can you be, Nancy? We're going to that bar right now and you're going to point them out to me, understand?"

She doesn't move.

"Now!" I yell.

While she goes to the bathroom, I grab my pistol from the closet. Even though it can't fire a bullet, putting a piece in someone's face still does something. I stuff it under my belt, and pull on my black leather car coat to cover it.

If any shit goes down, that'll end the discussion.

We're at the dive bar for half an hour and still nothing. She's been darting her eyes around like a frog watching for an alligator.

Finally, I gotta ask, "I thought you said they were regulars."

She gives me an apologetic look, glancing up from nervous eyelids.

"They were here, weren't they, Nancy?"

She lowers her head again. "A couple of minutes ago, Michael." I move toward the door, but she grabs my arm. "Michael, I didn't want to tell you because I know what you might do. Th—that you'd kill them."

You're right about that.

14

Apartment Shuffle

After Mother hears about me interfering in Nancy's life, I'm asked to move out. "Asked" is a polite way of saying she demanded it. The next day I take up residence with Morty at 5206 Snyder Avenue in the East Flatbush area. Morty bought a two-family home, he and his family on one side, Aunt Florence on the other. I grab a spot on his living room couch.

That first night, Morty comes to me after everyone's in bed. He has that "let's talk" vibe, the same one he gave me when I went back the second time to live with him in Florida when I was fifteen.

Shit, that was ten years ago.

"What's up?" I ask.

"It's uh, well, you know, kid, you staying here, that's okay for now. But it can't be permanent."

"Hey, I know that, Morty. I'll get my own pad soon. I just gotta get something going first other than this fucking construction job."

"Yeah. Well, thing is, Michael, I'm going to have to ask you for ten dollars a week rent."

I give him a "what-the-fuck?" look, but don't say a word.

"Michael, it's only fair. You know, for the food and everything else. Carol thinks it's right too."

"But what do you think, Morty?"

"Kid, I'm thirty-six years old. I've got a wife and two kids. I drive a cab. I'm getting by, but that's just about it. You know Carol. Anything that keeps my wife happy, makes my life easier. You give me ten bucks a week, my life's easier."

"Got it, Morty." I reach in my pocket and hand him two wrinkled fives. "I got a question for you. You don't have to answer if you don't want."

"What is it?"

"All those trips you made to Mexico last year when I was in prison, and the stuff you brought me. Who paid for it?"

Morty lowers his head. He knows what I'm dying to hear, but he speaks the truth, "Aunt Florence."

I gulp. "I thought so. Thanks, man."

Two weeks later, I move into a boarding house on East 21st Street, an old rooming house left over from the thirties where Murder Incorporated kept their whores. I take a brush and some paint from work, and I've got a clean, furnished studio apartment for fifty bucks a month. No TV, but that's okay.

It's July 1969, it's hot, and I'm in the best shape since I got out of the Army seven years ago. I keep my job in construction but change employers after two months. I go to work for Hunt & Goodman. A Black guy by the name of Jerry Hunt runs it with his partner, a Jew named Goodman. The whole crew is black, and right off, a few of them start grumbling about why the new opening went to some white dude. Goodman puts them straight when he hears about their beef. It's nice that being a Jew gives me a leg up.

I get back in touch with my childhood friend, Stevie Mandell. He's got lots going on, more than just his Hollywood star looks. When my piece of shit Pontiac dies, Stevie loans me a '63 powder blue Dodge Dart. That's the kind of friend he is. Aside from Morty, I've never been so close or trusted anyone more. We're like brothers.

I'm over at Stevie's a few nights later when he mentions the Berkowitz brothers are in town.

I got an instant headache. "Those fucking assholes. They owe me."

"What's that about?" Stevie asks.

"When my mother and I got busted in Mexico, she had to leave all her stuff behind in her Hollywood apartment when she headed back to Brooklyn after she got sprung. My sister Nancy didn't know any better, so when Harry and Ernie Berkowitz showed up at the apartment and offered to help, she told them it'd be okay. Problem was, after Nancy took my two younger sisters with her back to Brooklyn, they took everything and sold it, not giving my mother a penny."

Stevie grins. "So, Michael, what you wanna do?"

"I want them to feel some payback."

It doesn't take long to set up. Seems the two brothers are dying to unload some weed and I'm going to be their connection. It's the middle of the day when I pick up Ernie. He's gained a few pounds and got a rug since I last saw him.

It's best to cut a deal in a car than a public place. We ride around for a while doing some catching up shit. I'm not showing how pissed I am about what he and his brother did to my mother. The whole time I've got my piece under my ass, just aching for a chance to shove it in his face. When I pull over few blocks from his place, the real talk begins.

"So, Michael, you think you can get me a grand for these two kilos?" He smiles through crooked lower teeth.

"I know I can. But how good's the stuff?"

"Here," Ernie answers, handing me a brick.

I sniff it and wrinkle my nose like I'm not liking the odor.

"For you, Michael, since I know your mother and all, I'll cut you a deal. I'll take eight hundred for the two kilos." He winks.

You fucking wink as me and have the balls to mention my fucking mother?

"Where'd you say it's from?"

"Somewhere in Asia. What difference does it make?"

"Can I see the other brick?"

He hands it to me. I heft them in my right hand, then reach under my ass and pull out my piece. "I'm taking these, motherfucker."

He plasters himself against the door, his eyes all bugged out. "You don't want to do that, Michael. The people I got this weed from will come after you."

I crack him on his forehead with side of my piece. Not enough to make him bleed, but he'll have a lump for a week. "Get the fuck out of my car."

He grabs his head and stares at me in shock.

This is the last thing you thought I'd do, right motherfucker?

I whack his head in the same place and catch a few of his knuckles. He yelps. "You didn't have to do that."

"After how you and your brother ripped off my family, just be glad I don't kill you. Now, get the fuck out!"

Ernie exits the car. He cautiously juts his head in the window, his hand still on his head. "You'll be sorry."

I pull away from the curb and watch him in my rearview mirror as he stumbles in the middle of the street, still holding his head. I catch my smile in the mirror.

I take the two bricks over to Stevie's. He weighs them in at four-point-four pounds, a perfect pair. With a kitchen knife, I slice off a pound, and hand it to him. "Here's your cut."

Stevie shakes his head. "No, Michael. I got enough going on. Use this shit to get back on your feet, okay?"

"Well, if you won't take any, how 'bout rolling us a joint?"

Stevie makes one like a king-size cigarette and hands it to me. "Here you go, Michael.

I inspect it. It's filled with this green leafy shit that looks like home-grown pot. I plop on his couch, light up, and take a long hit. Then take another. When I let it out, I can't get up, like my body's made of lead. My head spins.

"Stevie, what the fuck is this shit, some kinda poison?"

He slaps me on the shoulder. "Hell no, it's Vietnamese grass, straight from the Mekong Delta."

I grin. "Well, I'm going to get at least a dime a bag for this shit, maybe more."

The Berkowitz brothers end up crying to their connection that I ripped them off. I tell their connection I have a Colombo family member who'll contact them and tell them to back the fuck off. I spend $300 to buy a gray '61 Pontiac with some of the profits and it's all profit.

I spend the night at Stevie's. In the morning, his older brother Eddie shows up. We call him Eddie la Phone because he's always on the phone. We're doing lots of memory lane shit when I tell him I'm hunting for some new action, something other than construction. Eddie glances at Stevie and grins.

"Michael," Stevie says, "it's time for you to get the hell out of that apartment you're in. I know a room for rent on Kings Highway. I'll speak to a friend of mine and get it for you for the time being. I've got so many things going on, and I need you near me, man."

"Sounds good to me, brother."

Eddie chimes in, "By the way, Hy Zeltzer's looking for you. Says he's got a trunk that belongs to you."

"Jesus, I forgot about that. Thanks."

Stevie asks, "What's in the trunk?"

"My armory." I chuckle. "I left it with him before I split for California a year-and-a-half ago. I've got my Thompson, an M-2, my .45 Colt, a couple other pistols, and loads of ammo."

"Sounds like you're ready to go to war." Ernie smiles.

"Yeah." I open my coat and tap the .25 Star in my belt, the same piece of non-firing shit I've carried for the past three months. "I'll see Hy tomorrow."

Stevie says, "Hey, you know Duke's home?"

"Yeah. He hasn't looked me up yet. He pissed off at me or something?"

"Nah, he knows you were away too, so he doesn't think you were laying on some beach while he was doing hard time in Sing Sing. You bugging out in court was genius. I bet he wished he would have thought of it."

We all laugh.

I add, "One thing for sure, his Italian princess wife made it clear she doesn't think much of my ass."

Stevie says, "Yeah, she doesn't like anyone who takes him out of the house. And I think she blames you for the death of Yella, her father. You caused him too much aggravation when you and Duke got pinched for robbing those drug dealers."

"Well, I felt bad about that, but I ain't making no fucking apologies. I'm an outlaw. When Duke came with me to do those stick ups, that's what he became. As far as I'm concerned, I already got too much guilt. I can't carry shit for someone else."

"Don't worry about it, Michael. Duke'll come around. I'm real tight with his wife's uncle, Larry Martieri, and she listens to him. He even wants to finance some of my business projects."

"Yeah? Like what?"

"He's got all these connections in the music world. That, I know for sure. We're going to open up a record store on Kings Highway, between 16th and 17th Streets. I checked out this store front yesterday. It's right near Charles Men's Clothes and the Kings Highway Bar. That's why I want you near me on Kings Highway, close to things. I also got this deal I came into with this guy that's in the know, named

Frank Abreano. They call him Frankie Hartz. He does cars. Cadillacs."

"Stevie, you remember I got busted for driving a hot car back in the 60s, don't you?"

Stevie nods.

"Well, we stole so many, Chevy and Buick changed the locks and ignition systems. What makes this guy's cars so good?"

"First off, he changes all the dashboard VIN plates, and he's got connections with the DMV in Albany. Once he puts these puppies on record, with new registrations and plates, they're as solid as they can be."

"Sounds bulletproof, man. Maybe I can get in on some of that action too."

Stevie grins and nods.

The next morning, I drive over to Hy's and lug my suitcase full of guns out to my car. After I drop it in the back seat, I open it. It all comes back to me. The bank robberies, the drug rip-offs, the gun fights, the kick of a gun when you pull the trigger, the explosion that makes everyone scream or fall to the floor. The sound a bullet makes zipping through the air and hitting its target. The tart sting of burnt gunpowder and oil in my eyes and nose.

Then there's the fear when I shove a piece in their face. It's all in here waiting for me.

I'm back in the action. Just like I want. Just like I need. Maybe I can get enough going to get Sheila and my kids back. Just maybe.

15

Back in It and Death

It's late September 1969, and it's getting ugly cold early in the morning. It's Brooklyn cold. I'm working on a building on the Upper East Side. It's six stories of turn-of-the-century decayed plaster and brick. Renovation. It's nothing more than taking an old turd and polishing it at three dollars and twelve cents an hour.

After a mid-morning coffee and bagel, I step out onto a second-story scaffold, and the whole thing collapses. I crash through the mess of wood and metal poles landing flat on my back. It knocks the wind out of me. I'm in good shape and know nothing's wrong, but it knocks the wind out of me. While I catch my breath, it's got me thinking.

There might be something here for me.

Everyone stops what they're doing and comes running over to see what happened. I get up slowly and collapse, grabbing my back, and moaning. I go on about seeing double and the foreman's having a coronary. I ask if I can call my doctor and I get helped to a pay phone over on the corner. I call Morty. He puts me in touch with Dr. Mo Renner, an old family friend. He says I shouldn't move and that he's sending an ambulance.

Ten minutes later, I'm on my way to a saint-something hospital nearby. They do all these X-rays, then put me in a private room. It's clean and nice. So, I decide to take some time off to watch TV and catch up on some sleep. When I wake up later that afternoon, there's a priest and two nuns standing at the foot of my bed all serious and praying. "What the fuck are you doing?" I ask.

The priest mumbles, "We're here to give you your last rites, my son."

"Last rites? Jesus, have you got the wrong room."

The priest wrinkles his brow.

I reach under my collar and pull out my Star of David, dangling it in front of his eyes. "I'm not one of yours."

The next morning, Dr. Renner comes by to check on me. "How you doing, Michael?"

I look around to make sure no one's listening. "Just like you said, I'm doing fine but not letting anyone know."

"Good. Now I'm going to recommend a specialist come see you, a Korean doctor." He winks.

"Sure. Whatever you say, Doc." Dr. Renner's an up-front kinda guy, been working for the *family* for years, and knows how to run the system. Morty's connection is solid.

So, this Korean in a white jacket comes in later in the day and does some karate chops on my legs and ribs, asks if it hurts. I roll over slowly and he feels my back. Since Dr. Renner told me what to do and say, my answers keep me in the hospital another four days, enough time for workman's comp to kick in.

I got my rent paid through the winter and I don't have to polish any more turds. That frees me up to hang out more with Stevie. I move into the apartment he told me about on Kings Highway. He's right, it's only a couple of blocks to the hardware store he's working, among other things.

It's been five months since I got out of prison in Mexico, and here I am at Kings Highway Hardware. I never knew there was so much money to be made off nuts and bolts, snow shovels, and bags of rock salt.

When I ask Stevie how he got the place, he just gives me one of his Hollywood-star smiles and says, "It kinda fell into my lap, you know?"

I stock shelves, nab a few shoplifters, run the register, opening and closing. I'm behaving the best I can, especially since I still have six law enforcement agencies eager to speak to or arrest Michael J. Hardy. But my name's Richard Mandell and that works just fine for me.

Five weeks later on November sixth, I go visit Grandma Edith, my "ma," in a nursing home. Grandma Edith along with Daddy Roy, my mother's parents, raised me until he died when I was twelve. Grandma Edith's the only real mother I've ever known, with Aunt Florence a close second. My mother, Shirley, not even in the picture.

Ma's in the rest home for some kind of rehabilitation. She perks up and beams when she sees me. It's been a long time since I saw her, before Mexican prison. Even though she has Morty as a son, and he's eleven years older than me, I'm still her boy.

She pats my hand. "It's so good to see you, Michael. I've been worried about you. How's my big boy doing?"

I may be six-one and 190, but I feel small when she says that. I look down. "Fine, ma. And you're looking good," I tell her and mean it even though she's in slippers and an old brown house coat.

I hang around through lunch and share her cherry Jell-O with mandarin oranges pieces. We watch daytime TV, *The Guiding Light* her favorite. We visit for a while, remembering so much of Daddy Roy, until nurses come to change her bedding. She gives me a big hug and tells me she loves me. I say the same.

I get a call from Aunt Florence at three a.m. the next morning. "Michael?" She pauses and sniffles. "Grandma Edith, your ma, she's gone."

"What? But I just saw her yesterday and she was fine." A cold air washes over me and I shudder.

"It was her heart, Michael," Aunt Florence says. "It just stopped."

I head over to Aunt Florence's place, next door to Morty, arriving at four a.m. He's stunned and can't stop crying. I've never seen him like that before. Aunt Florence is a wreck too. When my mother shows up at ten, after her breakfast, she takes it all in stride.

"She was getting up there, you know," my mother states. She won't give up her emotions to no one because queens don't cry.

Uncle Robert, Grandma Edith's brother, makes arrangements with Morty's help. Two days later we're at the I.J. Morris Funeral Parlor. Polished mahogany casket, brass, real nice. Everyone comes, including Marsha, Uncle Robert's girlfriend. I watch her lean into him and giggle, like there's something funny about Ma's life or what we're doing here. I'm gritting my teeth and about to do something when she catches my glare and stops.

The next day we head over to the cemetery with only three cars in the procession. I drive Aunt Florence and Uncle Robert, Morty with his family, and Mother with Rojullio and my sisters. A Beatles' song plays on my radio as we pull up to the grave site. I can still hear the lyrics. "Come together, right now, over me."

How fucking ironic.

I stand by the dark hole in the ground, Ma's casket hovering above it. A few dry leaves from a nearby maple blow into the cavity. I look over at my mother with her husband Rojullio, my sisters, Morty with his family, Aunt Florence, and Uncle Robert. I feel a tear about to fall and lower my head so no one sees, especially my mother.

Why do you have to be such a hard ass? And why do I have to be harder?

16

Busted but Fixed

I got to get something else going other than workman's comp and a few bucks from Stevie's hardware store. Every time I look at my gray '61 Pontiac sedan, I think of my trunk full of guns. I know it'd be easy to do a score but I'm trying to hold off. I know once I go down that road, I'm stuck there.

Stevie takes over another store, Ronnie's Gift & Card Shop on Kings Highway between 18th and 19th Street. A few weeks later, he gets the He & She Clothing Store, then opens Windmill Records, all four of his businesses now within a few blocks of each other.

One night as he's closing up the card store, I gotta ask, "Stevie, what's your scam, man? What's with all these businesses?"

"My partner, Larry Martieri, you know, Duke's cousin, he's bankrolling all this. He gets great deals."

"Deals?"

His eyebrows raise. "Don't ask."

"Why isn't Duke into any of this?"

"He gets a piece of everything, just like you. But he's got to keep clean, being on parole and all. That's why he's got some shit job working at Liberty Travel. Helps with his wife when she thinks he's behaving."

"Fucking Duke, man. Nice to see he's still got it though." I'd hang with Duke more, but his wife doesn't want him seeing me. As if I forced him to rob all those drug dealers with me and do time in Sing Sing.

Stevie's Windmill Records store is where the real money starts to come in. With the cab strike going on in the city, Morty takes a job at Larry Schafer Records and starts bootlegging forty-fives to feed Windmill Records. Morty's got to be careful. Larry Schafer has connections and he's also got a master phone booth key. Twice in one year he took road trips up and down the eastern seaboard and emptied out all of them. It took him over a month, but he came home each time loaded down with over $170,000 in quarters and dimes. Morty used to roll them up. It pissed off Larry big time when someone would use a slug, like he wasn't stealing himself.

I spend more time at Ronnie's Card & Gift Shop, and it's not because of Stevie or the business. Her name is Claudia Balen, a seventeen-year-old Jewish princess, and a virgin. That doesn't last long. Our passion's so strong, it's a memory I can still go to in a second. She lives with her parents a few blocks from the store, and we sneak over there every time they're out of the house. We almost get caught a few times. Eventually all that changes when I realize Claudia is the same age as Sheila when I fell in love with her. I see the same pattern I had with Sheila taking shape and can't handle that idea and the responsibility of a wife to come home to, or the children that would follow. So, I move on.

My '61 Plymouth's engine block freezes, and I pick up another set of wheels, a black '62 Pontiac. The months roll by and I'm bouncing between each of Stevie's businesses, helping out where I can. I'm seeing lots of girls and life's good. But my kids—I miss them and Sheila, yet I can't go there now. It could be better, but it's alright for now. I haven't been tempted to go into the trunk of my car, yet.

After work on Thursday, May 14, 1970, I give a lift to Chuck, someone Stevie knows, and I get pulled over for rolling through a stop sign. I'm not too worried because my ID says I'm Richard Mandell. I pass two joints I'm carrying to Chuck and ask him to sit on them. He seems cool with it. When the cop starts getting in my face, Chuck gets all hinky, then we're asked to step out of the car. The cop spots the joints. Chuck points to me to say they're mine. I don't deny anything.

Pussy.

I get booked into the 67th Precinct for Penal Law 220.05, possession of marijuana. They impound my car. I make my one call to Stevie, and he bails me out. I get my car back for fifty bucks and glad to see they didn't check my trunk.

Ten days later, I'm supposed to show up in court, and I'm hoping the cops haven't compared my prints to discover I'm Michael J. Hardy: a wanted felon in New York for armed robbery and escaping custody; a New Jersey parole violator; a US treasury counterfeiter on the run; wanted by the FBI for interstate flight to avoid prosecution; a grand theft auto suspect in Los Angeles; and wanted for questioning in Texas regarding my father's involvement in millionaire Ruth Holland's murder. Oh yeah, then there's my marijuana possession charge, but that belongs to Richard Mandell.

I'm wound up tight, all jittery. So, I visit two psychics, and they each tell me the same thing, I won't be going to prison now. However, my future is unclear. *Great.*

My public defender wrangles a continuance with the judge, and I walk out of the court a free man—for a while. I know I can never go into that court again. I got this heaviness building, the weight of all the people coming after me or wanting something from me.

A few days later on July 4, 1970, I drop off my trunk full of guns with Mickey to hold. He's a friend of Ira, my sister Nancy's boyfriend. I gotta do something, and that something is leave. I sign over my car and my Norton motorcycle to Stevie, and he hands me a wad of cash.

All over the city, families gather for barbeques and fireworks, while I hop a red eye Icelandic Air flight, eventually ending up in Stuttgart, Germany two days later on July 6.

I grab my olive-green duffel bag from baggage claim and find my way over to the Modernist Train Terminal. It reminds me of Grand Central Station in the city—loud, big, and busy. I stand in beneath a huge board suspended from the ceiling and stare at its clacking black tiles with their white letters. I read the names of places I've only heard about. Zurich. Geneva. Paris. Berlin. Rome. Moscow. Istanbul. People rush by, businessmen, families, students, priests. All on their way to some place they know, to a home. The tiles clack and flip over. Another train gone, another coming in. I got no idea where to go.

I shuffle up to a ticket counter and hesitate, trying to figure out what any of the signs or messages on the glass in front of me are saying. I glance up at the big board then turn to the bored ticket agent.

"Wo gehst du hin?" he asks.

I stare at him. "I, uh...." To my right, an old man dressed all in black with a long gray beard mumbles something in a foreign language into his window. I catch the word "Tel Aviv."

Israel.

"Tel Aviv," I say to the agent.

Two hours later, I board the Orient Express and take a seat by a window. For more than 2,500 miles I watch parts of a new world fly by. Towns. Villages. Cities. Hills, mountains, and valleys with rivers full of greens, blues, and browns. Natives. Peasants. Clothes I'd only seen in *National Geographic*, with head scarves, robes, and strange animals. I doze off and on for two-and-a-half days, squinting my eyes open from a dream-like trance every so often to view new wonders. I jump off the Orient Express in Istanbul and hop another train south. Since I'm an American, the transfer is easy, other people having to stand in endless lines.

It's early Thursday afternoon, July 9, when I step off the train in Tel Aviv. A searing heat unlike any I've known slaps me in the face. I also step into the middle of another Israeli-Egypt conflict, but that's not what's really going on. Like they've done for decades using other countries as their playground, the US and Russia have chosen sides and pit their aircraft and armaments against each other, bringing the entire region to the brink of another war.

Welcome to the Promised Land, Michael.

17

Israel

What kind of promises do you hold for me? I don't speak the language, already know I won't like some of their food, don't have any connections, and don't have enough money. But I'm Jewish and never felt so proud to wear my Star of David. I reach under my shirt to touch it and a shudder of longing comes over me.

You gave it to me, Ma.

A tired information booth attendant directs me to the Jewish Agency where they send all the wanna-be immigrants.

I fill out paperwork. I'm twenty-six years old, with blond hair and blue eyes, from Brooklyn. I'm Richard Mandell here. It feels like a betrayal when I write that name, not Michael J. Hardy, and not my Jewish family name Blaustein.

I'm ushered over to a desk where woman wearing a badge named "Deborah" waits for me. Dark brown eyes, short hair with black bangs, dimples, maybe thirty. She holds up my passport and looks over her black-rimmed glasses to compare the photo to me.

"What kind of skills do you bring with you?" she asks in perfect English with the sexiest accent.

"I've been working construction and spent a few years on a farm."

Her eyebrows raise. "A farm? Really?"

She asks a few more questions, finishes going over the form, and smashes a big red rubber stamp in the top right corner. I enter the country as an *Oleh Hadash*, a new immigrant. She says they'll hook me up to learn Hebrew at a school and get me a place to live.

I could have joined their Army, but I already did that once in the States without much luck. Besides, I wouldn't understand their orders and I'd probably get shot, something that's happened to me three times already.

They send me to Kibbutz Gan Dafna in the Golan Heights. It's a working farm where everyone tends the crops to pay for their room and board. When I step off the small bus, the earthy scent of dirt reminds me of my time at the Bordentown Reformatory on their farm in Jersey when I was nineteen and doing two-and-a-half years for twelve counts of armed robbery.

You better not have fucking graves detail here.

Recognizing I'm the only American in the group, the camp leader pulls me aside and explains in broken English, "Everyone work here. For best good. Together we work and share together." He lets his words sink in, or he's tired of speaking.

You running some kinda Commie place?

"Richard, after harvest, we sell crops to market. Then to store, yes? There to buy for ourselves."

"So, let me see if I got this right. You're telling me I get to work my ass off, and no matter how hard anyone else works, we all share the same, and get to shop together?"

He smiles, happy that I understand. "Is so."

Commie.

Their program isn't up and running, and since there's no work, I hang out with a dozen Israelis. They try to teach me some kind of card game, but between them yelling Hebrew swear words at each other, and the way they slap the cards on the table, I've got no idea what's happening.

In the late afternoon on Saturday, a light rain breaks the heat and a couple of us climb up on the roof. One of them brings along a transistor radio. As the sun sets over this strange land, I listen to the BBC for the first time and hear words in English I actually understand. It hits me.

I'm in fucking Israel.

Monday morning we're taken by bus to Kibbutz Gesher on the Beit She'an-Damascus Road. Our quarters are a simple bunkhouse with one bathroom. Reminds me of basic training. I hike up a small rise to look across the Jordan River at the thousands of Fatah fighters milling around. They're a mile from me with only the water and a mine field separating us. I find out right away that for twenty-three hours a day there'll be sporadic mortars and bullets flying through the air where we live and work in olive orchards. And for some reason I never understood, at two o'clock each day, for one hour, no shots are fired. There's dead silence. Almost like they've got to give their guns a rest.

For ten bucks, I buy a dagger from Ari, the guy who runs the kibbutz. I keep it tucked into a sheath in my back belt. I figure if one of the Fatah soldiers sneaks over and doesn't shoot me first, I'll poke a couple of holes in him and watch him bleed. I asked Ari for a gun, but he said he can't give me one because I'm not an Israeli, yet.

I've gotta kill me one of those motherfucking Fatahs.

Every morning before we start work, we wait while two huge Israeli half-tracks travel down the roads next to the orchards and spray fifty-caliber machine gun bullets through the trees, in case a Fatah soldier might be hiding there. There was once. I'm on alert no matter what, and during water breaks, I practice how fast I can get to my knife, like I did when I was twelve with my first switchblade.

I'm surprised I get accustomed to the shelling each night and the occasional stray bullet whizzing through the trees. Ezra, one of the guys working on the kibbutz, gets shot in the ass, but the bullet is so dead by the time it hits him, he only gets a little red welt. That doesn't stop him from hopping around and screaming like a little girl. Because of him, I'll eventually get kicked off the kibbutz.

The following weekend, we all take a trip to Jerusalem. It turns out to be the heaviest experience of my life. The Damascus Gate. The Jaffa Gate. The Tomb of King David. The room of The Last Supper. Mount Olive. I'm beyond overwhelmed, my mouth hanging open. So many names and places I remember from Boy Scout camp and in preparation for my Bar Mitzvah. Things I learned but could never imagine. The history washes over me. When I plunge into the catacombs, I imagine the voices of the thousands of dignitaries and slaves who walked on the worn cobblestones, causing goose bumps on my arms.

I end at the Temple Mount at the Kotel, the Wailing Wall, the last standing piece of David's Temple. Thoughts of my life and my Jewish heritage fill me, and I bow my head to immerse myself in deep prayer. As I mumble the few words of the Torah I remember, a ruckus breaks out with people running toward me and yelling.

They form a circle around me. Angry faces screaming in a language I don't understand. I fight to remain cool, but I'm getting pissed and about to throw down. Finally, a man realizes I don't speak Hebrew and raises his arms. The crowd quiets. He asks, "What you doing here?"

"I'm praying."

"You are on women's side." He wags his finger. "Not allowed."

The crowd calms down as I follow the man to the proper location. There I bow my head again for long moments of reflection. It's the first time I remember being completely at peace. No family pressure. No demands from friends. No law enforcement legions waiting to arrest me. It's just me, the wall, and my life ahead of me.

I can be anything here.

The moment passes too quickly when a loud voice chants near me, some guy wailing like he's the sorriest ass in the world. For a buck, I buy a small piece of thick paper and a pencil from a happy old man with a long gray beard who's missing a few teeth. I take my time to get my prayer right. "Let me make Grandma Edith, my ma, proud of me for once in my life." I roll up the paper, find a small crack high up on the wall, and wedge it in. I look up at the cloudless sky.

Did I ask good?

It's hours before we return to our kibbutz. Ezra is being the whiny little shit he always is, complaining about everything. When he isn't looking, I go through his stuff, take his passport, and hide it on a top shelf in a closet, under a pile of crap, just so I can see him gripe about something real. A week later he discovers his passport is missing and accuses me. I don't admit to anything, in fact, I offer to help find it.

Another couple of months pass with the same routine, work in the olive orchards, get shot at or shelled with mortars. It's after work on Friday, August 7, the Arab Sabbath, and I convince two of my kibbutz friends to hike up a nearby mountain with me. It's a four-hour climb to reach Belvoir Fortress, the ruins of a French castle built in 1168, left over from the Crusades. My feet throb by the time we arrive before sunset. We sit among the ramparts, huge blocks of cold weathered stone. I touch them and think of the men, maybe slaves, who carved them out of the earth over eight centuries ago to place them here.

That moment gets lost when someone lights up some hash and we all get high. After my last hit, I move away from them to sit on the far west wall and catch the final rays of the sun before it disappears. As the last light vanishes, I spot tracers from 50-caliber machine guns in the valley far below. From this distance, I can't hear a thing, but I can tell it's the Israelis pounding Fatah enemy encampments.

A cool wind snakes its way through patches of jasmine, and I breathe in its scent is delicious. My eyes drift to the battle below, and I finally get what's going on. I lift my voice to the wind. "Is this the same battle you've been fighting on this piece of land for a thousand years?" The valley gives me no answer.

I sleep huddled against a stone facade away from the wind and wake up chilled, thirsty, and with blisters on my feet. It's slow going to the kibbutz. When we arrive late in the morning, I find my duffel bag on my bed, stuffed with everything I own.

The kibbutz leader, Ari, positions himself on the other side of the bed, his arms crossed. "It's time for you to leave us, Richard."

"What for?"

"We found where you hid Ezra's passport. And there are other things. It doesn't matter. Now say your goodbyes."

I look around the room and spot Ezra in the shadows behind Abraham. He's not whining. Instead, he stifles a smile. Of all the things he could do, that pisses me off the most. I clench my fists and think of the dagger in my back belt.

Should I? Nah. You're not worth it.

I shake my head in disgust, pat a few buddies on the shoulder, and I'm gone. A couple of bus transfers later and I'm dropped off at the Tel Aviv beach. I look around and take it all in. It's mid-afternoon and the sun beats down hard. Lots of tourists. Surf pounding the sand. I heft my bag, full of mostly dirty clothes, and plod toward the water.

Might as well get my feet wet.

For the next few nights, I sleep on the beach. It's in the low seventies, so it's not too bad, but the sand fleas and rats are becoming a nuisance. So is my lack of clean clothes and a good meal. I've got $300 on me, but that's gotta pay for my plane ticket home. So, I hitch a ride into Jerusalem, find a blood bank, and give them a pint of Michael J. Hardy, enough to buy a few meals. Then it's back to the beach.

I hear word that Meyer Lansky is staying at a hotel a mile away. I met him dozens of times growing up. He always dressed smart, was short and quiet, but his eyes and everything else about him was intense, only business. My mother knew him real well too, handing payouts for him to dirty cops, politicians, and judges for over a decade, running suitcases of money to launder for the mob at casinos in Cuba, and running the largest bookmaking operation in the city and Detroit.

I head down the boardwalk and into his hotel lobby. I heard he left the US because it was getting too hot. Kinda like me, only a much, much bigger fish. I glance around. Americans, wearing gray suits and sunglasses, probably Feds, fill every corner. I return to the beach.

It's August 16, mid-afternoon, and I'm dozing, only moving if I have to swat a sand flea. A security guard runs up to me all excited. I can't understand his Hebrew, but he keeps pointing to the ocean and babbling. He grabs my arm and I follow him down to the water. He continues to point out to sea. Then I spot them, two sets of arms waving feebly. I hand the guard my passport and money, kick off my shoes, and dive in.

I reach a teenage girl out by the breaker line and realize her problem—she's caught in a nasty rip tide.

No wonder you can't get to shore.

She's glad to see me. "Bitte," she gasps in some kinda accent. I look maybe fifty feet further out in the ocean and spot the other pair of arms waving.

Great, a fucking foreigner.

I reach out my arm. "Take my hand."

She shakes her head, her eyes desperate as she twists around to spot her friend.

Louder and simpler now while I tread water, I mime what I want her to do while yelling each word slowly as if she's deaf. "Take my hand!"

The girl nods and grabs my hand. I look out to where the boy was waving. He's gone.

I take a few deep breaths and start to swim toward shore, now waving my arm at the guard. I try to sound brave. "It's not that far. Come on, let's get going."

It's over five minutes with nothing but my legs thrashing. I crane my neck to shore and I'm not any closer. The guard jumps up and down and waves his arms at me. I'm hoping to see some lifeguards or someone else who can help, but nothing.

I try to yell to him, but I can't. I got no wind. I'm forced to stop to catch my breath, but that's not working. I'm treading water the best I can, but my legs are burning, and I can't use both my arms to help tread because I'm still holding her hand. I look to shore. I'm gasping and begin to sink.

Sorry. I gotta let you go.

I release her and turn onto my belly to swim away. The girl calls to me, but I can't listen. I've got to save myself. A few seconds more of swimming and her frail voice pierces my heart. "Name of God, please."

I turn around. Her head is tilted so far back that only her mouth and nose are above the water. I dig deeper than I ever have in my life to fight through exhaustion and go to her. I hold her from behind, one arm around her waist and continue to tread water. She catches her breath, mine nearly gone.

Is this how I'm gonna end?

To give my legs a brief rest, I let myself go and sink under the water for a few seconds, then struggle to reach the surface. I've taken in some water, and it burns when it hits my lungs. I break the surface and are racked with coughs. The girl faces me and knows it's over.

Out of nowhere, an orange and white life preserver slaps the water next to me. I lunge for it, and motion her to grab onto the ring. It's everything I can do to hold on. Someone tows us toward shore until a wave picks us up and tosses us onto the sand.

I'm on my hands and knees, wheezing and coughing, water gushing out of me in deep spasms. Everything after that's a blur. I'm taken to a hospital and guess they pump my lungs and stomach in the emergency room. I look to my left to see the girl being worked on. She gives me a weak smile and her fingers faintly wave. Someone in white closes the curtain between us. That's the last time I see her.

Late that night, before I leave the hospital, the guard from the beach brings me my things. He asks me who I know, someone I could stay with. He's concerned. I remember Marim who I met at Kibbutz Gesher. He lives in Haifa. The guard gives him a call and Marim comes to get me.

On the ride to his place, I hang my head out the window, trying to force some fresh air into my lungs, but it's so humid, it's not working.

I stay with Marim for two weeks, but I'm getting sicker, and can't seem to cough the Mediterranean out of my lungs. I think back to the beach where I nearly lost my life and the waving arms of the teenage boy who didn't make it. I shake my head clear.

The faces of my two kids in Brooklyn flood my mind.
Time to go home.

18

Brooklyn Waiting

I sleep most of the way back from Tel Aviv to New York, wedging my six-one, 250-pound frame into a window seat. The only thing that wakes me up is my nagging cough. *Fucking Mediterranean.* On our final approach to the city, my stomach tightens as the New York skyline is framed in the tiny window. I wonder if there'll be a couple dozen cops or Feds waiting for me. I've given them seven different reasons to be there.

It's Tuesday, September 8, 1969, just after eight in the evening, when the wheels of the jet bounce off the runway and jolt me awake. Brooklyn. It's been waiting for me. The car horns, the cursing, the smell of it, like dirty concrete and asphalt has an odor. Sheila and my kids are here but she's with a fucking Puerto Rican cop. Then there's Stevie with all his action.

No cops are waiting, but Heddy is, and she smells real good, reminding me of what I like about being home. I called her and she picks me up at the airport. Heddy's the perfect Jewish American Princess in every way. And I mean perfect. Dark hair, dark eyes, looks like Natalie Wood, almost an exact replica of Sheila, my wife.

Heddy was a virgin until a few days after I met her. That was a month before I took off for Israel. She's been waiting for me to return. I think she's in love. Maybe I am. More than a few times I heard her pussy calling me from across the ocean. She still lives at home with her over-protective parents who don't think much of me. I can see why.

Because I walked away from my apartment on Kings Highway, I got nowhere to stay. My mother moved to California with my younger sister Debra. I won't go there. Morty already let me know I can't come to his place with all the heat on me. Stevie gives me a surprise though, his pad for the night, his own way of saying, "Welcome back, Michael."

Heddy stays the night and it's more than I imagined it would be. Several months of pent-up lust. It's different with her this time. Like I changed or she did. I don't know, but it's special.

The following day I go down hard, a virus infection in my windpipe with a raging 103-degree temperature. Seems like the Mediterranean hasn't finished with me yet, and it stays in me for two more weeks. I don't even touch the coke or weed Stevie leaves on the coffee table for me. That's how fucked up I am.

Stevie lets me stay at his place till I get on my feet. It's early October by the time I'm fully recovered. Aside from Heddy's pussy, I got nothing going. While I was away, Stevie gave his hardware store to his father, so I can't work there. I could hang out at his record or used clothing stores, but that's peanuts. I got no wheels since I sold my car and motorcycle before I left for Israel. I got no place to live. I got no money. And I haven't seen my kids in forever.

My guns.

I borrow Stevie's car and head over to Mickey's to pick them up. I don't really know him, but he's standing there trying to look all fatherly with his hands on his hips. "Sure you want this, Michael?" he asks, as I heft the suitcase.

The look I give him is my answer. The weight's right. They're all in here.

I call up Tony Gunn and Duke Cimineri and we have a get-together that night at Stevie's place. I pace his living room floor while they sit.

"This is how I see it. We can make money a couple bucks at a time by scamming people for records and other shit at the Thieves Market, or we can get something going with some *real* scores."

Duke leans forward with big concern on his face. "I can't go down that road again, Michael. I can't go back to Sing Sing. And my wife? She'll kill me, right after her father puts a couple bullets in me."

Everyone laughs and it breaks the tension. "We were stupid, Duke. I got sloppy and we got caught. We hit the same place twice. We won't do that again."

Tony asks, "What you got in mind, Michael?"

I keep looking at Duke when I answer, "Drug rip-offs."

Duke rolls his eyes and lets out a sigh.

"Hey, you know half the time the dealers are high, and they'll never go to the cops. And besides all the drugs and guns, they've got cash. Lots of cash." I rub my thumbs on the tips of my fingers, raise my brows, and squint my eyes.

Stevie adds, "We could use my businesses for alibis and to fence any of the drugs."

"Sounds good to me," Tony says.

I turn to Duke. "Well?"

He changes the subject. "I got something else going that could bring in some big money." We're all ears. "We just got in a shipment of thousands of blank airline tickets at the travel agency. They're just like cash."

I sit down and ask, "What we talking about here?"

"Well, if we do this right, we can fly anywhere for free and get a thousand bucks, maybe more for each unused ticket."

I do the math in my head. Just a hundred tickets at a grand each is a hundred grand. Before I can say anything, Stevie jumps in with, "Fuck yeah, that's cool."

I ask, "What do we need?"

Duke says, "If we're going to do this, we need two things—an authorization stamp, and you'll need to take some night courses to find out exactly how to process the tickets so we don't get pinched."

Nice thinking, Duke. You're all over it.

"Why don't you set it up, Duke? I know a postman who'll tip me off for drug rip-off since he knows where all the drug dealers live. We'll cherry pick some easy ones."

Tony asks, "What's his cut?"

I answer, "The usual. Fifteen percent."

Everyone looks to each other and nods. We've been friends since grade school and know if someone's full of it. Stevie asks, "Michael, you think you might go see Louis the Baron?"

"Yeah, already headed there tomorrow."

I'm feeling great. I got a crew now. People I can trust. Stevie's good to go, Tony will do anything I ask. And Duke? Duke's gonna take a little convincing.

I sign up to take hot cars from Liborio "Louis the Baron" Milito. It's a good deal at $600 apiece, my cost. He'll front me the first few because he knows my mother. We shake hands on the deal, and he adds, "Classy broad. Give a big hello to Shirley for me, will yah, Michael?"

I bob my head. *Classy broad? Really?*

I'll move the hot cars across the country to San Diego where my mother lives. Maybe I'll even drive out a few. The cars come with extra clean papers since Louis' got an inside man at the Albany DMV. The only way we can get busted is if the cops read the VIN off the engine or the rocker panel, but they always use the plate by the windshield. Most of the cars I'll get come with an odometer reading of less than 200 miles. To steal some, Louis' crew follows the new owner home from the dealership and steals them right after the owners go inside their homes. I'll put on another 3,000 miles getting them to California where my mother will sell them as used cars. She's got a connection at the DMV in Sacramento to seal the deal on their papers. Tight.

Six hundred for one of Louis' cars. Six hundred to transport each of them to San Diego, that is, if I hire someone. At forty cents a gallon, gas will cost about a hundred bucks, with hotels and meals for four nights another hundred, hundred fifty. If Duke gets the ticket scam going, I'll fly drivers back to the city for free.

Most of the cars will be Cadillacs. Their TV ads at the time say *"Standard of the World"* because they won some kind of award. New El Dorado convertibles sell for just under eight grand. My mother will be able to get six grand for a forty-eight-hundred-dollar profit and I'll split it with her. This is the first time I'll be in business with my mother. And this is *my* deal.

Maybe you'll like me now.

Two coast-to-coast road trips later in early November 1970, and I move into an upstairs two-bedroom place in Bell Harbor on Beach and 127th Street. Nothing but Jews and Irish in the neighborhood. Perfect for me, they don't like each other, and I look like neither. I buy furniture and a new beige VW, something that doesn't stand out. I get in touch with my wife, Sheila, through my sister Nancy. Sheila's still dating that fucking married Puerto Rican cop, but she agrees to let me see my kids.

Robert's five and Cheryl's three when they come over to my place to spend their first weekend with a father they barely know. I can't tell who's more nervous, like the first day at a new school where everyone's strangers. I take them to the park. We get hot dogs from a street vendor. We walk around, take in some sights, something to fill in the time.

When we get to my place, I cook up macaroni and grill some steaks. We spend the rest of the time watching TV. When I go to put them to bed that first night, Cheryl starts to cry and asks for her mommy. I don't know what to do, but Robert goes to her and gives her a hug and she stops.

You're a good brother, Robert.
I don't even know them, and they got no idea who I am.
I plan to change all that, kids.

November 25th, the day before Thanksgiving, Tony Gunn and I dress like undercover cops and rip-off our first drug dealer. Alfonse is his name. Half Puerto Rican, half something else. He looks like he hasn't cut or washed his hair in a couple years. He's so wasted, he doesn't even realize what's going on, watching Bugs Bunny cartoons the whole time we're there.

We score nine grams of coke, half a brick of weed, a couple pop guns, and $1,100 in cash. We'll clear maybe three grand when we're finished with everything. I leave Alfonse cuffed to his radiator, crying about his TV that I busted. Hey, he wasn't paying attention when I talked to him. I split everything four ways even though Stevie and Duke weren't along. That's how it's done. That's how you keep loyalty.

I'm back in the game.

It's all coming together now. I get to see my kids whenever I want. My apartment costs only a hundred seventy-five bucks a month. I pull down $2,400 every time a car goes to San Diego. I'm picking up a few bucks working at Windmill Records. Still banging Heddy, although she's starting to get all clingy.

Louie the Baron hooks me up to buy a nice hi-fi stereo console from Mary Capone, Al Capone's niece. Strange timing, because Stevie just introduced me to an old Sicilian named Pasqual, the guy who put the scar on Al Capone's face. You wouldn't know it by looking at him, Pasqual's so skinny with no hurt in his eyes.

Duke signed up Stevie, Tony, and me for night classes to learn about the travel business. Really, how to turn blank tickets into cash.

I can hardly wait to go to school with a Guinea and another Jew.

The first three Thursday nights in December we're out at a learning center on Long Island to get our airline ticket scam in action, all except for the authorization seal. Duke doesn't need to attend because he's been through all this before. Tony, Stevie, and I are good students, but we drive our teacher, Mr. Waters, crazy, interrupting him all the time with the same questions about the tickets and how they work. He tells us he'll get to that in week eight. I slip him a hundred so we learn what we need that third night. We don't care about certificates.

Christmas comes and I'm generous to everyone. My kids get lots of new toys and clothes. I let my sister Nancy move in with me in my other bedroom and I buy her new furniture. The new year comes, and the action keeps rolling. I'm working eighteen hours a day and the money's flowing. Duke scores a thousand airline tickets and gives me the combination to the safe at his work.

I head over early on a Saturday morning. I'm going to make it look like a real break in, everything all tossed around and fucked up. Before I get started, there's a knock on the front door. I peek out at a middle-aged woman shuffling her feet in the cold.

Shit, you saw me.

I yell through the locked door and tap on the glass where the sign is, "We don't open for another two hours, at nine."

She puts her lips to the crack in the door. "Please, can you help me? I've only got this morning to purchase tickets for my trip."

You got cash? Nah, let it go.

"Come back later."

"I'm not leaving," she yells.

Fuck.

I take a deep breath and open the door, a blast of January Brooklyn hitting me in the face. "Come on in then," I say.

I wait while she unwraps herself from all her winter clothes. She looks around at all the posters on the walls— Greece, Rome, Bermuda, the Orient.

"I'm Margaret Winslow." She sticks out her hand and I shake it.

"You can call me Richard, and you'll have to excuse me, I'm not dressed to see customers."

How the fuck do I get rid of you?

I motion for her to take a seat, and she does. "So, where you thinking of going, Mrs. Winslow?"

"Oh, I don't know."

I stand. "Well, why don't you come back when you've figured that out."

She doesn't move. She points to the Bermuda poster with its bright teal and starched white homes. "How about there, Bermuda?"

"That's not bad, if you don't mind hurricanes."

Her eyebrows raise.

"I sent a couple there last year for their honeymoon. The husband died when a palm tree fell on him."

"Oh, my." She adjusts herself in her seat and looks at another poster, Egypt with the Pyramids and the Sphinx. She points. "What about there, Richard?"

"Good choice. I'll just need to set you up with a bullet-proof rental vehicle. The only other drawback is you can't get travel insurance."

"What are you talking about?"

"Don't you know there's a war going on over there?"

I've got her just where I want and sense her start to crumble. "We do have some specials going on right now, like to exotic El Salvador."

She claps her hands together like she filled out a bingo row. "Oh, that sounds nice."

"You'll find the Spanish culture in the little villages there to be... real nice."

She sits up all excited. "Well?"

"Now where did I put that paperwork...?" I search a few desk drawers and stop. Even though the office is empty, I lean forward and look around the room like I don't want anyone to hear. She leans in for the secret only meant for her ears. "This deal is so good...," I hesitate.

"Yes?"

I whisper to her with concern, "If you don't mind maybe getting kidnapped."

She recoils like she just sucked a lemon and shakes her head. "That won't do."

I give her a sorry-ass face, like El Salvador's the last of the best bad places in the world she can visit. She tries to open her mouth to say something but stops.

I say, "Maybe...." She perks up. "Maybe, you know Mrs. Winslow, the Adirondacks are nice most any time of the year, and you can drive there." I look up at the clock. It's 7:20 and the morning sun is streaking through the windows. Her face is wrinkled with confusion, her eyes wandering around the room, trying to cling to something.

You need to leave.

She sighs and drops her hands in her lap. "Well, I think you're right. Yes. I guess maybe I'll be on my way then."

I nod, help her up and hand her all her winter clothes. By the time I close the door behind her, it's 7:25. I open the safe, take the authorization seal, and trash the place. I've worked up a good sweat by the time I walk out fifteen minutes later.

I'm not quite twenty-six, nine months out of prison in Mexico and already into some serious shit when I meet Salvatore "Sammy the Bull" Gravano, in mid-January 1970.

That's sixteen years before he becomes the second most powerful man in organized crime as John Gotti's underboss.

I'm hanging out in front of Windmill Records over in the 1700 block of Kings Highway, one of the businesses Stevie Mandell owns, when Louis Milito, an associate in the Gambino family through capo Salvatore 'Toddo' Aurello, walks by. This is the same Louis I've been "buying" cars from for $600. He took over Frankie Hart's stolen car business from him on his deathbed and runs an import-export business as a front. Louis' connected and was part of a crew called The Rampers, so he's heard of me and knows I'm good at what I do and not afraid to take on anything.

We talk about the usual this and that until he finally says, "I got a couple guys who used to work for me in The Rampers when they were younger. Sammy Gravano and Allie Cuomo. They're on their game. Right now, they grab cars for fifty bucks apiece. They need work. Got anything for them?"

I ask, "What are they about?"

"One's cruel and one's vicious."

I chuckle. "Which is which?"

Louis smiles. "You'll figure it out."

"What else they do?"

"Truck hijackings."

"Well, I don't do hijackings. Don't like the federal kidnapping charge that comes with them, and never had much luck either. Took a truckload of shoes once, but they were all left-footed."

"What the fuck?"

"Yeah, Louis. They keep hijackers from big scores by having another truck with only right-footed shoes. Hey, I'm good doing hijackings but only if it's a set-up where the driver wants a couple hundred bucks to hand over the keys. I do armed robberies. Do you think they'd be up for some stickups?"

"Yeah, I'm pretty sure. They're crackerjack. Take it from me, they can get the job done."

"Alright. Set it up."

Louis calls a day later and we're on. It's ten at night when I drive over to some no-name diner owned by Sammy and Allie on 4th Avenue, right by the Verrazano Narrows Bridge. I heard they bought the place for five grand and don't see where the money went. They probably squeezed the owner into making them some kind of "special" deal. There're red vinyl booths to the left, counter to the right, cash register by the door, and a big wall menu with the kind of food you'd expect. It smells like cigarettes and grease, old grease.

I take them in. Allie looks like your typical jabroni. Young, short, heavily greased parted black hair, white wife beater with slacks and suspenders. The banana boaters would call Sammy a "shit-a-face blond," good-looking, twenty-four years old, about five-six, jeans, white T-shirt, and black leather car coat. We shake. I can tell they work jacks and lug wrenches by their grips. You can know a lot about a man by the way he grabs your paw and looks you in the eye. Right away I see killer in Sammy's and wonder if he made his bones yet.

I'm sure you didn't whack as many as me.

I've dropped my gangster look of Italian silk suits, Roma shoes, and gold jewelry from the early sixties. It's not about how I dress that sets the tone when I meet someone. It's about the power I carry in my eyes, my fists, my pockets, maybe in the trunk of my car. But mostly how unafraid I am. They can tell. They can tell right away. A year in La Mesa prison in Mexico does that to a guy. Now I wear a better version of what I wore at thirteen years old. Jeans, black boots, T-shirt, and black leather jacket—the Brando look from the *Wild Ones*. I hide a grin.

I'm a much larger version of you Sammy, only you're Italian.

I ask, "What you guys looking for?"

"It's simple. We gotta make money," Allie says.

"Well, my crew does scores and brings in plenty of bread."

"What kind do you do?" Sammy asks.

"Mostly drug rip-offs. We like them because they're easy to pull off. And nobody goes crying to the man how we took all their shit. I set 'em up. Sometimes we even walk in with badges and guns like we're undercover cops. My favorite part is saying, Everybody down."

Sammy laughs. "No shit."

We talk for a while, compare who knows who, who's got the best brisket and Italian sausage in town. Finally, I say, "Listen guys, sometimes I get jobs my regular crew isn't into, or they're not available. That's when I can use some help. You up for that?"

They grin and nod. They're good to go. I end our time together with a day-old slice of apple pie and a cup of coffee.

You'll do just fine, because no one in my regular crew is ready to pull a trigger.

19

Explaining to Jimmy

It's May something 1991. I'm meeting with Jimmy for our bi-weekly get together at Wayside Super Max. He pressed the red button on his tape recorder. "So, that's how you met Sammy the Bull Gravano."

I'm a little annoyed Jimmy's so excited about Sammy.

What about me, motherfucker?

"Yeah. He worked in my crew on and off for three years."

"Worked *for* you?"

"That's what I said. You surprised?"

"Well, you know, he's the number two man in organized crime being John Gotti's underboss. That's a long way from drug rip-offs with you, wouldn't you say?"

"We did a lot more than drug rip-offs. A lot more. But I'll get to that later. Right now, I wanna get outta here."

Jimmy leans in and whispers, "You mean escape?"

"No. I'm tired of Wayside, nothing but low lifes. And the guards are for shit. How about LA County's millionaires' row?"

"Your bail's too low for that."

"Well, change it."

"Change it?"

"I'm not going anywhere, so increase my bail so I can get transferred."

Jimmy shakes his head in confusion.

"Jimmy, just get me over to millionaires' row. Better cells, better food, better law library."

"Hey, I'll take care of all the legal stuff."

"I know the place. Already been to County three times."

"Three times? When?"

I stick out a finger for each incarceration. "First was for the gunfight at Raleigh Studios when I got shot six times and was up for attempted murder of a public official. The second was for kidnapping and interstate flight. And once for parole violation."

Jimmy shakes his head and grins. "At least they'll know you there."

We spend the rest of our time talking through his latest motions and strategies. Something's got to change because I'm not going anywhere, and I feel like my soul is aging faster than my body.

I lay down in my cell, my frame wedged tight between my cot and a gray-painted cement wall. I think back to early January this year when I called Clara Black for a reading. She lives in San Diego and has been my go-to psychic over the years. At the time, I'd been in jail for two months and was feeling anxious. I asked her what was going to happen to me.

"Michael," she told me over the phone, "you're not going to get life and you're not going to get death. You'll do five years. And when you come out, it'll be like you were reborn."

Okay…?

"Anything else, Clara?"

"You have to forgive your son."

"What the fuck? He put me here. How do you expect me to do that?"

"You'll never be completely reborn until you do that."

Reborn—I like the sound of that. But is it worth forgiving a rat?

20

Cars, Planes, & the Bull

A week later, after I met Sammy and Allie, I'm in Monticello, about an hour and a half northeast of the city. That's where my future brother-in-law, Ira, has an apartment. I'm getting high on weed with Ira and hanging with Jeremy, some Jewish kid who owns a local kosher pizzeria. I met him earlier through Stevie Mandell.

Jeremy's full of himself and talks lots of shit. Finally, he says something that catches my attention, about the boyfriend of some girl he knows in the city who deals lots of drugs and has plenty of bread. When Jeremy's taking a piss, I lift the address book from his jacket, and then head to the city.

I'm living in Bell Harbor at the time in a two-bedroom apartment a block from the beach. I've got a little motorcycle thing going with my new Norton motorcycle, something I actually bought for myself as a gift. I get to see my two kids, but I'm still separated from Sheila. I'm not happy about that, but I told her it was okay for her to find someone else while I was in La Mesa. It's not really okay. In fact, it pisses me off.

I'm seeing lots of broads and doing what I want. Life is good. Not great, but good. My sister, Nancy, stays with me off and on. She's there when I get return from Monticello, just in from a trip to Jamaica with her friend, Samantha, who's also Jamaican. I get real pissed when Nancy tells me how Samantha had her smuggle a kilo of weed into the US for her.

"What the fuck were you thinking? You can get five years for that shit. If you want some weed, I can get you all you need."

"I'm sorry, Michael."

"You should be. Now, what I need is a coke connection."

"Samantha might have one."

So, I meet Samantha and let her know how pissed I am that she made Nancy smuggle drugs for her. She owes me. She tells me about a score, and I come up with a plan. I know my usual crew isn't up for this one because they won't go all the way if necessary. I go see Sammy and Allie over at their luncheonette.

"I got something for you guys."

"What's the set up?" Sammy asks.

"Four karate instructors in a third-floor apartment over on 14th. They've got lots of coke and cash. Two o'clock tomorrow afternoon. You guys in?"

They look at each other and nod. "Sure."

I'll bring Kevin Mazlow with me on this one. He's only sixteen at the time, but he's got raw potential and a set of balls to go with it. I met him while I was living with Marie Chances. I'd just got back from a trip to Mexico with her, paid for by her ex-husband's credit cards. I've got 144 switchblades I bought for two bucks each and run into Kevin in the neighborhood during a school day. He's sitting on the stoop to his apartment.

"You don't go to school, do you?"

Kevin shrugs his shoulders and kind of smiles.

"I've been watching you, Kevin. I know you're into stealing and doing dumb shit. So, here's what I think. Real soon you're going to get in a jam. If you want to keep doing these things, then make some real money, learn how to do it right, and do them for me. You want that?"

His eyes brighten. "Yeah."

"I'll make sure you make money."

He stands, shuffles his feet, and lets loose a shit-eating grin. "Okay."

I go in apartment, grab my box of switchblades, and return. "Okay, here's something for you. How much do you think you can sell these for?" I drop the switchblade in my pants pocket. Just like I did when I was twelve, I casually place my hand in my pocket. Then, in one fluid motion, I bend my knees, pull out the switchblade, and press the silver button. It snaps to life, the shiny steel ready. I make a few moves in the air like I'm slicing up an enemy.

Kevin's eyes light up. "Shit. Maybe fifteen, twenty bucks each."

"Good. Here's what we'll do. You give me ten dollars for each one you sell and keep anything over that. That work for you?"

"Sure." Kevin's smile tells me he's a good one.

Kevin's perfect for my first job with Sammy and Allie because he'll keep his mouth shut and follow directions. We drive over to where the karate instructors' apartment is and park up the street. Sammy and Allie parking down the street in a hot blue '70 Monte Carlo. We meet by a phone booth on the corner and stomp our feet in the January cold. Sammy and Allie will be going inside. I like our odds. Two guys from Bensonhurst with badges and guns versus four karate instructors high on coke.

I give Sammy and Allie official badges I got from Altman Police Supply. "When you walk in, flash these and say, 'Everybody down.'" I hand them four sets of cuffs. "If you need to use these, best to cuff them together, back-to-back." Sammy and Allie grin.

You're all over it.

We synchronize watches to the second, something I learned in the Army and use for jobs that require that kind of timing. I send them up. Then I motion to Kevin, "Go stand in the backyard down below the apartment window."

He gives me a *why* look.

I wave him off. "Just do as I say."

I stand by the phone booth with a direct line of sight to the rear of the apartment. I wait exactly four minutes, call the apartment, let it ring twice and hang up. Then I call again and Sammy answers.

"Well?" I ask.

"Some cash but no drugs."

"Really?" I smile.

"Cash, nothing else."

"Let's meet over at your place. I got a little surprise for you."

Kevin and I follow them over to their luncheonette. We walk in with a bag. They've already laid out the $3,200 they scored. I open the bag and dump six kilos of weed and dozens of bags of coke on the red Formica table.

"Where the hell...?" Sammy mumbles as he checks out the drugs.

"That's why Kevin was here. I thought they'd toss it out their back window when you guys busted in."

"Yeah," Kevin smiles. "It was raining drugs."

"I've never seen such tough guys piss their pants," Sammy laughs.

I split everything into thirds, a third each for Allie and Sammy and a third for me. They're satisfied, very satisfied.

I've got your loyalty now.

Sammy grins. "When you get another score like this, let us know."

"Sure." I take my cut and drive off with Kevin.

Kevin fidgets in the front seat until he's got to ask, "Where's my cut?"

"Listen, Kevin. When you got two hundred stickups under your belt and maybe rob twenty banks, then we'll talk about your cut. For now, just remember, you're learning, and you're with me."

At sixteen, Kevin wouldn't know what to do with all the cash and drugs anyway. Besides, he's my apprentice. I slip him forty bucks to keep him interested. "There's lots of people who'd pay big money to have me teach them what I know. Got it?"

Kevin nods.

We don't celebrate. I learned seven years ago not to do that after a big score. Like the night the Gotti brothers got into my shit and shot me twice. Now it's just business. I also know not to socialize too much with guys you do jobs with. Even guys like Sammy and Allie. The fewer links the better, because it makes it harder to do what's necessary, should the time come when loyalties dissolve.

Every few weeks over the next three years, we do jobs together, twenty-three in all. We even start to become a little friendly. I call Sammy "Sally" after his given name Salvatore. He calls me "Big Mike." At six-foot-one and 250 pounds, that makes sense.

After working with Sammy on a few scores, I realize we think alike. Old school street. Old school Mob. And he doesn't have the Jew prejudice with the Christ-killer mentality most Italians in the mob have.

When Maranzano laid down the rules for the way the five families would operate, you never deviated. That's how we ran. Like how we never talked about what we did. Never, even to friends, wives, or girlfriends. We never flaunted a victory over the government. And we didn't meet or socialize with people we worked with, because you never knew who was being watched or bugged.

Over coffee with Sammy one day, I made a point. "Here's the problem with some of the guys in the organization, Sally. They all think they're Al Capone. The whole structure of the Mafia and Murder Inc. was based on secrecy. Fucking secrecy. Some of them just don't get it. Jesus, you got guys like Joe Colombo picketing the FBI office. They're the guys who'll bring it all down."

"Yeah, I'm with you, Mike. The guys I grew up around that were in the mob, you knew who they were, but you didn't know who they were. If you know what I mean."

I laugh. Sammy and I think so much alike that we almost killed a cop, Angelo Bencivenga, a Mafia-connected Manhattan detective we worked with several times. I originally met him through Duke Cimineri, some kind of distant cousin of Angelo's.

Angelo owns the Solomar Travel Agency on the West Side of Kings Highway. Dirty cops end up having lots of shit on the side. After I got to know him, he even helped me with a little marital problem. I tell Angelo how unhappy I am that my wife Sheila is dating a married cop by the name of Fernandez out of the 27th Precinct.

Angelo asks, "What can I for you, Michael?"

"I want him transferred."

"What kind of transfer?"

"To the most dangerous precinct in the city. I want him to have an accident, a permanent accident. Maybe five or six weeks after he starts. You know, like something on the job."

Angelo grins. "Well, that would be Fort Apache in the Bronx."

"That's where I want him to go then. Now, what's a transfer like that go for?"

"I've got a friend of mine, Frank Sylvestri, in the sixty-ninth. He can usually get it done for fifteen hundred."

I nod. "Do it."

The transfer goes through, and instead of things going down hard for Fernandez, a few years later, he ends up becoming a millionaire from all the kickbacks he gets from the drug lords.

Our airline ticket scam is going great. I still don't like flying in planes, nothing but a big cigar tube waiting to be smoked.

Even though we ride first class, I clench the arm rests and sweat most of the way. We all have fake ID's. It's strictly business. No parties

I bring my mother in on the scam when we fly into LA. She drives up from San Diego and gets $500 for her cut because we write up first class, round-trip tickets to Honolulu. Since we don't use them, we cash them in, and I mean cash, $1,200 each. If they had those frequent flyer miles then, we would've broke that bank too.

Once Tony Gunn panicked because he left his wallet behind at the ticket counter. He whined, "I think they made me."

My mother looked to me and shook her head. "Your friend's got no balls." She walked up to the ticket counter and got her "nephew's" wallet.

Between the airline ticket scam and the hot cars from New York I deliver to my mother in San Diego, she's pulling down five grand a month—tax free. When Mother drove up to the Grand Central Deli in La Costa in a hot new Caddy, that was that. She got invited to all their parties and social events. Her pitch to people in La Jolla and La Costa was simple. "There's a dealership in New York that's going out of business and he's unloading his stock. You better get in on it now because they're going fast."

I meet her during one of my trips to LA when she came up from San Diego to cash two airline tickets. She's holding a baby in her arms.

I wrinkle my forehead. *What's your scam now?*

"Michael, meet your new sister, Edith Alice Gutierrez."

I reach out and touch her little hand. She's cute, with brown skin and dark hair. She gives me a gummy smile. "You had a baby?"

"Not exactly."

"What does that mean?"

"Well, Rojullio was slowing me down. Even though he babysits your sisters, cleans the house, even sleeping on the floor, he's a pain in the ass. I like it when he goes to TJ to stay at his apartment for the weekend." She puts the baby on her shoulder. "He wanted to have a baby real bad, and he still had a drinking problem. You know, for some reason, maybe it was because he didn't speak English too well, he thought I was thirty-four when we met—not forty-four."

I look at Mother and her eyes break away. *Bullshit.*

"Michael, he kept nagging me. So, I pretended I was pregnant and went to Tijuana. It took me several trips to set it up."

"You, in Tijuana?"

"Yes, Michael. I never thought I'd cross the border again after my time in jail there."

Your time in jail? What about my fucking year in La Mesa?

"I found a lawyer who got Edith a fake birth certificate for a thousand dollars." She patted the baby's head. "Her parents live in some cardboard shack."

"So, Rojullio thinks she's his?"

Shirley nods.

I weigh the good and bad of what she's doing. "It is kinda nice you named her Edith after your mother and all."

"Yes, Michael. I thought you might like that."

"So, where's Rojullio?"

She grimaces. "Well, that's another story. Maybe we should grab a bite."

I look at the airport clock. It's four hours before my flight to New York.

Over dinner she explains, "Rojullio got excited and wanted to celebrate, so he went on a drinking binge in TJ. Through all that, he forgot he lent his apartment to a friend who brought a drugged-up girl there for sex. Well, she died. Rojullio came home so drunk, he didn't realize she was next to him in bed, dead. In the morning he woke up to cops banging down his door."

"When'd all this take place?"

"About a month ago."

"Where's he now?"

"He's being held for murder. They're looking at him doing eight to twenty years, probably in La Mesa."

"He using my lawyer?"

"Yes."

I shake my head. "Jesus. Rojullio was a cop there."

She winces and smacks her lips, like the memory is sour in her mouth. "I remember La Mesa, all too well."

You remember? That's where I spent a year of my fucking life. Good luck, Rojullio.

A few months later on another trip to LA to cash in tickets, I meet Mother, this time without the baby. "Where's Edith?"

She's almost embarrassed, if that's possible. "The lawyer of the TJ couple said they wanted her returned, but I told them to forget it."

"So?"

"Well, I tried to get welfare for the kid, but her birth certificate wasn't kosher. So, I put her up for adoption and some white couple bought her."

That's how you made your money off her, isn't it?

"What happened to Rojullio?"

"After his conviction, I divorced him."

Rojullio ended up getting out in five years after a long trial and appeal process. He eventually plead guilty and had to let him go because he did enough time. I know, that sounds crazy, but that's how their justice system works down there.

Jimmy switches off the tape recorder. "Jesus, Michael. This was your mother?"

All I can do is shrug, nod my head, and look him in the eyes. I should feel something, but I'm kinda proud how tough she was.

"What else did she...never mind. I'm sure we'll get into more about her later."

We will, Jimmy. Yes, we will.

21

Shoot & Hijack

It's mid-February 1970 and I'm awake eighteen-hour days, the money sweet, action coming in from all sides. I'm working the Thieves Market with three different scams going—selling counterfeit movie posters like *Dr. No, Bullet*, and something with Jimmy Hendrix, providing *security* for an Afghan who sells leather coats but I'm moving a few out the back door, and the record store with bootlegged 45s.

More for convenience than anything else, I'm banging Pauline Fomero who lives next door to Sheila and my kids. Pauline's got a three-year-old daughter who's either sleeping or watching TV when I come over. Pauline talks too much, but she's got a nice rack. She always goes on and on about her husband, Tommy, and how he thinks he's something special, some kind of heroin and coke dealer.

A few weeks later, I go to pick up Robert for some father-and-son time. Susan, Sheila's skinny dyke roommate and babysitter, answers the door. Her face is ghost white.

You're scared.

"Sheila went to the market and left Robert over at Pauline's apartment." She gulps and looks at the floor. "And Michael, you might want to wait."

"Wait? What the fuck for?"

"Now, don't go getting mad, but Tommy's pissed and won't let anyone out."

"My son's in there with him, right?"

Susan's voice trembles, "Yes."

I grab her arm. "You're coming with me."

We go to Tommy's place. "Just knock on the door and stand in the front of the peep hole."

I've got my back against the wall, right next to the door, clutching my .38. I'm so amped and angry, my heart throbs in my ears.

She knocks on the door. Nothing happens. I squint at her and she knocks again.

Finally, Tommy yells, "Whadda ya want?"

I nod to Susan, and she says, "It's time for Robert to come home."

"No one's leaving here," Tommy yells back. "Not until Pauline tells me who she's been fucking."

Susan looks to me and I whisper her more lines. "Just let me come in for a minute to make sure Robert's okay."

There's some shuffling on the other side of the door. I hear the chain slide and watch the knob turn. The door cracks open. I push Susan aside and shoulder the door in, slamming all 250 pounds of my anger against it, the chain snapping like a twig.

I wade in. Tommy's on his back in the middle of the living room floor with a gun in his hand, a cigarette dangling from his mouth. He scrambles to his feet, and I run him up against the wall with my piece in the middle of his hairy chest.

I step away and he comes off the wall, his gun hanging by his side.

I jut out my chin. "Just let my son go and I'm outta here, Tommy."

His eyes are wide with confusion. "You've been fucking Pauline, haven't you?"

I look at him with disgust.

He raises his gun.

I squeeze my trigger, the roar ringing in my ears. My .38 wadcutter hits Tommy in his chest. He slams against the wall and slumps to the floor, grabbing his shirt, and looking down at blood that's starting to leak on his white wife beater.

I'm standing over him, staring at the mess. I yell to Susan, "Get Robert the fuck out of here—now!"

Behind me they scurry out. I toss the gun in Tommy's hand into a corner.

"I'm dying here," he wheezes, cigarette smoke leaking out of the hole in his chest.

Shit, Tommy, that's fucked up.

"No one's gonna die today, except you maybe from smoking." Tommy's eyes start to flutter like he's going to pass out. I slap him a few times. "Hey, you're not gonna die and you're not gonna say shit about this to anyone. Got me?"

"B-but you shot me," his weak voice answers, more smoke coming from the hole.

"That's right, motherfucker, 'cause you were gonna shoot me."

I turn to Pauline. "Call an ambulance." I freeze when Tommy's three-year-old daughter walks into the room holding a doll. She stands in the doorway looking from me to her father and back again, her face scrunching and about to cry.

Sorry, kid.

I run next door to Sheila's and find Robert. I kneel to look him in the eyes and take him by the shoulders. "I'm gonna have to go away for a little while, Robert. On a trip. You take care of your little sister, okay?" Robert nods.

I head over to the Grand Theater in Sheepshead Bay to figure out my next move. I call Stevie from the payphone in the lobby, and he says he'll come over soon. They're showing *Catch 22*. I don't like the movie. It's boring except when the propeller chops off the soldier's head. An hour later, Stevie finds me in the balcony, and we go out behind the theater. There's an open marsh that extends about half a mile to the beach. A few small sailboats dot the distance.

Who'd be sailing in this kinda weather?

Stevie looks at me concerned, like he did when we were kids and I did something crazy. "Michael, that was some wild shit with Tommy."

"Yeah, I know. But he wouldn't let Robert go and then the motherfucker pulled a piece on me. You believe that shit?" I pull up the collar on my coat. "You hear anything?"

"Nothing yet. I mean, they took Tommy to the hospital and all. He's not dead yet, if that's what you wanna know."

"Pretty much. Anyone after me?"

Stevie tilts his head to the side. "You mean a contract?"

I shrug. "Guess so."

Stevie shakes his head *no*.

I take my handkerchief and wipe down my piece, then bust it apart and heave the pieces into the marsh. The sailboats still move on the water. "Well, what'd you get me?"

Stevie grins, pulls a Smith & Wesson .38 police special from his belt. "Picked it up a couple months ago. Figured we might need one for something like this." He hands it to me along with two speed loaders.

I heft it in my hand. It feels good.

"Where you headed, Michael?"

Good question, Stevie.

"I'm not sure."

Stevie slips me a wad of cash.

I nod. "I gotta go," I say.

I make my way into the theater lobby and call Morty. He shows up fifteen minutes later and gives me a ride to Marie Chance's place in Spring Valley. The only worry I got is Marie ratting me out, but I'll watch her close.

I phone my mother in San Diego to tell her what's going down, but she already knows. When shit like this happens, word travels fast, even coast-to-coast.

"Michael, there's an APB out on you, *armed and dangerous*."

I finger my piece. *You're right about that.*

"Yeah. Got any ideas?" I'm waiting for her to line up a judge, maybe talk to the police commissioner, the mayor, or someone else she knows who can pull some strings.

"Just lay low. Maybe drive out a car. Stay on the road."

"Yeah, thanks. Gotta go." I hang up.

Next, I phone dirty Manhattan cop Angelo Bencivenga, my new go-to guy to fix things. He tells me, "I can bury your *wanted* poster, Michael."

"You'd do that for me?"

"Well, yeah, for fifteen hundred bucks."

Guess you aren't my friend.

I stay at Tony Gunn's girlfriend's place, over in Sheepshead Bay. After a couple of days of that, I pick up a hot car and head to San Diego. Nothing like 3,000 miles in a white-on-white-on-white convertible El Dorado to take your mind off all the shit gone wrong in my world.

I bring along a few of Duke's airline tickets to cash at LAX. When I drop the Caddy off at my mother's three days later, I give a call to mi patron, Patricio Baccera Ortiz, the gay drug lord who saved my ass while I was doing time in Mexico—and who I killed for a few times. He's still locked up in La Mesa del Diablo. He knows me as Richard Mandell.

"Ree-shard, es muy bueno to hear you. You no call you patron in long time."

I always like the way you mix English and Spanish.

"Yeah, it's been a while, mi patron. You miss me?"

He laughs. "No the same in La Mesa wit out you, Ree-shard."

He goes on to tell me some of what's happened since I left ten months ago. A shudder of excitement hits me. As dangerous as it was, I miss that action.

I tell him what went down in New York and how I've got to disappear for a while.

"How much dinero you get to shoot this Tommy?"

"Nothing. He kidnapped my son."

"That is good deal then. Listen Ree-shard, you want to make dinero?"

"What do you need me to do, mi patron?"

I can hear his lips smack as he smiles over the phone. He suggests we meet in person. I drive across the border into Tijuana to visit him the next day, arriving late in the morning. My stomach tightens as I walk into La Mesa del Diablo as a free man, every second of my twelve months there coming back at me, like a sour burp from a heavy meal.

Comandante Paco greets me with a stupid salute in the sally port, the corrale prisoners already poking their hands through thick chain link asking for dimes.

Jesus, nothing changes.

I notice Paco added some new ribbons to his khaki uniform, for what, I can't even guess. "Ree-shard, welcome to my new palace." He waves his arms out across the prison yard. A lot's changed. New buildings and carracas everywhere, the stores with neon signs. "Patricio has been most generous." His toothy grin looks comical now, so different than how I saw him when I first came to La Mesa, envisioning him as a shark. Now he's a mackerel.

Paco struts across the yard as he escorts me to Patricio's second story palatial carraca overlooking the prison, like I'm one of his boys who graduated and made good. We climb the stairs up to Patricio's suite where he greets us in his usual red silk robe and slippers.

"Ree-shard, so good to see you." Patricio hugs me hard and kisses me on both cheeks.

You really did miss me.

"You too, mi patron."

He stands back and takes me in, a big smile on his face. "New York is good to you, no?"

"It could be better, but it's good."

Paco's been hovering around the whole time, like a hungry dog waiting for table scraps. Patricio snaps his fingers at one of his servants and barks, "Juanita."

Paco's face light up when a stunning, petite, teen girl wearing nothing but pink hot pants, a matching tube top, and platform shoes wobbles out of an adjoining room, her eyes glazed, probably heroin.

In Spanish Patricio tells her, "Show Comandante Paco around, will you?"

She gives Paco a lazy smile, takes him by the arm, and leads him into the bedroom, closing the door behind her.

Patricio interrupts my dream-like gaze. "Ree-shard, you like?"

I grin.

"Maybe after Paco, you want some, no?"

"After Paco? Really?"

Patricio lets out a big laugh and motions for us to sit down at one of his patio tables already set with fine place settings and decorations, like I'm his honored guest. At the snap of his fingers, food and drinks arrive. "Lupe cook something especiale para ti. Chicken mole. I know you like."

Yes, I do, Patricio. Now what do you want?

As is his custom, we do small talk while we eat. God, I forgot how much I missed Lupe's fresh tortillas, rice and beans, and mole. We catch up on gossip, news from both inside and outside La Mesa, how he wished his gringo pistolero still worked for him because he has some competition that needs to be put in their place.

The dishes get cleared and the cigars come out. He gets up and I follow him to the railing overlooking Tijuana in the distance. We puff on Cubans for a few quiet moments.

I ask, "What can I do for you, mi patron?"

"See, this is why I like you, Ree-shard. You know me so well."

Time to tell me, Patricio. Come on.

"I have un pequeña problema. A truck I want."

"Should I ask what's in the truck?"

He taps his cigar ash on one spot of the railing and then another, as he says, "Just to take truck from here to there. Simple, no?"

We talk through the details, and it looks clean, for Mexico. I'll get $20,000 for the job but have to hire a two of Patricio's *trusted associates* at $5,000 each. It'll go down in a week. I can hang out in San Diego for ten grand. I got nowhere else to go.

It's after nine at night and I'm parked on the side of the Gabriel Leyva Road, the hood of a '57 Chevy we *borrowed* open. Down the street on the corner, Juan, one of Patricio's associates, leans against a light post, and smokes a cigarette. He signals the truck's coming by flicking the cigarette into the street.

It's on.

I crouch behind a pickup parked next to us while Jesus, the other associate, wearing a Federale uniform, walks into the middle of the street waving a flashlight.

The truck driver slows to a stop. Jesus walks up to the driver window and barks in Spanish, "Get out. I need to see your registration and lading."

The driver balks, but then complies. When he opens the door, I hop into the truck's passenger seat. Jesus and the driver get into some kind of argument. I thought my Spanish was pretty good after a year in La Mesa, but these guys are really going at it. Something about, "Gordito's going to be mad," then "Rafael will want an explanation." He's not going quiet.

The bad part of the heist is that the driver resists. After we grab the truck, we stop on a highway overpass. I put a bullet in the back of the driver's head and the two associates throw him over the edge. I drive the truck to a remote part of Tijuana, park it, and walk away.

22

Bagmen

When I get back to New York a few days later, I get a message to meet dirty Manhattan cop Angelo Bencivenga at his travel agency. On the drive over with Sammy, my little voice starts telling me maybe Angelo's not happy with how we've been splitting the money from some of our takes. I know we're doing it right, not that I like kicking back anything I've stolen to anyone. When you've done something big like kidnapping drug lords, you do the right thing or you don't do anything for much longer.

Angelo sits at his desk and lights a Camel. "Taking dirty money from cops has to be done right. No loose ends. Unlike anything you've done in the past, you have to be precise and extra careful in the sense that if you screw up at all, you'll be dead, or worse."

I call in Allie and Kevin to be in my crew. We're sworn not to tell anyone about this score. No one. Ever. We know that ripping off cops' dirty money is something they'll never let go. They'll exhaust every lead and track down whoever's responsible and make them pay, big time. I even heard of a cop who took that wrong turn once. They found him with a bullet in his head, parked in his running car on a Belt Parkway off-ramp.

We rehearse every move with two cars in an abandoned warehouse, going over possible problems that might come up. We get our timing down to just under thirty seconds, about the same time it used to take me to steal a car. Simple really, when you break it down. Overwhelm your target with surprise and force. If we need to talk, it's soft and quiet, single words, or hand signals to each other, nothing to let him make our voices. Never use our names. And nothing to attract attention from anyone in the neighborhood.

We follow the cop bag man on a run a week later to get down his drill. The score's supposed to be around $350,000. Angelo will give us the bag man's route and last pickup spot. We'll take care of the rest. From the score, Angelo will get 150 grand of which he'll kick fifty grand to Mimi, the local Mafia boss. We'll split the remaining 200 grand. Not bad for a thirty-second heist, if we can pull it off.

Our bag man will be a plain-clothes cop who's carrying a shopping bag with bagels resting on top of $1,000 wads of twenties wrapped in rubber bands. He'll have a .38 special in a shoulder holster and his hands will be full. That's good. Four shopping bags with a total of 350 wads of money will be in his trunk. There's absolutely no room for error. None.

It's a Tuesday night just before eleven. I've got a stolen dark blue Chevy parked eight spaces up the street from our heist. Allie's hanging at the corner. He brought his dog as a cover, a little Pomeranian named Buttercup—and it's like he's never actually walked the dog. I don't like having dogs or kids along for scores. Kinda like how W.C. Fields hated working with them in movies. But Buttercup is well-trained, small, and not a yapper, so we don't have to worry about any problems from that end.

Sammy, Kevin, and I wear clear plastic masks that make our faces look distorted, black beanie caps, and we're dressed all in black. We wait in the car, the engine off, slouched down in our seats, me at the wheel checking my side and rearview mirrors for the bag man to roll up. If someone walks by, they won't know anyone's in the car. We're amped. I hear the cylinder and hammer click as

Sammy keeps checking his gun. I finally have to say, "Leave it alone, already. We're set."

Stay cool.

"This fucking mask. It's hot," Kevin complains.

I snort. "Shut the fuck up, Kevin. This is how it has to go down. You know that."

Stay in line, Kevin.

This is the kind of neighborhood where people don't stare out their windows for too long when it's late at night. They don't want to see too much. They know there's more trouble if they witness any shit going down. Perfect for us.

Headlights.

"Down," I bark. Kevin and Sammy sink down farther, easy for them when they're both under five-six. I lean to the side onto the passenger's seat. I peek over the dashboard. A tan Plymouth Fury squeaks to a stop and double parks, leaving the car running. The bag man steps out.

"It's him," I whisper. He checks his surroundings for a few seconds, then heads up to the apartment and halts on the stoop. Nothing but your average forty-year-old cop with mutton chops looking to pad his retirement. He glances back at the sidewalk and street one last time. Satisfied, he goes inside.

I start the engine but keep my headlights off and look in the side view mirror. Allie begins to walk Buttercup down the sidewalk.

A minute later, the cop exits the apartment with a grocery bag in one hand, car keys in the other. He looks around again, then strides straight for his car. Allie's a few cars away with his dog, behind the cop. I pull out.

This is fucking it.

I drive up and stop next to the cop's car just as he's placing the grocery bag in the trunk of his Plymouth. He turns to check us out, and just as he does, Allie throws a black bag over his head and shoves a gun into his ribs, saying. "Quiet and you won't get hurt."

With the dome light off, Sammy and Kevin jump out of my car and grab the four grocery bags from the trunk and put them in our car. Allie cuffs the cop behind his back with the cop's handcuffs and takes his gun.

"Do you know who you're fucking with?" the cop muffles through the black bag. Allie smacks his head with his gun and the cop grunts.

With the cop disarmed and disoriented, we okey-doke him into the trunk of his Plymouth and close it. We all pile in the Chevy, Allie bending down to pick up Buttercup just before I pull out.

I lean over to the passenger's seat and say out the window, "Enjoy your nap," as we pull away.

After a block, everyone laughs, finally letting out some of the tension that's been building all night.

Fucking yeah.

I park behind of Angelo's travel agency, making sure no one's watching. We bring in the shopping bags, and take off our masks, tossing out the day-old bagels, and dumping all four bags on an empty table. Angelo slaps us on the back and can't stop dancing around.

"Fucking incredible. Fucking incredible," he keeps babbling. "I can't believe you guys pulled it off. Did anyone see you?"

"We're clean," I answer.

Then Angelo gets all serious. "You know, if this fucking leaks out, there's nothing I can do to protect you guys. You're on your own. The only way anyone'll ever find out is if someone in here says something." The room goes quiet. "We can never do that. Right?"

Everyone lets out with a little "Yeah."

"Never," I add when I look around at my gang.

I hand Angelo his bag with 150 rolls for him and his connection. He hugs it like a big teddy bear with a Cheshire cat smile going on. "Wanna do this again, Michael?" Angelo tosses out.

Greedy cocksucker, aren't you?

"Sure. But not for a couple months. They're gonna be ready for us if we do it too soon. But we're down for it."

We carry out our $200,000 in two bags and head over to Sammy and Allie's luncheonette to split it up. It'll be eighty grand for me, and I'll give a little taste to Kevin, with sixty grand each for Sammy and Allie.

We do this twice more over the next six months and know we've pressed our luck. One million dollars total. There's never been anything sweeter than taking money from dirty cops. We almost pull one on Stanton Island, but there's only three ways out of that shit hole. Too much risk, even for the money. It's not that I'm afraid, I just don't want to die at the hands of some dirty cops.

It's the clean ones I worry about most.

23

Tyrone

It's the day after Thanksgiving, November 1970. I pull up in front of Angelo's travel agency and turn to Sammy. "Let's play it tight with Angelo. I don't know what the fuck he wants, and I don't want any surprises. You down with that?"

"Sure, Big Mike."

We walk in and Angelo waves us past the old ladies to the back room. Smells like stale coffee and mimeograph paper. I glance around.

You never know.

We go through a few minutes of *how's things?* before Angelo gets down to it.

"I like working with you guys. There's no bullshit. So, here's a score that's going to bring in a cool million dollars. I'll take two-fifty. You guys split the rest."

Fucking about time!

Out of the corner of my eye, Sammy sits up, all attentive.

Stay cool, Sally.

"What we gotta do?" I ask.

"Kidnap a drug dealer by the name of Tyrone. I'll get you detective badges. You pose as cops. Keep him under wraps for a day or two until the money drops. I'll take care of that end. Then find a good place to leave him."

"What exactly do you mean by *leave* him?" I ask.

Angelo squints at me, no doubt surprised I'm going there. "This ain't no hit, Michael. Just ransom."

"Okay. So, where's the grab?"

"He lives in a sixth-floor apartment in Manhattan over near 127th Street and 7th Avenue. We'll make sure is wife and kids will be out of the house. Just Tyrone at home."

"Sounds simple enough," Sammy says. "We'll need a place to keep him on ice."

"I got that covered," I add and turn to Angelo. "When?"

"This weekend work for you guys? Either Friday or Saturday night."

I look to Sammy. His face gives me my answer and I say, "If it was summer, I'd wait to plan it out. Too many porch monkeys watching our asses. Since it's too cold for people doing shit outdoors, we're in."

Angelo grins. "A few more things, I'll provide back-up for you at the pick-up. If I do my job, you won't see me. And, you're gonna like this, I've got taps on all his phones. So, if his wife decides to tell someone else, like his associates or the cops, I'll know what's going down, and we'll be all over it. But I doubt she will. Why the hell would a drug dealer's wife call the cops?"

You're all over it.

"Nice set up," I say.

Angelo hands me a diagram of Tyrone's apartment and we're out of there. As we drive away, I turn to Sammy. "Let's keep this one tight—just you, Allie, me, and Kevin. Sound good?"

Sammy nods.

I decide we'll do the grab Saturday night. It gives us another day to plan and set things up. I empty the trunk of a hot blue Plymouth to make room for Tyrone. I visit my connection in Bensonhurst who has an empty basement apartment we can use. It'll cost me five hundred bucks and that includes a phone, mattresses, card table, and no questions.

Kevin will wait in the car. Me, Sammy, and Allie will dress in suits with detective badges and guns. Three against one makes for good odds.

We show up at Tyrone's apartment just after eleven Saturday night. We're cool and we look the part. Sammy even got a haircut and his nails done. I can hear the TV from the other side of the door when we knock on Room 621. Tyrone sees our badges through the peephole and lets us in. Tyrone's about six-foot-two, maybe a buck-seventy, with a huge-ass afro making him look seven feet tall.

"Turn around," I tell him.

He pauses until Sammy reaches up and puts a piece to his head. "You heard him."

Allie cuffs his hands behind his back and pushes him onto his white Naugahyde sofa. I take in Tyrone's apartment. He's got some serious design shit going on. Not my style, too much gold sparkle in the furniture and paintings. I look at Tyrone. He's trying to figure us out. He's dressed in beige bell bottoms with a yellow polyester shirt with wide lapels, a few pounds of gold around his neck. His nose has a little white dust on the edges and the coffee table has a rolled-up bill.

So, this is how a fucking drug lord lives.

While Sammy and Allie stand over him, I close the curtains and check the rest of the apartment for anyone else and to see what he's got laying around. I come back with a blue silk pillowcase filled with thirty-five grand and two kilos of coke.

He's confused and looks from Sammy to Allie to me. "Why you taking my shit and cuffing me? I ain't late on no payments."

"Shut the fuck up," I bark at him. "Now, get up. You're coming with us." I nod to Sammy and Allie who help him off from the sofa.

"What the fuck!" Tyrone says.

Allie reaches up and whacks him on the side of his head with his piece again. "What did he just say to you, motherfucker?"

I look at my two little guineas standing next to skinny Tyrone with his giant afro. I hold back a smile. While Sammy goes into the hall to see if it's clear, I wipe down the place, just in case. We follow Sammy past the elevator, not wanting to run into any residents, and take the stairs down five flights.

We exit a side door of the building without running into anyone, right out to the car where Kevin's waiting with the trunk open. He puts a black sack over Tyrone's head. Tyrone looks funny with his huge afro, like he's an alien. I lean in and whisper, "You make any noise or scream, and you're not coming out of this trunk alive. Nod if you dig it."

His head bobs up and down. Kevin okey-dokes him into the trunk and closes the lid. I smile.

I love the sound a guy makes when he falls in a trunk.

It's almost midnight when we arrive at the Bensonhurst apartment I lined up. Sammy and Allie check the street for anyone walking a dog or looking out a window. I signal Kevin and he gets Tyrone out of the trunk. We slip into the basement apartment through a side door.

The room's still the same as I set it up the day before. Two mattresses on the floor, windows covered, a porta-potty, a TV, a green card table with a phone on it, a steam heater, and four chairs. It's musty, just like a holding cell should be.

First thing, Allie puts a belly chain with handcuffs on Tyrone, and then chains him to two huge cast-iron sewage pipes on a wall. Kevin has Tyrone face the wall, removes the bag, and puts a blindfold on him. Then Allie adds a mouth gag.

Nothing like a Black drug lord who can't talk shit or see shit.

I tell Tyrone, "You behave, and in a day, you'll be back to doing whatever it is you do. Tell me you understand me."

He grunts.

Like we went over, my crew keeps our talk to a minimum, mostly hand signals, and never using any names. I lift the phone and dial Angelo. "Package arrived."

I hang up and motion to Allie and Sammy, tapping my watch and holding up eight fingers. They nod. Kevin and I leave. On the drive back to my place I remind him, "We need to be back here by eight with food. Rest good. You're gonna need it."

The next morning, we show up with sandwiches and coffee. Sammy and Allie look like they haven't slept all night. That's good. Tyrone twists his head. I can tell he's straining to hear, anything to give him a clue as to where he is, who we are, and what we want. He'll find out soon enough. Allie unchains him from the pipes but keeps his belly chain and cuffs on.

I point at Kevin, "Time for our guest to do his morning dump."

Kevin's face recoils at the thought, but he leads Tyrone to the porta-potty, pulls down his pants, and sits him down. A couple of minutes later, Tyrone finishes with a grunt. Kevin looks at me with a do-I-have-to? look.

"You're the fucking apprentice," I snarl and point to a corner. "Gloves are over there."

Kevin shakes his head in disgust. "Fuck. Shit. I mean, really shit. You mean I got to wipe his black ass? Fuck!"

Kevin finally cleans up Tyrone and brings him to the table. Allie removes his gag but leaves his blindfold on. Tyrone stretches his mouth, trying to get the feeling back. He's got the nervous stink of fear on him.

"You hungry?" Sammy asks.

"Yeah," Tyrone answers.

"Open up." Sammy says and feeds him a turkey on rye. After two hungry bites, Sammy holds up a Styrofoam cup to Tyrone's lips. "It's hot."

Tyrone sips it. "Got any cream or sugar?"

I bark, "What the fuck did you say?"

"Uh, nuttin'," Tyrone answers.

"Good. Now listen. You're gonna call your wife and tell her to get a million dollars together."

"What's this, some kinda shake-down?"

Like he enjoys it, Allie smacks Tyrone on the side of his head again with his piece. Tyrone shirks, ready for the next whack.

I continue, "She's got twenty-four hours. I hope you're on good terms with her, Tyrone. You're gonna find out how much she loves you, that's for sure. Now, ready to make the call?"

Tyrone nods.

While Sammy dials, I add, "Tell her if she goes to the police, we'll know. Then you'll die and so will she, and so will your two kids. Tanya and Reggie, right?"

He stops breathing.

That's it. That's what'll get to you.

"There'll be one advantage though. We'll make sure you all share the same hole we dig for you."

The call goes well. Tyrone follows our directions perfectly. I listen in with my ear next to the phone, his afro itching my face, the stench worse this close. Tyrone's a believer. More importantly his wife is, and she says she can get the money, but it might take a little longer.

"As soon as you can, Baby," Tyrone adds. "These guys ain't fucking wit me."

With that, I hang up the phone. Allie gags him and chains him back to the pipes. I call Angelo, "Call's been made."

"I heard. Good."

Sammy and Allie crash on the mattresses while Kevin and I watch TV. It's Sunday morning, so it's mostly preachers going on about sin and shit, trying to scam people to give 'em money.

What a fucking racket.

I go out around one in the afternoon to pick up some chicken parm from a local restaurant. The same drill continues until the next morning when Tyrone makes his second call to his wife.

"You got it together, baby?"

"I need another day. Tyrone, you sure you want to do this?"

Before he can answer, I jump in, "What the fuck are you waiting for? Maybe you should just bust up some of the plaster board in your walls."

Tyrone tenses.

So, that's where it's at.

I whisper into the phone, "Get it to us first thing tomorrow, or start looking for a new husband."

I call Angelo while Kevin and Allie gag and chain Tyrone again. "You heard. Yeah."

I hang up and pause, then walk over to Tyrone. "If your wife doesn't come through, you're gonna get a legal separation from her—the hard way. Got it?"

He nods.

It's Tuesday morning at eight o'clock when I place the third call to Tyrone's wife, this time while he's still hanging on the wall.

"I've got the money. Now what?" she asks.

"You'll receive another call. Do exactly what he tells you and you'll be seeing your lovely Tyrone again before you know it. Don't fuck up."

"Okay."

I call Angelo. "It's all yours."

Now we wait. This is the hardest part. All this work, and if the drop goes bad, we're fucked. But for a million bucks, there's a lot of things we'll wait for. At 3:12 in the afternoon, the call from Angelo comes.

"It's all there?" I ask.

"Yup," Angelo answers.

"I'll let you know when we're done here so we can meet."

I give a thumbs up to my crew and walk over to Tyrone. "Well Tyrone, I guess your wife still loves you. Personally, I don't understand why, especially since you got such a small pecker. Or is your little turtle just scared?"

Everyone laughs, except Tyrone. We wait another six hours, just after nine o'clock when it's dark, quiet, and traffic's gone. Sammy and I wipe the place clean. As Allie and Kevin put a bag over Tyrone's head, I tell him, "We're gonna drop you off and you're gonna forget all about this. Like a friend of mine once said, you're going to get amnesia, hard. If you don't, we know where you live and how to get back at your family. Got it?" Tyrone bobs his head. "Consider this adventure the cost of being in your line of work."

Sammy and I make sure no one's around when Kevin and Allie take him out of the basement and deposit him in the trunk again with a thump.

Beautiful.

I drive us over to the old West Side Highway and stop underneath. No one's around. Kevin opens the trunk and drags out Tyrone. I nod to Allie, and he unchains him, but leaves the bag and gag. Tyrone stretches his arms and legs, trying to get the stiffness out, but he remains all tensed up, afraid we'll pistol whip him, or gonna pop him. I add to his discomfort by taking out my piece and pulling the hammer back right next to his ear. "Walk slowly in the direction you're headed for fifty steps. If you stop before that, or take the bag off your head, we're gonna use you for target practice. Got it?"

Tyrone grunts an answer.

We get in the car, and I watch him through the rearview mirror as we drive off.

Back in the neighborhood, I stop at a phone booth and call Angelo. "We're done with our delivery. Ready for visitors?"

"Sure."

We head over to Angelo's travel agency where we split up the take. A million bucks. The most cash I'd ever seen. Mostly hundreds, with some fifties, and few twenties. Two hundred forty grand each for Allie and Sammy. I take the extra twenty to give Kevin a little taste, maybe buy him a new car and some clothes. At seventeen years-old, what does he know about spending twenty grand?

The good news is that Tyrone will never coming looking for us, because he believes we're cops. The bad news? There's no bad news. In fact, we do two more of these within the next eighteen months. God bless drug lords and their devoted wives.

Jimmy switches off the tape recorder and scribbles a few more notes. It's the little things I notice about him when we meet in LA County Jail. The manicured nails, perfect reddish-blond hair combed back, a new matching tie clip and cufflinks every time we meet.

You own a jewelry store?

He looks up. "West Street Jail, is that where you met Rudy Giuliani?"

You're impressed.

"Yeah, Jimmy, but a lot more than meet."

His eyebrows raise. Jimmy puts his Mont Blanc inside his suit, and slips his yellow legal pad in his briefcase, latching it shut. He stands. "When we get together in two days, I'd like to hear about that. I should also have a lot more of your murder case to discuss as well."

"That bitch, Marcia Clark, up to something?"

Jimmy puts up his hands, like he's surrendering. "No, not that I know of. Just some strategies we need to go over."

I nod. "Works for me."

In my cell that night, someone down the hall talks in their sleep, another snores, two others empty their bladders, and someone coughs up a lung.

Will this be all I'll hear for the next ten years?

24

LA County with Jimmy

It's takes until June 1991 for Jimmy to work his magic. He gets my bail increased which gets me into millionaire's row in LA County. I know, it sounds crazy to *increase* my bail, but the food's better here, the guards already know me from my three previous stays, and the law library is one of the best in the world.

Jimmy and I are about to start another one of our sessions, when there's a knock on the door. A guard steps in and whispers in his ear. Jimmy nods at the guard and turns to me. "I've got to take another client. Unexpected. You'll have to wait outside in holding."

Another fucking client? I don't move.

"Please, Michael. It should take just a few minutes."

The guard leads me out the door while some rag head walks in. I turn to watch Jimmy through the glass after they close the door. The skinny terrorist sits down and starts yelling at him. Jimmy keeps his cool, places a few papers on the desk and holds out his Montblanc. Even from here I can tell it's just his standard contract.

The soundproof walls can't hold the Arab's hatred. "Blatt, you're nothing but a cock-sucking Jew. You're all the same. It's too bad the Nazis didn't do a better job killing all of you when they had the chance." He slams his hand on the table for effect.

Jimmy tilts his head to the side, glances back to the window to see if the guard's watching, and spots me. I catch an almost-smile at the corners of his mouth. In one motion, Jimmy smashes his Montblanc through the hand of the Arab.

Fucking way to go, Jimmy!

Now the rag head really has something to complain about. He grabs his bleeding hand and hops around the room screaming. "You fucking stabbed me! You fucking stabbed me."

The guard pokes his head in the room, and I edge over to listen in. "Everything alright in here, counselor?" the guard asks.

"Just a little client control problem. I think we're okay now." Jimmy grins.

Jimmy stands there all calm-like holding the pen until the Arab signs the contract, blood dripping on the paper

The rag head storms out of the room holding his bloody hand and looks back into the room, muttering under his breath, "When I get through with you, I'll have you disbarred, or worse."

He eases into a chair across from, stares at his bloody hand, rocking back and forth, and moans. "Fucking Jew lawyer."

The guard's waiting for me at the door to the conference room. I step up to the Arab on my way into the room. I bend down and whisper, "If you say anything about what just happened, and I mean anything, they'll be scraping your sorry sand nigger ass off the bathroom floor."

I leave him with his mouth hanging open, walk into the room and take a seat. There's still a little blood on the table. Jimmy and I don't say a word while we wait for the guard to come back with a towel to clean it up. I look at Jimmy. He's all business, arranging papers, but he's more than that.

I got me one fucking great lawyer.

Neither of us says a word about what happened, but there's a new level of respect going on. Jimmy goes through some upcoming motions. "Michael, it's been over seven months since your arrest and things are beginning to shift in our favor. I told you time was on our side. The longer it takes, the better for us."

"Yeah, but I'm fucking tired of waiting."

"I believe it's all going to come down to either us cutting a deal for voluntary manslaughter or we go to trial."

"I'll take a trial."

Maybe you can stab the prosecutor's crippled hand with your pen.

"I thought you might say that, so here's a few things for us to consider. First, we never know what kind of jury we're going to get, and jury trials are unpredictable. Second, my best guess is that we've got a fifty-fifty chance of winning. And then there's...," his voice tails off.

"There's what?"

"Putting you on the stand."

"I don't wanna get on the stand. If I don't, they can't ask me about my past, right?"

"That's why I think we're at fifty-fifty."

"Okay, check this out, man. If we go to trial and lose, do I still owe you fifty grand?"

Jimmy looks at me and shakes his head and chuckles. "It doesn't work that way."

"So, how does it work, Jimmy?"

Jimmy gives me a *really?* look. "Michael, a young woman, alone, buried like a dog in your backyard, by you, and your son. Can you see the kind of picture the DA's going to paint?"

"So, what's my defense gonna be?"

"The DA's going to come at you with everything, and they have every right. They've got a dead body which has to be accounted for. They'll play all your TV appearances from Geraldo, Brokaw, and Montel, where you bragged about your life of crime and doing hits."

I try to lighten the mood. "I was just acting. Not bad, eh?"

"As evidence, they'll submit all your records of violence and your fifteen, uh, sixteen years of incarcerations, and all the fights you got into while you were inside. By the time they finish, you'll be lucky the jury doesn't try to hang you in court the same day."

"What about my character witnesses?"

"They only come into play during the sentencing part of the trial, and you've only got one that's any good. By the way, why does someone like Nick Pileggi want to vouch for you anyway?"

Because we're friends, motherfucker.

"I guess because we're both from New York. Also, he worked as a reporter in the city and handled the crime beat. We got some kind of connection. I don't know, maybe it's because I'm the only gangster he knows who's not locked up for life, or dead. With his juice, he also thinks he can get me some kinda movie deal with Disney, for part of my life."

"Disney? Your life?"

"Yeah. He thinks a movie could be made about the time I kidnapped my daughters from MacLaren Hall and had the FBI and everyone else chasing us all over the country."

"A movie, Michael?"

"Yeah. Why are you so surprised?"

"Well, your life isn't exactly Disney material. What's Nick getting out of this?"

"Nothing. Look, he still talks to me. Sometimes I give him ideas or lines for his books and movies, you know, here and there. I don't bullshit him."

"Well, it's time for us to cut the bullshit, Michael. The deal they're offering could go down quick, so we've got to be ready."

"Let me think on it, Jimmy. I believe we can win this case."

Back on my cot that night, I run through everything that's brought me here. *Numbers.* They're coming back at me again. I just turned forty-seven and I'm feeling it. My left-hand aches, probably from all the times I hit or stabbed someone. The hundreds of people I robbed, mostly at gun point. Then there's the eleven times I've been shot, flat-lined twice, tried to commit suicide two times, had my hands on over a million dollars more than once, and watched it all evaporate. I've spent sixteen years in prisons and jails.

Fuck, that's a third of my life.

My three kids. Really four, but I don't count Mark because I haven't seen him or Dorothy in twenty-five years. At least my motherfucking-rat-of-a-son's doing hard time in Corcoran. Every day I pray he'll fuck up again and go away forever, or maybe someone will take him out. My oldest daughter isn't making any better choices. Then there's my youngest, Debra, she's thirteen and my best hope for something good coming out of my life.

It's too bad you gotta be in foster care right now, baby girl. Maybe it'll toughen you up for the life ahead of you.

It did for me.

25

Heddy

It's a few weeks later in mid-December 1970. I'm pulling jobs with my regular crew, as well as Sammy and Allie, and running cars to California. Lots of money coming in. And I'm still seeing Heddy. I finally admit I love her. She's everything I want—class, great looking, sweet, she loves me hard. But there's something that happens to me when I get too close though, like I'm compelled to leave to be with Nancy Jonas and her ass.

A couple of times I drive out to California with Nancy to deliver cars to my mother. I can see Mother doesn't approve of her by the way she ignores Heddy, but she doesn't get in my shit. Mother lost that right since I spent a year in La Mesa for her. Because I'm bringing her all her action now, she gives me a pass on her opinions.

New Year's Eve rolls around back in the city. I think of all the good things going on in my life and Heddy's at the top of my list. So, I propose to her while we're out at a club. It's real special. I pay the band to play "We've Only Just Begun," and we slow dance. I'm still officially married to Sheila, but I can take care of that with a quick trip to Reno. Besides being in love with me, Heddy's real smart too. She teaches school and starts night classes to become a lawyer.

She's so excited, she sets it up for me to have dinner with her father who owns a couple dry cleaners. Just us two. I know he's friendly with the Tommy Lucchese family,

Carmine Tramunti heading it up at the time, but I don't know how friendly. We meet at a four-star Italian restaurant, my way of showing respect.

I've got on a new suit and saying all the right things. "Your daughter, Heddy, she's really special to me."

He studies me with intense dark eyes, graying hair, glasses, and wearing a thousand-dollar suit. "She means everything to me, Michael."

I clear my throat. "You know, we've been going out for almost eighteen months now."

His eyes are intense, burrowing into me. "So she says. And this is the first time we meet?"

You busting my balls already?

"Did you see the ring I got her?" It's a two-carat rock.

"Yes. That's nice. Hey, look, Michael, I've got to be honest with you. I really don't see how this will work out between you and Heddy. There's just too many differences between you two."

"Whadda ya mean?"

He leans forward. "How much time you got?"

So, you are gonna bust my balls. I nod for him to continue.

"She's a practicing Jew, you're not. You come from a broken home, she doesn't. Your mother, well, you know about her and connections better than me. You already have children; Heddy doesn't have any. And you've got a truckload of trouble waiting for you."

I raise my eyebrows.

"I checked. I found four warrants for your arrest, and I suspect there's more where those came from. On top of all that, you're still married. Want me to keep going?"

I'm getting real pissed, but don't say a word. I swallow hard and wait for what's next.

Motherfucker, you think you can talk me out of marrying Heddy?

He pauses to light a cigarette and blows the smoke into the air above him. Then he looks me straight in the eyes. "Michael, here's the bottom line. You've got a daughter. If she was twenty years old like Heddy, would you give her your blessing to marry someone like you?"

My first reaction is *What the fuck's wrong with me?* I take a measured breath. For once in my life, I think like a father, and think of my daughter, and all the hopes I have for her.

You're right.

"Probably not."

He nods his head and grins, like he just won the lottery.

I'm really no good for her, am I?

I wave over the waiter and when he goes to hand the check to Heddy's father, I grab it. Without a word, I peel off two hundred-dollar bills and drop them on the table, one final insult to him. I walk out.

I don't see Heddy for a couple of days. She keeps calling and coming over to my place knocking on the door, but I avoid her. I just can't get her father's words out of my head.

Who the fuck does he think he is, saying I'm not good enough for his daughter? She loves me.

Most guys would buy candy and roses to win a girl's affection. I track down Heddy and grab her off the street. "You're coming back with me to Bell Harbor."

Some people might call it kidnapping. I call it love. I drive her over to my place. After our time in bed, I tell her I can't get her father's words out of my head. I take her home.

With tears in her eyes, all she can say when she gets out of the car is, "Goodbye, Michael."

It hits me how I tried to remake Sheila in Heddy, but that'll never happen.

Then I do something I never do. I get drunk, and I mean sloppy drunk. I call Heddy and she comes over. I don't care what she thinks. It's over between us anyway.

She's crying and all loving, just another reminder of why she's too good for me, just like her father said. She's saying shit like we ought to elope, maybe move to California away from her family. I toss the ideas around in my head, some of them sounding real good, and take a shot of whiskey.

Maybe you're playing me. My mother warned me about women like you.

Through all her tears and talking, we calm down, long enough for me to make love to her. She's amazing the ways she gives herself to me. Later we argue about her father. I don't remember what I said but she tries to slap me. I take a few hits, but that's enough, so I smack her—hard.

She grabs her purse and stops at the door to look back. I yell something nasty at her, something that'll make her stay away, like how much I love fucking Nancy Jonas' ass. She sobs as she runs down the hall.

Why do I have to be such an asshole?

I'm so depressed, I stay in bed for a few days. No matter how much coke I snort, or how many women I fuck, the misery won't leave.

I'm finding love a hard thing to understand.

26

Last Jobs with Sammy

The last time we get together with Angelo, we almost kill him. He asks me and Sammy to come over and see him, says he's got something special. We meet him at our usual place, in the back of his travel agency. He pours himself a big mug of coffee and throws in five scoops of sugar, not offering us any. He sits in his tufted maroon leather chair behind his beat-up mahogany desk and smiles.

I know that look, Angelo.

"Listen, Michael, Sammy. I have this ex-partner of mine, name of Dewey Morrow. He and I were bagmen up in Harlem for ten years. He lives near Spring Valley, you know, up in Rockland County. Here's his address."

He hands me a piece of paper. "I want you guys to rob him."

"Rob him?" I ask.

Angelo tosses in another scoop of sugar, stirs his coffee, takes a sip and winces in disgust, plopping his cup on his desk. "Yeah. He must have close to a million dollars in his house, maybe more."

Sammy sits up. "How do you know this, Angelo?"

"Because he's afraid of banks and he's afraid of internal affairs finding out about his money or any kind of holdings. Me, I got everything in the name of my in-laws, so I have it all buried in some name or another and that works. Plus, I own land in New Mexico under my father-in-law's name."

"What kinda cut we talking about?" I ask.

"Since you guys are doing the heavy lifting, let's do the usual, twenty-five percent for me. The rest is yours."

I look to Sammy, his eyebrows rise. I nod to him, then go back to Angelo.

"Listen, it's one thing to go and hit some guy, even a cop on the street and okey-doke him into a trunk for an hour or two. But I gotta problem hitting a guy in his house with his family there, especially if he's a cop. He's more likely to fight for his family and refuse to cooperate than some guy on the street. Plus, that's home invasion, kidnapping, and whole shit load of other charges."

"Michael, this one's a pushover. I guarantee it."

"Do you know where the money is?" Sammy asks.

"No. Probably somewhere in his basement. It doesn't make any difference."

You fucking with me, Angelo?

"And why not?" I ask.

Angelo grins. He drums his fingers on his coffee mug, taking his time. "His fourteen-year-old kid has diabetes bad, and he needs insulin twice a day. All you guys have to do is keep the kid's insulin away from him until Dewey coughs up where he stashed his money. You know he will."

You're really fucked up.

"Yeah, sure, Angelo," I say. "Me and Sammy are gonna get something to eat down the block and we'll be back in a while after we talk this over."

Angelo nods. "Okay, Michael."

As we head for the back door, Angelo tosses out, "Remember guys, seventy-five percent of a million dollars is seven-hundred-fifty grand."

I wave back at him. We walk down the street and stop outside a corner bar. We look around to make sure no one can hear us. I slam my palm into the brick wall. "I don't fucking believe that guy."

Sammy barks, "I'll tell you what his story is. That cop is one cold-ass motherfucker. Doing that to his ex-partner and putting his kid in the middle. I say we go back there and whack him. This guy must think we're thugs from Bombay who kill children."

"After that shit, I wanna kill Angelo, too. Believe me. But that's out of the question, Sammy. Listen, let's play this off and find some reason we can't do it and just bow out quiet like. What else can we do? You think I don't want to take him for a ride? That wouldn't be smart 'cause we'd have heat coming at us from all sides."

"Jesus, we can't even make this fucking guy disappear. It's like he's a made man being a fucking Manhattan detective with fucking connections."

I glance up and down the street, like my answer's hiding somewhere in the city. I finally say, "Someday I'm gonna fix his ass for making that mistake in judgment, thinking we'd do that to a kid."

"Yeah. Someday."

There's always been rules, Angelo. You never break the rules.

It's summer 1971. I'm on another job with Sammy. I bring along Nancy Jonas. She's my gun moll because I'm a felon, holding my .45 for me, and she does anything I ask. Plus, she's got the world's greatest ass to do it with, and it doesn't cost me a penny. I find a guy named Thomas out of Jeremy's Monticello address book and set up a score.

"I want to buy a couple kilos of coke," I tell him.

"Why don't you come over to my place on Avenue P and 18th Street now?" he asks.

It's muggy, hot, and rainy when Nancy and I pick up Thomas. He's about forty, got long brown hair, and smells like money. I tell him I need to stop by Cassidy's apartment, a girl I know. That's where I have Sammy, Allie, and Kevin waiting to take him down. After I pull up and park, Thomas tells me he first needs to go to the Lower East Side, a heavily cop-patrolled area to pick up some extra bread.

What the fuck?

When we get there, tells me, "I'll just be a minute," and walks into some apartment building. I'm double-parked and a little worried when cops drive by, but I just wave to them like everything's cool. After forty-five minutes, he still doesn't come out. I'm pissed, so I leave.

I go back to Cassidy's apartment. It's small. Just one bedroom, a living room and kitchen. Bars on the windows but no screens. She's got flower-power shit all over the walls.

I'm drinking a Coke and sitting around with Nancy, Sammy, Allie, Kevin, and Cassidy on a couple of broken-down sofas. I'm trying to figure out my next score when there's a knock on the door. It's Thomas with a cigarette dangling from his mouth. I pull him inside and get right in his face. "Why'd you fucking leave me holding my dick, asshole?"

"Well, I had to scope things out." He taps his ashes in my Coke.

I pull out a .45 and press it into his jaw. "Listen to me, motherfucker. You just took me on a wild goose chase, and now you put your fucking ashes in my Coke?" Now I got Thomas' attention. He's scared, his eyes bugging out. "You're gonna fix this. Start dialing."

His fingers shake as he opens up his black book and calls every one of his contacts to have them come over because he tells them he's got two kilos of coke. Nancy's loving the action, her eyes all wild and excited, hanging on me.

She whispers in my ear, "Take me in the bedroom and fuck me good, Michael. Any way you want."

I shrug her off. "I got business going on now."

She's cool with it, but her blue eyes let me know any time and any place she's ready. She walks toward the bedroom and disappears around the corner.

What a fucking nympho.

Twenty minutes later, people start showing up. We pat them down to make sure they aren't packing and have them sit on the floor, leaning against the walls. While we wait for the two kilos of coke to arrive, I have everyone chill out as more people keep showing up. Thomas spends most of his time apologizing to everyone and telling them the score's coming soon.

You sold it good, Thomas.

It's getting so crowded and hot, I have Nancy and Kevin go out for drinks and pizzas from Scarola's, the best around. When they come back, I place Kevin by the front door, the only way out. He's holding my Thompson machine gun. Sammy and Allie hang out with their guns, making sure everyone's cool. I got my chrome-plated Colt .45. The one bathroom in the place is getting a workout. I even send Kevin out to get more toilet paper.

Twelve hours in and I finally make a little speech to the seventeen people who've showed up—so far. "Listen, unfortunately, you all walked into some shit where you can't leave until we leave. If even one of you tries, we're killing everyone. Got it?"

Nervous nods around the room, "We're cool, man. We're cool," come from our guests.

The call Thomas said was coming, finally arrives, after twenty-four hours of waiting. By now we're up to twenty-three rank guests, and I stuff them in the bedroom, Kevin standing guard by the door.

Before I shut the door, I tell them, "You're gonna be quiet and not say a thing. This'll all be over in half an hour."

We wait. Seems like that's all we've been doing. I stand in a corner of the living room facing the front door, but with my eyesight toward the bedroom. Sammy's on a chair, his piece out of sight. Allie's on the sofa next to Nancy in her bell bottom jeans, tube top, barefoot, smiling at me through her long blonde bangs with those blue eyes.

Thomas answers the knock on the door and lets the two punk-ass dealers in. They're both in their twenties, bone skinny with afros, but they're white. As soon as Thomas closes the doors, our guns come out. One of them is carrying, so I take his 9mm off him. The other has the two kilos of coke. We shove them both into the back bedroom and close the door on them.

I yell through the door, "No one comes out for twenty minutes. We'll be watching."

We walk into the living room and wipe down the place. Allie stops and asks, "Hey, Michael?" He points to the bedroom. "While we're here, why don't we take them all down? They probably got at least a couple grand between them."

I look at him and shake my head, "No fucking way. End of conversation."

I see disappointment on his face but don't care. We all leave the apartment and take off in separate cars.

As I drive off with Nancy, she asks, "Why didn't you want their money?"

"Nine years ago, I went along with two guinea partners when all we were supposed to do was grab a drop box from a fucking bar in Jersey City. Instead, we robbed twelve people. That ended up costing me two-and-a-half years of my life in prison for the same stupid shit."

Nancy glances over at me. There's that look in her eyes again. She reaches down, unzips my pants, and puts her head in my lap. We creep through rush-hour traffic on Kings Highway. I lean back, grab a handful of her blonde hair, and let her do her thing.

A few months later, another job comes out of the Monticello address book. This broad in Manhattan on the East Side has a boyfriend with lots of coke and cash. I line up Sammy and Allie, but no Kevin this time.

I phone the broad. "Jeremy said we should call if we were in town. We'd like to score some coke, a couple kilos."

"Sure. Why don't you come over now?"

I already know, but she gives me her address.

I go up to her fifth-floor apartment by myself, while Allie and Sammy lay back in the stairwell. I've got my .45 tucked into my belt and cover it with my black leather car coat. I knock, say who I am, and she lets me in.

I pull my piece on her and for some reason she's not that scared, but she's hot. About twenty-three, about five-foot-eight, long blonde hair, red miniskirt, white halter top, no bra, full lips. I walk her through the place to check it out and open closets to make sure no one's hiding.

I ask her, "What's your name?"

"Susan."

"Okay, Susan. What's the setup?"

"My boyfriend's got the stuff. He's gonna call. Then he'll show up ten minutes later."

Allie and Sammy knock on the door and I let them in. She starts shaking a little bit now with three of us in the room, especially the way Sammy's checking her out.

"Nobody's gonna hurt you," I say, and that gets Sammy to stop staring.

The phone rings and I whisper to her, "Don't fuck around and you won't get hurt." I put my gun to her head and listen into the receiver when she answers. She smells good, like a rich white girl from the East Side should.

"Yes, they're here. And they showed me the money. Yeah. We're cool, baby. We're cool." She hangs up.

"Good."

"What now?" Sammy asks.

"You and Allie wait down the hall in the stairwell and come in right after him, okay?"

After Allie and Sammy leave, the girl turns to me, "You do realize the kind of karma you're racking up in your life for this, don't you?"

I smile. "Yeah, but it's my karma. All mine."

Ten minutes later, almost to the second, I hear running down the hallway. The door bursts open with Sammy and Allie dragging in her boyfriend. Sammy smacks him around with his piece and the boyfriend grovels on the floor. Sammy yells at him, "What the fuck? You were gonna leave your girlfriend here alone with us, motherfucker?"

The boyfriend's maybe thirty, brown hair, and dressed like some rich kid who's trying to act like a drug dealer. I watch him cringe when I open his leather satchel.

Fucking great score.

I pull out three kilos and twenty thousand dollars and place it on the glass table. I snap open my stiletto and taste each. Two of the blocks are coke, but the third I can't make out. "What's this shit?"

"Heroin. Pure heroin," the boyfriend whines. Then he adds, "You could step on it maybe fourteen, fifteen times. That's a million dollars you're holding there."

Sammy and Allie's mouths hang open. They're staring at the shit. "Tie him up," I say and take the heroin toward the bathroom.

"What the hell you doing?" Allie asks.

"Flushing it."

"Aw, come on, man," Sammy pleads.

I stand in the doorway of the bathroom and look back at them, their eyes all lit up with the idea of a million bucks. "I don't mess with heroin. It robs the soul. Davey Goldberg, my mother's boyfriend, taught me that years ago. Anything that happens to anyone from this shit leaving my hands, I'm responsible for. It's like a bomb you throw out a window. I'm calling the shit on this, brother. That's the way it is."

Sammy and Allie know not to press me. It takes three flushes to get it all down. I walk back into the living room. They've got the boyfriend tied up and gagged good.

Sammy turns to me and asks with a smile, "Mind if I take the broad into the bedroom?"

You've got to be fucking kidding me.

I look to the boyfriend and his eyes are wild. The girl, just as bad. I turn to Sammy, "Right now, they're not gonna say shit. You do this, and she'll go to the hospital. Then it's rape. And then we're fucked. And that's the last time we'll do anything together. Jesus, we got twenty grand and two kilos of coke. What the fuck else do you want?"

That shuts up Sammy and Allie. But it gets me thinking, and my little voice whispers to me—*watch them a lot closer.*

The biggest score we never did is forty-two kilos of coke along with $250,000 in cash. My postman connection tells me Harold Fuchs is holding that much in his apartment. Harold's a pussy and it'll be an easy score. If we handle the cutting and distribution of the coke, this'll make us multi-millionaires.

Maybe I can retire.

I'm driving over there with Sammy, Allie, and Kevin. My little voice tells me I'm hungry for a Sabrett's hot dog. At the Optimo Cigar store on Broadway and Canal, there's a sidewalk window, so I pull over. It's ten at night and steam pours from the opening when the vendor pulls out dogs for everyone. It's my crew, so I'm buying. We stand there eating on the street. I look at my guys.

There's nothing like taking down a big score on a full stomach.

For some strange reason, I'm getting turned off about this job tonight. It isn't the size of the deal that has me hinky. Something's just not right. I shovel in the last bite of my second dog and wash it down with a Coke.

I mention it in a way that everyone knows I'm not a pussy. "Guys, I'm not feeling this score right now."

They look at me and shrug their shoulders. Sammy adds, "Whatever."

I'm surprised, none of them's too hot to go on the job either. "Let's hit him tomorrow. The money and coke ain't going anywhere."

I was wrong. The money and the coke went somewhere—to the cops. We found out the next day that Harold's apartment had been bugged and under heavy surveillance. He ended up getting arrested that very night we were going to take him down. The headlines of *The Times* read "Coke King of The City Busted."

Our last stick-up together is taking down Samantha, the Jamaican friend of my sister Nancy. Samantha lives in Far Rockaway in a fourth-floor apartment and is supposed to be holding at least a grand and lots of coke. It's nine o'clock on a cold January night in 1972. My crew consists of Sammy, Allie, and the Kevin. Kevin waits in the lobby on a bench pretending to read a paper.

Like you can read.

The three of us take the elevator up. I look at Sammy and Allie. They still wear that cheap Italian cologne and grease their hair back.

Don't you guys know that style's been dead for ten years?

Because Samantha knows me, I stay in the landing to the side of her apartment way up in the stairwell with my piece. Sammy and Allie carry .38s and badges. I hear them knock on the door and enter. Some loud voices, then it's quiet for a few minutes. Finally, a door slams and feet move down the hallway and into stairwell toward the lobby. I follow.

I'm just about to catch up to them around the last corner when they stop and turn on me. I walk right into Sammy and

Allie pointing their guns in my face—so I draw down on them. Kevin walks up behind them and doesn't get what's going on. Neither do I.

What's up with this shit?

No one says a word. If it comes down to it, we're gonna let our pieces do the talking. Our guns remain pointed at each other like we're waiting to see who blinks first. We're frozen like that for maybe twenty seconds, when Kevin finally breaks the tension. "C'mon, let's get outta here."

I cock my head to the side. We all lower our pieces and tuck them away. But our eyes remain on each other longer. Too long. We drive separate cars back to Sammy and Allie's luncheonette to split up the score.

"That's about eight grand in drugs and eleven hundred in cash," Sammy says.

We grab our splits and I head out with Kevin. As we drive away, I say, "The score feels light."

Kevin nods. "Yeah."

"I tell ya what, the next time we do a score with them, and we can prove it comes up short, I'm gonna whack them. You down with that?"

"Yeah, I'm down with that."

You're ready, Kevin. If I wanted to re-kill Lincoln, you'd be down with that too.

I never do another stick-up with Sammy or Allie, but I do work with them on the side through the Five Fingers Car Theft Ring. Maybe it's good we never pull another job together. We might have had to see who'd draw down on each other again, and this time, who'd pull the trigger.

I wouldn't have blinked, but that coulda been ugly—real fucking ugly.

27

Nabbed

I'm on such a roll, money coming in so hard, I see nothing but green, and it blurs my vision. My mother starts making mistakes, big mistakes that'll bring everything down. I feel it, but I don't see it.

She connects with Lester Auerbach, her new slave-of-the-month. She met him when her brother Morty and Lester drove cabs in the city. Lester's short, paunchy, Jewish, ugly like a gnome, and he stutters. He's got bad habits too, like scratching his nuts in public. She brings Lester into everything she's doing, showing him how our airline ticket scam works, and telling him about our hot cars.

So, Lester ends up finding this rich broad, Barbara, in La Jolla, California. She's interested in buying a new Cadillac for $6,000, but she wants to come to New York to see the car in person and drive it back. Lester convinces Mother it's a good idea, so she has me get her free first-class airline tickets to fly Barbara and her out and leave Lester behind to watch my sisters.

The good news is Barbara's got a cashier's check to purchase her black and gray Cadillac Brougham with only sixty-two miles on it. The bad news is that Mother throws me in the middle of her scam. I've been invisible. None of her west coast buyers know my name or what I look like.

I pick up Mother and Barbara from Kennedy. Barbara's maybe fifty and looks like the wife of a plastic surgeon, all put together with big dyed blonde hair and she wears a couple thousand in jewelry. Mother's hair is flaming red as always, and by what she wears, it looks like she's trying to compete with Barbara. She's doing a good job of it, too.

To save money, Mother gets someone she knows to loan her an apartment in the city to conduct business and so she doesn't have to pay for a hotel room. She stays in the apartment while I walk Barbara to the bank two blocks away where she cashes her check. It's supposed to be simple. She signs a few papers. We get the money. Barbara gets the keys to the car. She drives it to La Jolla. Everyone's happy.

When we get back to the apartment, Barbara says, "I don't know, Shirley. It just feels like…like something's not right." She's clutching her purse like it's her virginity.

I give my mother a what-the-fuck? look.

Mother gets in Barbara's face. "What's not to like about this? You've seen the car. The paperwork's good. All you have to do is sign. You know it's a good deal."

"Well…," Barbara's voice fades like her excitement.

Mother leans into her. "Well, what? I fly you all the way to New York, first class, I might add. And now this?"

Barbara lifts her chin, all defiant. "You can't make me do what I don't want to do."

Oh, yes, I can.

Mother's voice rises. "We made a deal and you're going to honor it."

Barbara steps toward the door and I move in her way. Her 110-pound frame doesn't stand a chance.

I look to Mother, almost like I'm waiting for permission to do something more than get in Barbara's way.

She turns to Shirley. "What is this anyway? Are you threatening me?"

Mother puts her hands on her hips. "There are no threats here. This is just you following through on your promise to complete our business transaction. Now gimme the money."

Barbara doesn't move.

I yank the purse from Barbara and toss it to Mother.

She pulls out the money and gives Barbara her purse.

"Sit down," I tell her.

Barbara fumes and whines but realizes she's not going anywhere until she accepts the deal by signing the owner papers. They're on the table in front of her, the pen waiting to be picked up. I move closer, crowding her chair. She signs.

I give her the keys, walk her down to her car, and send her off. "Have a nice trip." I wave to her as she pulls away.

When I get back up to the apartment, Mother has my three grand in twenties on the table. I don't need to say anything. She knows I'm not happy.

As I grab my cut and move to the door, Mother puts her hand on my arm, and gives me a sad little smile. "Michael, can you take me to the airport?"

You're playing me again.

"Yes, Mother."

Two weeks later, Mother flies Jim Trubee out from San Diego using another one of my first-class tickets. She stays back in San Diego this time, maybe because she's guilty about the deal with Barbara going sour. Trubee is another one of Lester's moves. Just like Barbara, Trubee's supposed to drive his car back, see the USA. I get him a motel room and bring Stevie along. Trubee's a dimwit but a good-looking guy. Tall, dark hair, almost movie star-like. He and Stevie hit it off, but that won't be enough to close this deal.

Trubee's got the cash, $5,800 for a maroon El Dorado with white leather interior. I park it in the motel lot and bring him down. He loves the car, touching it like it's the first night of his honeymoon. It's got eighty-two miles on it. He hesitates. I can tell he's getting suspicious because the deal's so good.

"I don't know," he says, fishing. "Can I meet the dealer and talk to him?"

What the fuck?

I smile, like it's a normal question. "That's what he pays us for, to handle his business. Besides, his lot's closed. He's just trying to move his last few cars. The paperwork's clean and ready to sign."

"I need to make a few calls up in my room. Mind waiting in the lobby?"

"Sure," I say. After he leaves, I turn to Stevie. "Something's not right. Think he's undercover?"

"Nah."

"When he comes down, if he's still backing off, let's walk away."

"I'm down with that," Stevie says.

We wait half an hour then head up to his hotel room. Trubee's gone. Lester calls me a few days later to tell me Trubee took a plane back to San Diego. I unload a pile of shit on him and let him know. "That's it, fucking Lester. No more flying people back."

It's the morning of May 1, 1972, when I get a call from my uncle Morty. "A federal indictment from California was just handed down for your arrest. Shirley and Lester got busted too, for something called the Dyre Act."

"What's that?"

"Moving hot cars across state lines."

Mother, arrested? Oh, shit.

"Gotta go, Morty."

I hang up and stare at the phone as if it's going to give me answers. It's after five in the afternoon and drizzling when I arrive at Nancy Jonas' home in Spring Valley, north of the city. I tell her what's going down and she's in.

An hour later, I've packed the backseat of my VW with clothes and camping gear. We're going on the lam, maybe to Michigan, where she's got a sister. I told her not to make any calls until we get to a phone booth on the road. I'm wearing a raincoat over my best maroon silk gangster suit with brown Roma shoes. I've got a couple grand on me, the rest I left with Stevie to hold until I let him know where we land.

Nothing else will fit in the small trunk in front. I've got one more load to get, to grab my trusted travel companions, my hefty, sawed-off M-2 machine gun, and my Colt .45. When I slam down the hood, three G-men are there, two with hands under their coats.

"You're under arrest, Hardy," one of them says as he throws me on the hood, cuffs me, and shoves me in the back seat of a gray unmarked Ford sedan.

"It's about time," I mumble.

I sit alone and contemplate what got me here. All my outstanding warrants, and the recent shit with Mother and Lester. I'm feeling it all start to come down on me. If I was a ship, I would have just rammed into a huge iceberg. I lean my head back, take a deep breath, and stare up at the brown-stained headliner above me.

What prisoner put this shit here?

I wonder who to call to get a good lawyer. I lower my head and notice a key in my handcuffs.

What the...?

I glance out the rear window at the three agents. They're Manny, Moe, and Jack to me. They rest their hands on their knees as they celebrate my arrest, their adrenalin still on high. They look like they're left over from the Dillinger era. Tall, late fifties, thinning hair, with the same gray suits and thin dark ties, like they got stamped out at the J. Edgar Hoover factory.

I look at my cuffs, then back at them again. They've wandered off a ways, looking up at Nancy's place, not paying any attention to me. Keys are in the ignition. I check on them again, and they're farther away.

Are you fucking with me? If I take off, will I run into a roadblock at the bottom of the hill, full of nothing cops with guns? Fuck it!

I uncuff my hands, reach in the left pocket of my raincoat to pull out a .38 snub-nose Smith & Wesson, and smile. *You didn't even pat me down.* I peek out the rear window again and they're even farther away jawing at each other, now laughing.

How far do I wanna take this?

A few minutes later they're back at the car. Two of them jump in front seat, the third in the back with me.

I hold up hands to show them the unlocked cuffs and dangle my .38 by its grip—by the way, a stolen detective's gun. I grin. "I think you guys forgot something."

They look at each other and blush, realizing how close they came to a major fuck up. Not a single word out of Manny, Moe, and Jack as it takes almost an hour before we pull up to the FBI building at 26 Federal Plaza near Broadway.

I'm fingerprinted and deposited on a dull gray metal chair next to Manny's desk. He tidies up some papers then leans over to me all friendly. "Now, Mr. Hardy, uh, mind if I call you Mike?"

I smile and nod. I know what he's trying to do, but I want to fuck with him. "Sure."

"So, Mike. Can I get you some coffee, a Coke, or anything?"

"Nah. I'm good."

He tries to hide his grin, like he just talked some school kid out of his lunch money. "You know why you're here, don't you?"

"Not really. I thought I'd wait for you to tell me."

"A friend of yours," he glances at his notes, "told us where to find you."

"Isn't that nice."

"So, I'm going to ask you a few questions, Mike. Is that okay?"

"I guessed you would. But check this out, man. I'm not saying shit without a lawyer."

He recoils, like he took a bite of some rancid meat. He tosses me in holding cell, basically a small room made from thick gray chain link. I fall asleep. He wakes me up a few hours later to ship me over to the West Street jail. I'll be arraigned before a federal judge for extradition to California.

I'm not gonna fight it, so I use a public defender. I don't remember his name.

Two things happen the next day, on May 2, 1972. First, my Great Aunt Florence has a stroke and dies on her kitchen floor. That happens right after Mother calls her to tell her we both got busted. When I hear that, my blood boils.

You'd do that to Aunt Florence? What the fuck were you thinking?

Second, the head of the FBI, J. Edgar Hoover, dies. There goes an era. I think of all the criminals Hoover put away before me. A noticeable buzz runs through the West Street jail. Talk of a vacuum of power ripples through the place and how that might benefit prisoners with pending cases. I wish I was over at FBI headquarters to watch Manny, Moe, and Jack cry.

My public defender lets me see my indictment. Not pretty. It's from the Southern District of San Diego and lists twenty-eight federal counts for car theft and interstate transport of stolen goods, plus conspiracy to commit murder, and organized crime on top of that. I added them up. Each count has about five years attached to it—140 years total.

I'd been running one of the fingers of the largest car theft ring in America dubbed by the press as "The Five Fingers" with cars going to Canada, Chicago, the South, California, and Mexico. The mob gave up-and-comers fifty bucks to steal late model GM cars off the street. They'd drop them at a warehouse down by the docks where their dashboard VIN numbers were replaced with ones from junk yard cars. A DMV connection in Albany got spiffed to clean up the paperwork as far as New York State goes.

Worked perfectly. Except someone ratted me out. Otherwise, I wouldn't be sitting in a cell with a twenty-eight-count indictment stuffed up my ass. That someone had to come from San Diego because that's where the charges originate. I find out months later while I'm in court, in a side comment from Tom Coffin, the assistant federal prosecutor in San Diego, that someone was Mother.

Fucking bitch.

Looks like she was trying to cut a deal to get her sentence reduced, at my expense, again. After screwing me over by having me take the rap for her counterfeiting in Mexico, she promised she'd never do that to me, again.

Mother never did prison time before, maybe just overnight stay in jail until one of her mob lawyers got her out. She always had a judge fix charges against her and helped me out a couple times. But that was New York six years ago and she's in San Diego. Mother doesn't have any juice there. I understand why she did what she did, but that didn't mean I had to like it.

The Feds need to get me to San Diego and I'm trying everything I can to slow them down. I even stage a fall down a flight of stairs and fake ankle and knee injuries. They put me on crutches.

I tell them, "I can't be chained," and that "I'm afraid to fly." It's my best performance since I went crazy in court and was sent to the New York State Mental Hospital in '68, diagnosed as insane.

So, they agree to take me cross-country by car, escorted by marshals.

That'll give me time to figure out my next move.

28

NYC to SD

Marshal Jim West arrives at the West Street jail to pick me up. He stands at my height, six-foot-one, but has dark hair. He's got the same name as the lead character from *The Wild Wild West* TV show from the sixties. He's a light-hearted kind of guy, but he carries a .44 Magnum, so I know he means business. He ignores my injuries and places standard-issue chains on my ankles, waist, and hands.

I'm placed in the back seat of a gray Ford sedan. No door handles. No window cranks. Our first stop is the Baltimore City jail for the night. Jim West tells me, "I hate to do this to you, Mike, but I gotta drop you off with a bunch of blacks."

I look around. I'm the only white guy in the dormitory. "Gee, thanks, Marshal."

No one gets in my shit, so I don't care. I eat my rubber chicken dinner and get some sleep. One thing about that jail, it was hot as hell.

My next night is Bloomsburg, Pennsylvania where Marshal West picks up a draft dodger and bank robber. I'm not too social so I don't remember their names. Nice breakfast of grits, eggs, and toast. I take the window seat. We stop for lunch at a McDonald's, and I pound down two Big Macs. Meals and watching interstate pavement become the highlight of my days if I'm not dozing.

Late that afternoon, we pull into the Milan, Michigan sheriff's station.

Right away the fat sheriff tries to fuck with me. "Print him," he tells two deputies and grins at me.

"Fuck off. I gave my prints to the FBI in New York."

The deputies grab me, try to twist my arms, but I don't budge. For a while I don't know what the sheriff's going to do or how far he's going to take it. He puffs out his chest to show me his shiny little badge. I don't care.

I know my rights. No punk-ass sheriff in the middle of bum-fuck America is going to mess with me.

He finally barks, "Hey, wise ass. If you don't give me your prints, I'm not lodging you."

I look to Marshal West. His face is scrunched up like he's got heartburn. He's got to be thinking that if I don't stay here for the night, he's got to find me lodging someplace else and that'll be a pain. He leans over and whispers, "Hey, Mike, make it simple for me, would you?"

Dinner is hot dogs, potato chips, and green Jell-O.

Marshal West puts me on the chain the next morning. The sheriff grins at me as we shuffle toward the door.

"Nice place you got here," I toss at him.

He slaps a night stick in the palm of his hand trying to stare me down. I smile knowing he can't, and won't, do shit. I can tell he wants me to stay in his custody a little longer so he can show me how friendly he can be.

My last stop with Marshal West is the St. Louis City jail. He's been here before and winces when he tells us, "Sorry guys, it's not gonna be any better than last night. Good luck."

As they check us in, they hand me ten worn, red plastic coins, kinda like poker chips, to buy shit. This place is really fucked up. Stinks like dirty underwear. While we wait to be processed, loud bangs come from outside. I know that sound. *A forty-five?*

The place goes crazy with deputies running all over. We can't do anything but sit and watch them go nuts for an hour. Turns out, a prisoner they just released got shot on the front steps of the jail. He didn't make it.

After we're processed, they take us to a cell block with twelve prisoners. The place is all black. I got no problem with that, until four young ones approach us.

"Dis be our show. Dig it?" one of them says.

Really?

I check them out. Nothing to talk about. Skinny. Junkies or pimps. Not a problem if I can get any of them one-on-one. The biggest one, with a huge-ass afro, does some kinda jive-ass strut up to my face. A giant palm tree comes to mind, but with a gold-capped tooth. I give him a little grin, he relaxes, then I swing my left hand hard into his face and he goes down. I start wailing ass and kicking, almost blind, when the other three jump in. I don't hear the other prisoners yell, but I catch their mouths moving, almost like slow motion.

During the fight, I throw the TV at one of them and it explodes, glass flying everywhere. I catch the guards standing by the gate enjoying the show.

You love this shit.

Some white Jew-boy from Brooklyn putting a hurt on four pain-in-the-ass Blacks.

The guards finally have enough, take me out and put one of the *show* boys, Leroy, in a cell with me. I guess they think I'll teach him some manners.

I can do that for you, Leroy.

Here I am stuck with this punk ass. He's got a welt his face where I hit him. He grins, trying to be all friendly. "You got any of dem coins?"

I look at him without expression. I see he's trying to read me. I toss my plastic coins on the dirty gray wool blanket on my cot. "Sure. Go ahead. Take one. In fact, take them all."

He balks.

I step in his face. "What's the matter, motherfucker? You don't want *my* coins? They're not good enough for you. Know this, if you take just touch one, you're gonna pay."

He backs away like a frightened little girl. "Guard. Hey, guard. Let me outta here."

As they escort him away, I yell, "Sleep fucking well, Leroy."

I get the cell all to myself. I'm here ten days waiting for the next marshal to arrive, and without any trouble going down. That's what happens when you establish who you are when you walk into a shit hole.

Marshal Luther Robertson picks us up for the next leg of our journey. He's tall and serious with a handlebar mustache, a good ol' white lawman from Dodge City who loves everything about the old West. He even carries a long barrel, six-shot Colt. Same passengers, same drill. I keep looking for chances to escape, waiting for Marshal Robertson to fuck up or get lazy, but he does everything by the book.

Our next stop is Marion, Illinois, at their underground super-max penitentiary to drop off one bank robber and pick up another, Warren Briggs. He's really something. During our ride, we talk for hours, and I find out what a gentleman he is. Intelligent too. He invented a laser beam that could kill people, and also a desalinization process. He's the first man ever to escape Marion. He told me how he kidnapped a girl after he got out, and he was so nice to her, she didn't even press charges.

Marshal Robertson drops off Briggs at Leavenworth, Kansas, then says goodbye to me and the draft dodger at the Kansas City jail. We're there over a month. It's cool. We have a whole floor to ourselves. Color TV, good food. Get to work out a little. Finally, some judge in San Diego sends an order to get me there as soon as possible, that I'm holding up his case.

Who the fuck does he think he is?

Two days later, Marshal Cliff Kline from San Francisco picks us up. He's one big fucking blond dude with a face full of teeth and a deep voice. Certifiable with nickel-plated .44 magnums resting on both hips. He drops us off at the Oklahoma City jail our first night. The next morning, we head to Abilene, Texas, where we're locked in a storeroom because there's no room in their jail. It has regular bars which could easily be cut if I had a hacksaw, but if I got out, I don't have any money to go anywhere or do anything. We sleep on cardboard boxes that night.

Next, he takes us to the La Tuna, Texas federal prison. Now, this place has some style. I find out it used to be an old Spanish monastery. It's located right on the border of Texas and New Mexico, and it's low security.

A cellmate tells me, "They want you to escape so they can catch you, then hit you with some serious time."

Supper's tasty—beef enchiladas, rice, beans, and tortillas. I get seconds. They have me shower and change out of my gangster suit into khakis. It's about time. I'm ripe. We get put in C Block, where fat Vinnie Teresa is held way in the back. He was in the Boston mob. I was hoping to talk to him, but it didn't work out.

I do meet Cisco Torres from the Black Liberation Army. He and his brother Gabriel were arrested for killing five cops. He's nothing but a wise-ass Puerto Rican talking lots of shit, and I don't like his Maoist politics. He quiets down so I don't have to do anything about him.

It's huevos rancheros for breakfast and then Marshal Kline points us west and we're flying. That is, until a Texas ranger pulls us over. I watch Kline get out of our car when the ranger walks up. "You were doing ninety-five miles per hour in a fifty-five zone. Driver's license please."

The marshal pulls out his wallet and hands over his driver's license. "I'm US Marshal Cliff Kline out of San Francisco with federal prisoners in the back of my car. We're on our way to San Diego. I don't want to be late."

The Texas Ranger bobs his head like he's sizing up his options. Without a word, the Texas ranger hands the marshal back his license and walks back to his car. We spend a cold-ass night in the Tucumcari, New Mexico jail.

We're scheduled to be in Phoenix at the Pima County jail at the end of the day. It's noon Sunday morning when we roll into Tucson to stop for lunch. We've been good, giving Marshal Kline no shit. He pulls up in front of a restaurant and shuts off the engine.

"I know you guys are tired and hungry. Here's the deal. I want to go to the steak and brew house here. If you behave, I'll buy you lunch."

We look to each other and nod in agreement. Our ankle and waist chains jingle as we shuffle into the restaurant. The smell of charbroiled steak overwhelms my nose. The place has wagon wheel lights on the ceiling and red and white checked tablecloths. Everyone turns to look at us, a local church crowd filling the restaurant, their Bibles next to them on their tables. Within ten minutes, we got the place to ourselves. Looks like they didn't want to be too close to sinners, not while they're having their after-church Sunday dinner. My porterhouse steak and baked potato never tasted so good.

We stay the night in Phoenix, then travel on to El Centro, California. Nothing much to say—boring as hell. The next morning, we head out to our final stop, the San Diego County jail, the place I've been dreading for 3,000 miles with 140 years of federal time facing me.

I get out to stretch my legs and look up at the huge gray structure poking through the evening haze. I can't help but wonder what's in store for me.

Marshall Kline tugs on my arm, "Come on, Hardy. It's the end of the road for you."

I hope not.

29

More with Jimmy

Jimmy shakes his head, maybe in amazement. "Okay, Michael. You've got another kidnapping charge from…" He skims over more papers. "When was it, nineteen-eight-three?" Jimmy finds that one further down on my third rap sheet. "It looks like you only did about a year for that. How come?"

"Because it was Debra Ann, my daughter, I kidnapped. Right after her juvenile court appearance in LA, they decided that rather than give her back to me, they'd hand her over to the State and put her in MacLaren Hall, kinda like an orphanage. They said neither me, my wife, nor my mother were fit parents." I slam my fist down on the table remembering how it felt that day. "It wasn't fucking right, Jimmy. Not at all. Jesus, she was only five."

A guard comes to the door and taps on the window to check things out. Jimmy nods to him that it's okay.

"What happened next, Michael?"

"They brought her into court where she had to listen to all the shit that's wrong with us. Debra Ann kept looking over at me. My oldest daughter was there too. She told me during an earlier visit that she'd been in MacLaren Hall, and all the nasty shit that went down there, mostly by the people in charge. Rape. Torture. They had a room, a dungeon…" I shake my head in disgust. "I watched the court-appointed social worker take Debra's little hand. When Debra turned to look at me—that was it."

"What'd you do?"

"I'll tell you what ended up happening. I got that fucking place shut down, I did."

Jimmy frowns like he doesn't believe me. "Okay. So, how'd that happen?"

"There was a national manhunt going on for me while we drove across the country. So, I called an *LA Times* news reporter and told them why I kidnapped her and what was really happening at MacLaren Hall. He checked on it and printed it up. Well, that started a big investigation, and by the time I got to LA County a few months later, it was all over the papers. Eventually, they shut the place down."

Jimmy lets out a little smile and scribbles a few notes. "A bright spot in your past, Michael. That's good. We can use that to counter some of what the prosecution's going to throw at us."

"Yeah. What's the latest with them anyway."

"Marsh Goldstein wants to meet tomorrow. Says he's got a new proposal."

"And?"

"I keep telling you we've got time on our side. The longer it takes for them, the softer their case becomes, and they get distracted by their other cases. I think you'll like the deal they give us."

"Deal?"

"I'm guessing he'll ask for twenty. I'll counter with five. We'll probably meet somewhere in the middle."

I slam the table again. "What the fuck? I'm not gonna rot in a fucking cell while you do some Monte Hall shit with my life."

"It's not like that, Michael."

"Sounds that way to me, Jimmy."

"I told you before. They push. We push back. They pull. We pull back."

"Look, in four more months, I'll be in here a year. I'm rotting in here, Jimmy. I know we can't go to trial, but what about cutting a deal, a deal I'm in on?"

"That's not how it works, Michael. You can't be in the room."

"I don't give a shit about that."

"You should."

I toss in my cot that night. Every noise in the place has me on edge. A guard's rubber soles squeak on the linoleum floor as he makes his rounds, a prisoner coughs, someone takes a leak. I think back to kidnapping my daughters and what we had to do to survive all the way from LA to Brooklyn. Car theft. Driving back roads. Buses. Trains. Selling jewelry. My wife with Johns. Some hustles.

Sad thing is, six months before that, in the office of a Hollywood studio, I dictated the entire manuscript of my life to Jim O'Hara, actress Maureen O'Hara's brother. He had it transcribed. It *was* with me when we were on the run, all wrapped up neat in a small cardboard box with brown twine around it. That was supposed to be my ticket to a book or movie deal.

That got lost along the way. My life. My entire fucking life, left under the seat of a white '79 Lincoln Continental somewhere in Colorado.

Just before I drift off to sleep, one final thought hits me.

It's kinda sad, the shit we leave behind.

30

SD to NYC

It's late June 1972, as I settle in my cell in the San Diego County Jail. That's when it hits me. I spent my twenty-eighth birthday in the Kansas City Jail a month ago. No calls. No cards. Not even Aunt Florence's one dollar I get from her for every year. Because she's dead. My mother killed her.

News of my crime preceded me. The San Diego Union Tribune's headlines wrote about a "New York Mafia Associate" being held in the San Diego County Jail. I kind of like the notoriety, but it doesn't last long in a place like this. No special treatment, no special food, no conjugal visits.

I call up my gun moll, Nancy Jonas, and have her drive out my VW from upstate New York. After she gets here three days later, she sells it for $1,600. I use that as a down payment for a local lawyer. I forget his name or what he looks like other than that he's loud, or deaf, or both.

Visits with Nancy are nice, but I can't touch that ass from the other side of the glass. So, after a week of hanging around, she uses one of Duke's airline tickets for a first-class flight back to New York. Now I'm really by myself.

My lawyer thinks he's got some angles to get my 140 years down to something more reasonable—maybe twenty years. "Mister Hardy, there are a few inconsistencies with their procedures in your case and, well, there's a lot of pieces still up in the air. The federal prosecutor let me know he could do a lot more for you if your New York end of the operation were brought into the picture." He clears his throat and gives me a weak smile. "If you know what I mean."

"You want me to fucking rat?"

His answer doesn't matter because I'll never do that. Two days later, he disappears. Maybe he watched too much TV news and was afraid of any ties I might have to the Mob. He keeps my money.

Motherfucker.

None of my mother's New York connections are any good in San Diego, so mob lawyers are out of the question. I also guess they don't want to stick their fingers in this mess in case I cut a deal. With the Feds working to build their case against me, I get a new attorney, a public defender. I think his name is Matthews. He's short, bald, and old. He's alright, but he's not gonna get me what I want, so I go hard at the law library. I get word that my mother's trial is underway and there's some extra Feds waiting around because they want to use her testimony against me.

Thanks, Mother.

Lying back on my small cot in a third-floor cell I share with three low-lifes, it dawns on me—everyone's backing off. Even Stevie, Duke, and Tony. Not a word from them, and that means no money. I get little sympathy from Uncle Morty, considering his sister, my mother, is on trial. It's like he finally got tired of all my shit. With Aunt Florence gone, my friends out of the picture, and all the mob connections dried up, I'm on my own.

Not a surprise, but I'm not getting along with the deputy sheriffs in San Diego. Then there's US Marshal John Luffoon. He's huge and one nasty motherfucker. He's riding my ass and sides with them. He doesn't like my attitude, and I don't like that none of the deputies shows me any respect. Maybe it's because I toss out some select "fuck yous" at them or disobey their orders. The only reason they exist is to piss me off anyways.

My attitude becomes too much, so Luffoon has some deputy sheriffs toss me in a rubber room, a floor-to-ceiling padded cell that reeks of disinfectant. Just bread and water. No books. No TV. Only a hole in the middle of the floor for me to take a shit. Even the Army brig in New Jersey in 1961 was better than this place.

Jesus, that was eleven years ago when I was seventeen.

They finally let me out of my rubber room for an exercise break and I get into it with three deputies. They've been waiting to get a piece of me. Two of them slam me against a wall, the other has his baton out. For a second, I flash back to the wall in the Tijuana jail four years ago, and the two-by-fours the Federales used on me.

Art Falcona, a good-hearted deputy sheriff with huge ears, swings by. "What you fellas up to?" he asks the three of them.

One of them snaps back at him, "We're teaching Hardy a lesson."

Art crosses his arms and nods at them. "And what kind of lesson would that be?"

The deputy sheriffs back off and take me to my rubber room. That night, Falcona brings me a tuna fish sandwich and some magazines. He must have said something to someone, because three days later, he lets me out of the rubber room.

"Hardy, keep clean and take it easy, okay?"

"Sure. Hey, and thanks for everything."

Things are going good until lunch three days later. I leave my seat to get a Coke and come back to find some big-ass Chicano with greasy hair sitting in front of my tray. I look around the room to see if any guards are watching.

I loom over him, and say in a low voice, "You're in my seat."

He grunts, not even looking up. "No, puto."

My Coke finds its way on top of his hair. It's on. He jumps up and almost knocks over the table. When we start going at it, a small race riot breaks out between the other prisoners. All the beefs they have with anyone come out now. An alarm sounds and guards pour in from everywhere. I've got my new *friend* on the ground and throwing everything I can at him. Guards drag me off him. The whole place gets shut down for a few days until everything calms down.

They decide to give me my own cell. Exactly what I wanted anyway.

A week passes and still no word from Stevie, Duke, or Tony, like I got leprosy. We're partners in everything we've been doing for the past two years, and I've given them a cut of all my action, but they don't want a piece of this shit. Prison scares them, especially Duke after his three years in Sing Sing. They must be afraid I'm gonna roll on them or something. I thought they knew me better.

Another week passes, and I get a simple letter signed by Louis the Baron, Sammy, and Allie. They give me their best wishes. "Hope you're doing alright, Michael. We're here for you." The sentiment is not lost on me. Between the lines they're reminding me not to say a word. I imagine they've already moved their operation and made plans to slow it down, should I say the wrong things. If I do, the next letter they send me will mention my wife and kids, and anyone else I care about, and how I'll never see them again.

I spend my time in the law library, meeting with my public defender, and watching TV in the break room. By now, everyone's heard about me, the crazy Mafia-connected car theft ring operator, so they steer clear. Nearing the end of what will become my five-month stay, word comes down that my mother got eight years. She'll be doing half time.

You shoulda got more.

That probably means I'll get fifteen or twenty years, because the cars came from me, and I won't rat on anyone.

Lester Auerbach, Mother's worthless slave, gets ninety-days study at Terminal Island. I think they should just put his ass away forever for being so fucking ugly. Ed Mann, the DMV guy in Sacramento gets two years because he turned states' evidence.

I get rid of my public defender and hire Louie Wentzell. I got no idea how I'm gonna pay him, but he thinks I got deep hidden pockets, and I think he's fifty pounds overweight. He works a deal which will take my twenty-eight charges down to four. That'll give me twenty years in a federal pen. At half time, that's ten years. I'm not thrilled about it, so I got to come up with something else. The idea of giving away ten years of my life for some insured chunks of metal doesn't sit well with me, and that my mother put my ass in here makes it even worse.

While I'm taking a shower the day before I go to court, I come up with an idea that can stall the proceedings and give me a chance to reduce my time, maybe even escape. I spend the day in the law library.

The next morning in court, Judge Thompson asks, "Mr. Wentzell, is your client ready to take a plea?"

Wentzell rises and is about to respond, but I stand up, "No, your honor. I'm ready to go to trial."

Wentzell turns and whispers to me from the side of his mouth, "What are you doing, Hardy?"

"You'll see."

Judge Thompson raises his eyebrows and looks over at Tom Coffin, the Assistant US Attorney, who shrugs.

The judge continues, "Alright then. Is the US government prepared?"

"Uh, yes, your honor," Tom Coffin answers, as he scrambles to organize the papers on his table.

You think you're prepared, motherfucker? Watch this.

"Your honor," I say.

The judge looks to me and nods.

I hold up two sheets of handwritten paper. "I'd like to submit my witness list to the court."

The court clerk approaches and takes them from me. He shows them to the judge and then to Tom Coffin. They look at each other confused.

While they're trying to figure out what all this means, I lean into my lawyer and whisper, "When they're finished talking, ask for a Rule Twenty-one-B."

"To where?"

"New York."

Judge Thompson clears his throat. "Will both the prosecution and defense please approach the bench?"

My lawyer joins Coffin in front of the judge. I strain to listen.

"Mr. Wentzell, is this what I think it is? Is your client honestly asking this court to subpoena fifty-seven witnesses from New York to testify here?"

"Yes, your honor," Wentzell answers. "All of Mr. Hardy's involvement, uh, I mean *alleged* involvement, is in the State of New York. If his case is to be tried here, we require these witnesses to be present here in San Diego before we can move forward."

The judge and Coffin look to each other again. My lawyer turns and winks at me. I can hardly wait.

Here it comes.

Tom Coffin asks, "Surely this can be trimmed down some. Say, to ten or fifteen witnesses?"

Wentzell counters, "If it pleases the court, Mr. Hardy can substantiate the rationale for each witness and their testimony."

"Counselor," the judge says, "I'd like to speak with the assistant US attorney for a moment."

"Yes, your honor."

Wentzell comes back to my table and can hardly contain himself. He leans down and whispers, "Great work, Hardy. I think we'll get a change of venue at least, maybe even reduced charges."

So, what am I paying you for?

The judge puts his hand over his microphone while he talks to Tom Coffin, jabbering away for a few minutes. He looks up. "Counselor, will you and Mr. Hardy please approach the bench?"

I'm feeling confident when I take the ten steps, but don't want it to show. We stand before the judge. He takes off his glasses, rubs the bridge of his nose, and stares at me. I give him nothing back, no reason to move to anger or retribution.

"This request appears to have some validity. That being said, it makes it somewhat untenable for this court to continue, having to subpoena this many witnesses and have them all travel here from the State of New York to testify. Any ideas, counselor?"

Wentzell answers, "Well, I believe my client might be willing to take a Rule Twenty-one-B, plead guilty to five years each for four counts, but serve his time in New York State."

The judge looks to the US Attorney. Tom Coffin nods. "The federal government can agree to that, your honor."

The judge waves his hands like he's trying to shoo away flies. "Everyone step back then." We all move to our tables and wait. "Let the record indicate that Michael J. Hardy has taken a Rule Twenty-one-B and pled guilty to four counts of five years each, which sentence is to be carried out in the State of New York." The judge bangs his gavel.

I smile and slap my lawyer on the back.

Tom Coffin approaches and shakes Wentzell's hand. "Nice move, gentlemen."

I chime in, "Thanks. By the way, I hear there's a commission in New York City that's supposed to clean it up, you know, the dirty cops and politicians. I know some bad ones. You think that might cut me some slack?"

"Maybe. A US attorney by the name of Giuliani is going after everyone." Coffin starts to move back to his table but stops and turns. "Oh, I think you might want to know something." He gives me a little fuck you smile. "It was your mother who told me that if I wanted to know about the car ring, I ought to talk to you." He pauses to watch my reaction. I give him nothing. "She's really something, isn't she?"

Yeah. She's something alright.

Four days later, two US Marshals pick me up in their dark unmarked sedan with another draft dodger and bank robber sitting in the back. Seems like that's the standard set of criminals being transported these days. I got the window as usual. The trip starts with the driver barking, "We're doing five hundred miles a day, gentlemen, so buckle up."

Our first stop for the night is Las Cruces, New Mexico in the city jail, a total of five guys in a 100-bed dormitory. Just an overnight stay then it's back on the road, all the way into Fort Worth. It's so crowded in there; we're put in a segregated dormitory on the women's side.

We wake up the next morning to a breakfast of eggs sunny side-up, grits, bacon, and coffee. As we're packing to leave, an older woman prisoner with bright red hair knocks on the big window separating our dorm and theirs. We turn and watch six women flash their sagging tits at us and laugh.

Fucking Texas hospitality!

We smile about that all the way into the Little Rock, Arkansas jail. The following day we travel to Memphis, Tennessee where I'm told I'll have to wait ten days for my next marshal. That means I'll spend Christmas and New Year's here. They place me in a cell block with a bunch of blacks, all with their own TVs and radios blaring. It takes twenty minutes before they're driving me crazy.

I call over the lieutenant deputy. "This noise is for shit. Can you put me someplace else?"

"Sorry, you've got to stay here, Hardy. Marshal Luffoon noted on your paperwork that you're a troublemaker."

"Okay. So why don't you just put me in the hole? It'd be better than this shit."

He tries to hide a grin. "Look, I can't, because you haven't done anything."

"Then why don't I just spit on you?"

That question gets me transferred to a different cell block with twenty guys, nineteen white and one Black. And wouldn't you know it, he gets into my shit about my cigarettes. Funny, because I don't smoke, but I know the value of bats, that's what they call cigarettes, in jail. I shove. He shoves back. I'm about to go a couple rounds, when he throws what I think is water in my face—but it's watered-down bleach.

I cough and sputter. "What the fuck?"

He comes at me with a Bic pen and stabs me everywhere while I try to kick the shit out of him, but I can't see a thing.

Three deputies come in to break up the fight. They got worry on their faces and keep repeating, "Oh, shit." I can tell they're scared. They get paid $125 a day for federal prisoners and don't want to fuck up their meal ticket.

They lead me to a sink where I rinse my bloodshot eyes for a few minutes. I try to rub off all the ink from the pen stabs. There must be ten of them, all oozing a little blood.

Motherfucker.

They take me across the street to the homicide bureau where the sheriff's lieutenant sits me down. He's skinny with big red sideburns. "So, Hardy, do you want to press charges against this nigger?"

I like you guys.

"No. But as soon as my eyes clear up, put me in a cell with him and I'll kill him."

He laughs. "We'd like to, more than you think, but you know we can't. Just between you and me, if you did kill him, we wouldn't press charges. That nigger raped some doctor's wife, then killed them both."

"Where's he going?"

"To the electric chair."

"Sorry I'm gonna miss seeing him fry."

For the next leg of my cross-country trip, we switch marshals again. I get a strictly-by-the-book angry one named Smith. It's like he's constipated or worse. We stop in Boonesborough, Kentucky for the night. One more long ride and I'll be back at the West Street Federal Jail where it all started eight months before.

31

Brooklyn & Giuliani

It's Monday night, January 8, 1973, when US Marshal Smith pulls up to the West Street jail. I wipe the fog off the inside of my window with my sleeve and stare out through the cold mist at the two-story concrete-and-brick building. It doesn't look like it was once a brewery owned by Dutch Schultz. After his arrest, the government confiscated it and turned it into a jail.

This New York night can't decide whether to snow or rain, but it slaps me hard anyway when I step out of the car, a reminder I've been gone eight months. Bostonians would call this weather raw. In Brooklyn, it's just fucking cold.

Home.

Marshal Smith leads me into the building, hands in my paperwork, and signs me over. Not a single word from the guy, like he's mute or just tired of driving around criminals like me.

I get dumped into a holding cell while they process my paperwork. Two gray-haired guards, the kind who've seen it all in their forty years on the job, wander over and stand in front of my cage to check me out. One slurps from his "world's best daddy" coffee mug. They smile at me like they just caught a big fish. That means they saw my rap sheets. I smile back.

Stand back boys, 'cause this big fish is going fishing.

There're lots of famous people with me in the West Street jail, but I've got more important things on my mind right now, like getting a lawyer. The next day, I grab Murray Mogel, a public defender. The only thing I use him for is to make a phone call.

The following day I'm brought into the counsel area of the jail, a room with six cubicles separated by low walls, each with a small wooden desk and four black metal chairs. It smells like lawyers and prisoners, a combination of hope and lies. A guard escorts me to a cube where two Feds wait. They're both hatted-up and wear trench coats, old school, like all they watch is *Columbo*. They stand over six feet tall and each of them has got that Charles Durning kind of gut going on, like they've been feeding on lots of Giuliani's bad cops and judges.

We sit down and they introduce themselves. "I'm George Ahrens and this is Inspector Harold Hess." Ahrens' voice comes out raspy, probably because he's a two-pack-a-day guy. "Seems your lawyer called Tom Coffin, the US attorney in San Diego, and asked him to phone Rudy Giuliani. He's the US attorney for the Southern District we work for. Coffin said you might have some dirty cops you can give us."

I look at them. They're intense. I nod slightly.

"Well, do you?" Hess asks.

Give them the minimum, Mike.

"If there's a way you can get me outta here, I'll lay it all out for you."

"Maybe. First tell us who you got in mind?" Ahrens asks.

I lean in and so do they. We're so close, I can tell what Hess had for breakfast, a Denver omelet, and I have to back away. I whisper, "Well, to start, I got Angelo Bencivenga and his partner Jack Rosenberg, if you want them."

I watch them glance at each other and smile.

You know them. Good.

"Can you get them on tape?" Ahrens asks.

"Sure."

Hess nods. "Okay, we'll get you out of here then."

While I wait the two days it takes for them to make arrangements, I ask around. Ahrens was a patrolman in the 77th precinct in my neighborhood where he was known as a straight shooter. Hess worked another beat. They joined the Feds a few years back and have been making waves, helping Rudy Giuliani bring down some big names. Dirty names.

West Street jail has the best casting ever. I'm here off and on for the next twenty months in max segregation, where everyone's doing short time or awaiting trial. Guys like Johnny Dio, a capo in the Lucchese crime family, who's big with the labor unions. About fifteen years ago, he didn't like what *Daily Mirror* reporter Victor Riesel said about him, so he threw acid in his eyes and blinded him. After Johnny's lawyers got him off for that, he got convicted for extortion and tax evasion, spending more years in prison. After he got out, he moved into stock swindles. That's what landed him back here awaiting trial, which will end up getting him nineteen years.

Henry Hill's inside and nothing but a skinny little punk, just like Joe Valachi and the other rats who squealed on the mob because they couldn't take the heat. Henry became famous after Nick Pileggi wrote *Wiseguy* last year. I heard they're going to make a movie about him. Henry never made his bones. All he did was stand off to the side and watch better men do their work—maybe drive their cars, like some kinda fucking chauffer.

There's Big Paulie Vario and his brother Peter, both members of the Lucchese family. Carmine "Mr. Gribbs" Tramunti who ran the Lucchese family, he's real friendly. Over lunch one day he mentions how he knew my mother and then tells me the real truth about how Lucky Luciano got arrested and deported. Rounding out my celebrity Mafia jail mates are Junior Persico, the boss of the Colombo family and Huey Macintosh, Junior's bodyguard. These are guys I can talk to, but don't plan to have any run-ins with while I'm inside.

I get to hang with some other serious criminals, like August Ricord. He's the dope king of South America, part of the French Connection, and wanted by the French for collaboration with the Nazi's during WWII. Christian David's inside as well, August's bodyguard. He's also wanted by the French for killing two Sûreté agents. Over dinner, Christian tells me how he took a drink in a Buenos Aires bar one night and woke up the next day in the West Street jail.

"Must have been one helluva drink," I say and smile.

Jesus, I almost forgot, E. Howard Hunt. I share cell S3 with him for a while. He is one cold-ass motherfucker. All his years in the CIA, his involvement in the Bay of Pigs, as a Whitehouse plumber, and Watergate. He was even suspected of blowing up a plane that killed his wife. All those years doing all that shit, and he's supposed to be tough, but he gets transferred here from a DC jail because two Blacks there kicked his ass.

I get to meet the most dangerous man in America, Garrett Trapnell. He hijacked a plane out of Kennedy Airport and shot up a bunch of federal agents. I almost laugh when he tells me he was rejected for membership in the neo-Nazi and National Renaissance parties for being too extreme. After West Street he went to Leavenworth. From there, he talked some broad into stealing a helicopter to pick him up from the open prison yard. She pulled a gun on the helicopter pilot who took it away from her and killed her. Then her daughter hijacked a plane trying to get him released.

No woman's ever loved me like that.

He was the last man to be sentenced for life to absolute solitary confinement in the federal system.

Ahrens and Hess come pull me out of West Street just after ten in the morning and take me to their offices in the World Telegram and Sun Building, by the Brooklyn Bridge. We talk for an hour and they're liking what I'm saying.

Ahren's stomach growls and Hess' answers. "How 'bout some lunch, Hardy?"

We walk over to Aldo's on Broom Street. There's something about a first meal after eight months in jail, everything tastes better. This one's eggplant parmesan. The side of fettuccini with marinara gravy puts it over the top along with the hot buttered rolls.

For the rest of the afternoon, it's more talk in their office. Ahrens' hand cramps up because he's writing so much, and he has to stop to shake it out. I tell them enough to make them happy, but not too much. I want to keep this going. The ash tray's full by the time they haul me out of there and back to West Street. I don't ask, and they won't tell me what happens next. It's all up to Giuliani.

Three days later, I get the call and they come pick me up on a Sunday afternoon. Apparently, they checked out my story and told Giuliani I'm the real deal. He signed papers that release me to their custody and give me immunity for anything—except murder. First thing, they have the guards at West Street unchain and uncuff me, then we head over to the Office of the First Deputy Commissioner's Special Force.

When we walk in, Ahrens shows me the cot they set up in the corner of the office. He points to an end table. "We rented a TV for you, Hardy. Over on the desk by the phone, there's take-out menus. Chinese, a deli, Greek, and Italian. Pick what you want for dinner, and they'll deliver. We're buying." He smiles.

You guys are all right.

I look around the room. Some kinda plant in one corner next to a table with magazines. A brown Naugahyde sofa. A picture of the New York City skyline's on a wall.

Can't you just look out a window?

On the desk, there's a small glass bowl with a goldfish in it, the kind you get at a county fair if you toss a ring on a Coke bottle. "Who's that belong to?" I tease.

Hess shrugs his shoulders. "I don't know. It's been here ever since we moved in. One of the secretaries feeds him."

Ahrens gets all serious and lowers his voice. "Hardy, we need to talk. Grab a seat."

"Okay," I say, sitting on the sofa.

"We could put you on the chain and go through a whole lot of security protocols, but we'd rather not."

I smile. "I'm good with that."

Hess asks, "Can you promise you won't try to escape?"

I look from Hess to Ahrens. "You got my word."

They both shake my hand to seal the deal. "Order what you want and settle in tonight. We'll get started first thing tomorrow morning, okay?" Ahrens asks.

"When do I get to meet Giuliani?"

Hess glances at Ahrens, then comes back to me. "We'll see how things go first."

"Sure. By the way, what day is it?"

"Sunday," Ahrens says.

"What am I supposed to do all night?"

"Watch TV, read a magazine, sleep," Hess says, as they grab their hats and coats and are gone.

After I get Kung Pow Chicken, I go through all the shelves and drawers. Nothing I can use. I end up watching *The F.B.I.* with Efrem Zimbalist, Jr. and his team catching criminals.

You wouldn't have caught me if my mother didn't give me up.

The next morning, we begin. They're loaded with files on both Angelo and his partner, like they've been planning this all along. They just needed a little push. That's me. With my immunity, I give them lots of details about some of the shit I pulled off with Angelo. I keep my crews out of the picture. No Stevie, Tony, and Duke. No Sammy, Allie, or Kevin. The Feds seem okay with that. For once they don't give a shit about what I did, they just want dirty cops.

They seem particularly interested in the three times I hit police bag men. I lay it all out for them, how Angelo gave me the routes and the last pick-up spot. They laugh when I tell them how we okey-doked the bag men into the trunks of their own cars.

"A million dollars total?" Hess asks, shaking his head.

"Yeah, but each time I had to mix up how we took them down so they wouldn't be ready for me."

They look to each other and share a smile.

You're impressed.

I tell them how Angelo set it up for me to kidnap Tyrone and two other drug lords for a million dollars ransom each. When I describe how I pulled off the jobs, they can hardly stop laughing. "Shit, Hardy. That's almost like you did a community service," Ahrens says.

Thanks, George. I never thought of it that way.

They take me shopping a couple times and I finally get a little wardrobe. Since I have so much to talk about, they bring in a policewoman, Maggie, to take dictation. Never had that before. She's not much to look at, but I've been locked up so long, it's the little things that get me going, like the way she crosses her ankles. She's got great ankles. Kinda nice to have a broad write down everything I say. Just to see if she's listening, I even throw in a couple of things that make her blush. This goes on for several weeks while they plan their strategy for how to set up Angelo.

By now, I've pretty much got the run of the place, even going down to the cafeteria with one of the guys for coffee in the morning. I look at all the people working here and how they only exist is to catch people like me.

Shit, with the right clothes and a shiny badge, I could do your job.

One night while everyone's gone from the office, I call Stevie Mandell. I'm careful what I say in case the phone's bugged.

"Hey, Stevie. It's me, Michael."

"Jesus, Michael. How are ya?"

"Fine. I'm out on bail. How you doin'?"

"I'm okay." His voice is tentative.

"Whatcha doin'?"

"Ya know, this and that."

"How's business?"

"Good, real good. Hey, it's nice to have you back, Michael. I'm working some things. Why don't we talk in a few days and get some shit going?"

That's all you got to say after eight months, motherfucker? All the while I'm locked up and my mother too, and you didn't do shit to help us.

Between his words, I feel Stevie wondering why I got out on bail and my mother didn't. Unlike my mother, though, I didn't give up anyone for the car theft operation, and I don't intend to. The operation's still going strong, just not shipping cars to California. That finger got amputated.

"Sure, Stevie. I'll check back with you in a few days."

32

Dirty Cop & Judges

It's Groundhog Day, February 2, 1973, and it's been raining all day like a son of a bitch, a raw New York rain. After lunch, Joe Jaffe, Giuliani's new go-between for my operation, comes to visit Ahrens, Hess, and me in my room and he's soaked. I catch him checking out my cot and living arrangements in the Office of the First Deputy Commissioner's Special Force, and no doubt wondering who the fuck I am.

He's average looking, but intense, like Giuliani's already infected him with his extreme justice disease. Jaffe waves Ahrens and Hess into an adjoining room for a few minutes, then they return.

Jaffe sniffles and clears his throat. "Hardy, we'd like to work with you. But there's some things we need to go over first."

I nod. *What now?*

"First, we want you to make contact with Angelo Bencivenga, get comfortable wearing a wire around him, get him relaxed and talking a little. Small stuff for now. Meet with him a few times to see how it goes. Think you can do that?"

I bob my head. "That's why I'm here."

"If that goes well, we need you to clean up your outstanding warrants and other violations before we go further. Sound good?"

Out of the corner of my eye, I spot Ahrens and Hess bobbing their heads, like they want me to take the deal they're a part of bad, maybe get them a medal or promotion.

This is my ticket out of prison and I'm going to ride it as long as I can. Sound good? You bet it sounds fucking good.

"Works for me."

Those few things Giuliani needs me to clean up are a nasty pile of shit. Jaffe goes over my escape from the New York State Mental Hospital including interstate flight to avoid prosecution. Then there are my charges of impersonating an officer and armed robbery of dozens of drug dealers, where they tried to pin over a hundred crimes on Duke and me. My federal counterfeiting charge is still floating around since I left La Mesa prison in Mexico. There's my most recent twenty-eight counts for grand theft auto and assortment of other crimes. Added onto that, jumping bail a few times and my parole violation from New Jersey left over from ten years ago.

You must want Angelo bad.

Jaffe ends with, "I'll leave it up to Inspector Hess and Ahrens to walk through the details with you."

He grabs his damp raincoat, heads to the door, and turns. "We're counting on you, Hardy. This guy's a bad one. And we want him."

You get rid all my shit; I'll give you the fucking Pope. I just want outta here so I can even the score with Henry, Stevie, and everyone else who screwed over me and my mother.

In the afternoon a couple days later, I make the call to Angelo. Hess and Ahrens are on the line listening in with their tech guy taping everything.

"Michael! Jesus, it's good to hear you. I heard you got pinched."

I look over at Hess and Ahrens. They're like two expectant parents. One's drumming his fingers, the other's biting his.

"Yeah, but nothing's sticking. I'm out on bail."

"That's good." There's a long pause.

You're cautious. I can use that.

"Thought I might come by your agency, see what's up, maybe get something going."

"Sure."

"How 'bout Wednesday evening, Angelo?"

"Seven work?"

"Yeah. Great. See you then."

I hang up. Hess and Ahrens let out deep sighs. They look at the clock. Hess says, "Let's order in some dinner and start planning this thing out."

Angelo's favorite place to conduct business is in the back of his Solomar Travel Agency on the west side of Kings Highway. The front of the office is occupied by three old ladies on telephones, with a bunch of posters hang on the walls, but the back room is where the action happens. A few million dollars passed through Angelo's hands there the past few years when I worked jobs with Sammy the Bull and Allie Boy. Cash—all cash.

After talking about my insight into Angelo's operation, Hess says, "We'll get a wiretap for all the phones in the place."

We finish for the evening, and as they're about to leave, I ask, "I gotta be honest with you guys, I've been locked up almost a year. I need to get laid. Hell, it's been so long, even Maggie, your policewoman, looks hot to me."

Hess and Ahrens share a laugh and look at each other. "You know, we aren't allowed to set you up with anyone, Hardy," Ahrens says.

"I know. Mind if I get out tomorrow night for a few hours?"

"Sure," Ahrens answers cautiously as they grab their coats and hats. "But be back bright and bushy tailed in the morning."

After they leave, I call Duke. We catch up for a while, then I tell him about my problem and ask, "What can you do for me, brother?"

"Call me back in a little while."

An hour later, Duke tells me, "Eight o'clock tomorrow night, Fairmont Hotel, room four-fifteen." I can hear his smile through the phone. "You're gonna be happy, Michael."

"Thanks, man."

I bring joints Stevie gave me to the Fairmont. I knock on the door. A petite Asian broad with perfect teeth and bright red lipstick greets me. She takes my hand and leads me in. "Hi, Michael. I'm Lily."

She smells like clean sheets and jasmine, wears black heels and a skimpy black dress.

I hope there's nothing under there.

Her touch is so light, I begin to stiffen. I look over at the bed and there's another broad, a tall Sicilian, on her knees wearing a bra. Panties, and nylons. Some kinda music's playing on a radio but I'm not hearing a note.

"I'm Patty," she smiles, kinda swaying.

As I'm checking her out, Lily undresses me. When she finishes, I gently take the spaghetti straps of her black dress and pull them over her shoulders. She wriggles and lets her dress fall down around her ankles. Nothing but heels, clean shaven, just what I need. She kneels down in front of me and smiles. I keep my eyes open 'cause I don't wanna miss a thing.

I arrive at the office late the next morning. As I hop off the elevator, I spot Hess and Ahrens with their hands on their hips, squinting down the hall from their office door.

You guys look like worried parents waiting for their daughter to come home from a date. How nice.

Hess starts in just as I get to the door. "We got a lot to go over before you meet with Angelo tonight."

"Aren't you going to ask me how it was?"

They both give me a *really?* look. Ahrens says, "We'll assume it went well, Hardy."

Just then, Maggie walks in with her pad and takes up her usual seat. There's absolutely nothing hot about her today, especially not her ankles. I grin realizing how the two girls from last night erased my memory of any other woman who I thought was sexy since I got out.

We get down to business. They've got maps of all the streets surrounding Angelo's travel agency. They've already driven around the area a few times so they know what the traffic's going to be like and where they can watch the building from the front and rear without being spotted. I draw them a layout of his office, the alley behind, and note the exits.

Ahrens points to a spot on their map. "We'll drop you off a few blocks from his office. We'll be in our van. Just be cool. We'll be listening in if anything goes wrong."

"It's going to be all right, Hardy," Hess says.

You think I'm worried?

"I'll be fine, guys," I say.

My meeting with Angelo isn't much to talk about. Lots of chat around what's going on, almost like he thinks I might be wearing a wire. I don't press him, and he relaxes. I let him know I'm staying at my Uncle Morty's place while I wait for my lawyer to do his best to get all my car theft counts dropped.

"What about your other warrants?"

Fuck!

I can't show it, but I didn't see this coming. "Most of them were under an alias and they haven't figured that out yet. The others are so old, they're not getting too excited about them. And since my mother's already doing time for her side, I guess they're not too worried about my end."

Angelo's eyebrow goes up, "Really?"

"Hey, that's my best guess. Look, while I'm out, I wanna get some action going. Think you can line up some scores? I'll bring in my crew."

Angelo nods cautiously. "I could do that. Gimme a couple days to set up something, then call, okay?"

"Sure, Angelo."

That ended my first taped conversation with dirty cop Angelo Bencivenga. When I shake his hand, I can't help but think, *you were going to fuck over your partner just for a score, motherfucker. You deserve this.*

I get back to the van. Hess and Ahrens are beaming as much as Feds can. "Jesus, Hardy, is this guy the real deal, or what?" Hess asks.

"I told you he was. He really didn't say shit this time, but I'll get him to spill."

On the ride back to the office, Hess and Ahrens are busy planning my next meeting with Angelo. They're happy. That means I'm happy.

Over the next two weeks, I meet with Angelo three more times. They're loving what I'm getting him to say. The last conversation really gets Hess and Ahrens hot.

"Michael, your friend Yvonne is really something," Angelo says. He barely saw her before and haven't seen him look this turned on, even over a big score.

"Yeah, isn't she?"

"You know my secretary?" He's almost drooling.

"Patty, right?"

"Yeah. I got this thing. I want to see Patty with Yvonne. You know, together, naked on a king-sized bed in a hotel room."

I smile. "A little two-on-one action, Angelo?"

He blushes. "No. No, I just want to watch them go at it."

I got you.

I nod and smile. "I think I can set that up, but I need a favor."

"What?"

"I got another score coming up, but I need a piece. Got nothing to put in my hand, man."

"No problem. I'll fix you up. Might take me a while though."

"That's cool. I'll call in a week to see how it's going."

First thing the next morning, Jaffe, Giuliani's guy, comes in. He can hardly sit still. "Hardy, you've done good. Real good. We catch Angelo giving you a hot gun, that'll be the start of a shit storm we'll bring down on him. Now, it's time to clean up your warrants."

"Well, how we gonna do that?"

"Right after lunch today you're going to stand before Judge Gurfein."

"I'll let my lawyer know."

"No lawyers. Just you, the judge, and Mr. Giuliani."

I go to open my mouth and Hess steps in. "Hardy, just do as he says. You're gonna like this deal. A lot."

While I wait for Giuliani to show, Ahrens tells me about Judge Gurfein. "You're not going to want to fuck with him, Hardy. Word is, he was the liaison between Lucky Luciano, Thomas Dewey, and the Secretary of the Navy, responsible for mapping out the invasion of Sicily during the war."

This judge must be fucking something.

Giuliani's no nonsense when we walk into court together, like I'm some garbage he's gotta kick to the curb. There's no one there except the three of us and the judge's clerk, not even a court reporter. Judge Murray Gurfein looks to be in his mid-sixties, thin, mustache, and glasses. I can tell he and Giuliani have worked together before by the way he waves him to his bench and Giuliani hands him a wad of papers.

Gurfein glances over them for a few minutes, looks to me first, then back at Giuliani. "You sure this is what you want, Mr. Giuliani?"

"Yes, Your Honor," Giuliani replies.

The judge fans through the stack of papers again and shakes his head. It's gotta be my rap sheets and all my warrants.

"This will bring down one very bad cop. Maybe more, Your Honor," Giuliani adds.

Gurfein picks up his pen, glances up at me, winces slightly, then signs, and hands it to his clerk. "So ordered," he says, then he's up and out through a back door.

Giuliani hands me a piece of paper and explains, "This is a twenty-five-hundred-dollar signature bond, Hardy. There's no cash involved."

No shit!

"Okay."

"Sign here."

Giuliani hands me a pen and I scribble my name, the easiest signature I ever made. On the way down the court hall, Giuliani leans into me and whispers, "You do this right, Hardy, and you'll walk with five years' probation."

Five years' probation? Good, then I can go after Henry, Stevie, and all those guys for fucking over me and my mother.

"Thanks."

"Don't thank me," he snarls, "just get me that cop."

On the courthouse steps, Giuliani hands me over to a detective who's been waiting. "Go with Detective Stubbs, Hardy, and do what he says. It's time to clean up your outstanding warrants and pending cases."

"As long as you don't waive extradition to Jersey," I say.

"We won't do that. You'll take that up with Judge Rothwax."

No handshake. No thank you. Giuliani just turns and walks away.

Detective Stubbs doesn't look like a detective with his plain suit, thick glasses, plain tie, and dead pan expression. *You should be an accountant.*

First thing, we grab a couple of slices at a pizza place a quarter block from 100 Center Street, the Tombs, where I'll be staying.

Stubbs adjusts his glasses on his nose. "You're gonna be busy the next few days, Hardy," Stubbs says.

"How so?"

"Well, tomorrow morning, you'll be going from court to court to get rid of your stickers. We'll start with Judge Culkin in Manhattan Criminal Court to clean up your case from sixty-eight."

"What about my lawyer?"

"Mr. Kaplan will be here first thing in the morning. He's been briefed on everything."

Why am I the last to know?

Judge Gerald Culkin is something. Pacing behind his bench, puffing on a cigar, his huge belly visible even through his black robe. He's pissed and he should be. We've been in his court two hours already. It wasn't supposed to go down this way.

"Your honor, the people have witnesses and evidence," the assistant DA pushes.

"So, where are they?" Culkin asks.

"If the court can give the people a few days, maybe a week...," the DA's voice fades under Culkin's glare.

Culkin stops at his bench. He grabs his gavel, hovers it in the air while his court clerk runs up to the bench with a calendar and points. "Monday, March fifth, nine o'clock. So ordered." He bangs his gavel and that's that.

My lawyer leans into me. "Looks like this one'll take a little longer."

"I thought this Giuliani had some pull."

The following Monday, the assistant DA isn't doing much better. "Your honor, I'm a little embarrassed, but we can't find the witnesses. But we have the weapon. May I get a postponement to bring it to court?"

"You're trying this court's patience. I'll want to see this evidence of yours on...," The court clerk steps up to the bench again with the judge's calendar and points. "In two days, on Wednesday, March seventh at three o'clock. You think you can do that?"

"Yes, your honor."

Three o'clock Wednesday rolls around and it's the same drill. The DA's red in the face. "I'm sorry, your honor. The weapon can't be found. It seems it may have been taken as part of the French Connection heroin deal. But we have Mr. Hardy for escaping the state mental hospital."

I jump up. "No, I didn't. I got lost and wandered away after you had me certified insane."

"That's enough out of you, Hardy," Culkin bellows.

My attorney tugs on my arm and I sit down.

Culkin lights his cigar, stands up, and paces for a minute. He stops and waves us all up to the bench. "Conference. You too, Hardy."

The assistant DA glares at me, but Culkin cuts him off. "What do the people want?"

He's defeated but gives it one more try. "The people will agree to two counts of nighttime armed burglary, and the defendant can walk."

My lawyer whispers to me, "Take the plea."

I whisper back, "Okay."

We meet back in Judge Culkin's court late the next Monday morning. He's pacing behind his bench again with a huge stogie, this time puffing like a locomotive, an angry one. As he talks, he shoots glances at me. "Okay, kid, this is how it's going be. I'm going let you choose: five years' probation or three years on the rock at Riker's Island."

I lean in to say something to my lawyer, but the judge continues.

"If you screw up, I'm sending you up state for five years. So, you better not screw up." He turns to his clerk. "Let's put him on second call."

Culkin looks down at me and exhales a lungful of thick smoke. "Go have a baloney sandwich and come back after lunch, Mr. Hardy. Then we'll take care of this."

I go with my lawyer to see the probation officer during lunch, so no sandwich for me. After second call, I'm back in front of Culkin. He's seated and staring at some papers. My stomach's growling and it's not just because I'm hungry.

Culkin motions with his hand like a choir director. "Mr. Hardy, stand up. I see the probation department isn't going touch you with a fifty-foot pole." He clears his throat. "This does not please me in the least." He takes a deep draw on his cigar, then taps the ashes in his tray. He looks up at me and shakes his head. "I have no alternative but to give you an unconditional discharge."

Culkin bangs his gavel. The assistant DA jumps up to say something, but Culkin stares him down. I'm not a hugging kinda guy, but my lawyer gets one from me anyways.

Detective Stubbs escorts my lawyer and me upstairs to Judge Rothwax's court. This one's simple. He confirms that I'm a fugitive from justice for a New Jersey parole violation from ten years before. He sets a ninety-day period for the state of New Jersey to come get me. If they do, I'll spend another twenty months in the Bordentown Reformatory.

I don't think I can handle graves detail again.

I walk out of the courthouse into the late afternoon air and take a deep breath. I look behind me at the gray concrete building, its weight somehow lifted off me. Aside from Jersey, all I got to worry about is the car theft charges, but I can wipe those out if I give Giuliani to Angelo.

I'm a free man for at least ninety days. All I gotta do is stay clean. What's good is I got time enough to inflict payback on some people who deserve it. My anger doesn't allow me to see into the future and know what that's gonna cost me. But if I could, I wouldn't care anyway.

33

90 Days

It's April 7, 1973, exactly one year to the day since Joey Gallo got gunned down in a restaurant in Little Italy. I remember it well because it was his birthday and I thought that was a real fucking shame.

I'm living back in Spring Valley with Nancy Jonas and her ass. Kevin's along too, ready to start pulling down scores when I set them up. Nancy brings in a few dollars dancing, shaking that ass at men who throw money at it while I try to figure out my next move.

I'm having some problems with my .45 lately. They can be a pain in the ass. A week ago, I'm switching my half-cocked piece between my hands while I'm driving my Volkswagen. I go to take the hammer off safety when my car hits a bump. The gun goes off and blows out the center of the steering wheel, plastic everywhere, my ears ringing for two days.

This morning, when Kevin comes in my room to wake me up, I'm startled, reach under my pillow for my piece to take the hammer off safety, and it slips again. This time the bullet goes through Kevin's pants and into the wall. I get up, all groggy, stumble into the next room and find three-year-old Claudia, Nancy's daughter, laying in her bed with her eyes wide open, a bullet hole in the wall next to her head. Nancy walks in and just gives me a look.

I'm shook up bad and go into the bathroom to be alone. I stare at my face in the mirror. Fu Manchu mustache, light blue eyes, round face, combed-over blond hair starting to thin. That's my face, but not what I'm feeling.

If you killed her, you'd have to eat a bullet, Mike.

I nod in agreement, take a deep breath, and acknowledge how lucky I got. Whatever promises a psychopath like me makes to himself, I try one.

You got another chance. Make this one work.

A few days later, I take ten bucks and head over to Rosemary's place a few blocks away. She's always got some weed to sell. "How much for a quarter ounce?" I ask.

"How much you got?" Rosemary answers, as she itches her red head real hard like she's trying scratch her brain.

What a skank.

"Ten."

"Gimme it and I'll get you your weed tonight. Come by at seven."

At eight that night, I swing by. Screen door's open, so I walk in. She's got two Black guys with her, maybe her pimps or lovers, it doesn't matter. She's laying across them on her broken down, stained blue velvet sofa. The TV's on and I can hear Jack Lord on *Hawaii Five-O* yammering about "Book 'em, Danno." She wrinkles her forehead trying to figure out who I am.

"My weed, Rosemary. Where is it?"

Her friends sit up a little. She slurs, all high on something, "Come back later."

I step forward. "You said seven. Later's now."

"She told you to come back later, honky," her friend with the crooked teeth says.

"I ain't talking to you, nigger."

Now I got their attention. They push Rosemary over to the end of the sofa like she's a pile of dirty clothes. She moans, all confused. The other one leans toward the coffee table. In between the beer cans, full ash tray, and chip bags, I spot a 007 knife.

What are you, some punk hoods?

"Rosemary, if you don't have the weed, just gimme my ten bucks back."

"Junior's got yo money."

"Which one of these assholes is Junior?"

She laughs, all high. "He's not here, silly. We don't have no money."

One of them stands and moves toward the closet—the one with the bad teeth moves for the knife. I reach behind my belt and pull out my piece.

"Siddown. And you," I say to the other, "get your hand away from the fucking table."

They comply. Even Rosemary perks up, her eyes wide.

I wave my gun from one to another. "I'm going to ask you again, real slow, so you can understand. Where's my fucking ten dollars?"

All of a sudden, money's in their hands. I grab a ten. I probably could've taken a hundred, but I leave.

Just as I get back to Nancy's, police sirens close in. I grab some clothes and run out the back door. I hop in her car and drive out of town. First thing I do is find a pay phone to call George Ahrens and tell him what went down.

"Jesus, Michael, what the fuck were you thinking?"

"Hey, she was trying to rip me off. And those Blacks—"

"For ten dollars?"

"Hey, no one cons me, man."

"Why don't you just come into the office? We got some work for you."

An hour-and-a-half later, I walk into the Office of the First Deputy Commissioner's Special Force, a place I lived for over a month. No more cot or TV. I'm out on a $2,500 signature bond. All I got to do is clean up my shit, and stay out of shit, for the next ninety days and help them get

Angelo. Ahrens is by himself, and he's pissed, arms crossed, a scowl on his puss, shaking his head.

"I talked to the police chief in Spring Valley." He shakes his head. "We got to back up there tomorrow morning, Hardy."

"Where am I supposed to sleep?"

"That's your problem. This motel is closed."

I stare at him. "What time tomorrow?"

"Be there at nine. And see if you can keep from screwing up," he glances at his watch, "for the next ten hours, okay?"

With that, he walks out.

I spend the night at Morty's and head back to Spring Valley the next morning just like Ahrens asked.

"Let's take care of your ten-dollar problem," Ahrens says, stepping out of his car in front of the police headquarters. "And one more thing, don't say a word, not a fucking word. Let me do all the talking. Got it?"

"Yeah."

"I mean it, Hardy. You can't go fucking this up."

Jesus, get outta my face.

We visit with the chief of police for a few minutes and then walk over to the court together. Apparently, the long arm of Giuliani reaches all the way to Spring Valley into their courtroom. During the night, the broad dropped the charges against me for armed robbery. Seems they shook prostitution and dealing in her face. The judge releases me on my own recognizance.

After Ahrens gets back in his car, I lean in through the car window like I'm taking his order at some drive-in. "I know. I'll keep my nose clean."

"For the next eighty-nine days, you better." Ahrens peels out in his unmarked black Ford Fairlane, leaving me with a face full of exhaust.

I pack up everything and tell Nancy, "We're going back to the city. There's no action here."

We drop off her kid at her mother's and bring Kevin with us. We all move into Theresa Gonzalez' house, a broad I've known for a while. She and Yvonne are the ones Angelo wanted to watch with his secretary. They're best friends. I just never got the lesbo thing. I even tried to fuck it out of Yvonne, and she seemed to like it, a lot. But she always went back to Theresa.

We pick up all the camping shit I left behind over in a Sheepshead Bay apartment in case I need to make a move and get out of town. I call up Stevie and Henry Kofflert answers, like he's his fucking secretary.

"He's not here right now, Michael."

"Hey, let him know I called, Henry. I need to get some action going."

"I'll let them know."

"Just have him call me, okay?"

"I said, I'll let them know," Henry snaps as he hangs up.

I stare at the phone.

I am bothering you or something, motherfucker?

Right then, Henry moved up to the top of my list. He's ahead of Sammy and Allie. He's even ahead of Stevie.

I loved you like a brother, Stevie, but then you disappeared when I went in for eight months. You fucked me. And my mother.

My plans are taking shape. I have Nancy get me my guns, and I spend the afternoon cleaning them. Theresa's got a worried look on her face when she sees all the parts scattered across her dining room table. My sawed-off M-1 with the M-2 auto-trigger housing gets the most attention.

She points at it. "What's that for, Michael?"

I glance over at Nancy, grin, and slap a clip into it. "Duck hunting."

Theresa lets out a nervous laugh.

"Hey, Theresa, if you gotta problem with this, talk to Yvonne."

Three days later, it's on. Theresa helps out by getting her friend's second-story apartment to use while she's out of town. Then she calls up Henry and has him come over. Says she's seen him around and wants to get to know him better. Since Henry probably hasn't gotten laid in ten years, he jumps at the chance.

It's nine in the morning and I've got Kevin with me. "Kevin, I'm gonna show you how to do righteous payback. This motherfucker, he hung up on my mother twice when she called him from prison." Just saying those words again has me seeing red. "Henry's gonna bring them all over here. All of them. Sammy and Allie, Stevie, anyone else who ever tried to fuck me and my mother over. I'm gonna kill 'em all."

Kevin grins and nods. He's not afraid. In fact, his eyes are lit up like a pinball machine. I've got everything spread out on the cherry dining room table—handcuffs, rope, pillowcase, matches, knives, gags, guns.

You're gonna pay, Henry. You're gonna pay big time.

I pace the living floor like a lion waiting to feed, the thick orange shag carpet getting stomped on by my 250 pounds. I'm holding my sawed-off M-1. Kevin's by the kitchen window looking out at the front walkway. He's got my .45. I look at my watch. It's 9:12.

Motherfucker, you better show up.

"It's him," Kevin whispers. He's bouncing.

Today could be your day to kill someone, Kevin.

I stand by the door and listen to Henry's feet echo on the concrete courtyard below, stop, then continue up the stairs.

That's right, room 213's right up here.

For just the briefest of seconds, my wife and kids flash in front of my eyes. Almost as fast as they appear, they're gone and replaced by me standing in front of a judge, a pile of dead bodies next to me, evidence of what I plan to do. I shake my head clear and get back to business.

Henry's feet stop in front of the door. He knocks.

It's on.

I nod to Kevin, and he covers me with his piece. In one motion, I swing open the door, grab Henry by the thick gold chain around his neck, and yank him into the apartment, tossing him onto the floor. His face. I'll always remember what it looked like. Confusion, surprise, and fear. I close the door and point my M-1 at his chest.

"Michael! What the hell?"

"Henry. So nice to see ya too."

"Whadda ya want?"

"Payback."

"What the fuck for?"

"That you don't know, Henry, that's your biggest fucking problem."

Henry scrambles to his feet. His eyes widen when he sees the dining room table. "How, how big a problem?"

I smile and step over toward the table. "Take whatever you're thinking and multiply by ten."

It's eleven hours, a kung pao chicken and Italian meals later. Henry tries to say something, but I can't understand him with the gag in his mouth and the bloodied blue pillowcase over his head, handcuffed to a chair.

"Henry, you ready to make some calls now? Is that what you're trying to say?"

The pillowcase doesn't move, except for around his mouth where he's breathing, the damp fabric going in and out, gurgling noises coming from him.

You're thinking.

Finally, his head shakes slowly from side to side.

"Wrong answer." I whip him in his chest with my belt buckle and he lets out his standard grunt. I'm starting to make up new shit now. I haven't gone to the matches and knives yet. That's for later. "We can keep going, Henry. All day. All night. It's up to you."

It's eight o'clock and the *Carol Burnett Show* comes on. Me and Kevin laugh our asses off for an hour. I look over at Henry and shake my head.

Fuck. When you gonna break?

Carol does her final sign-off with a tug on her ear. I pull up a chair next to Henry. I nudge his ribs to wake him up. I know a couple are broken. He moans. "Henry, I'm asking you again. This time, polite like. You finally ready to make some calls?"

Right away he shakes his head *no*.

I say to Kevin. "Bring him to the bathroom."

Kevin smiles and uncuffs Henry. Henry has a hard time standing after being in the chair so long. He stinks too, like he shit himself. Between his busted jaw, broken ribs, and swollen eye, he's missing a few fingernails. And by the swelling in his right thumb, I guess I broke that too when he tried to block the rifle butt.

I pull back the lacy white shower curtain and get what I'm hoping for, a thick pipe coming from the wall with a shower head. "Get me the rope and the knife," I tell Kevin.

By the time he comes back, Henry's already handcuffed again and standing in the tub with his arms over his head. "Henry," I say, taking the rope from Kevin, "since you messed yourself, I think it's time we cleaned you up."

He grunts something I can't make out. I know it's not about making the phone calls. I've given up on that. Now it's just payback for what he did to my mother.

After I cinch him to the pipe, I turn on the cold water. "Refreshing, isn't it, Henry?"

Another grunt and he shakes a little. I turn to Kevin. "Stay with him. I'm gonna watch *Dan August*."

A half hour later, Burt Reynolds slaps around some street punk, trying to get him to confess to something.

You make it look so easy.

The show ends at ten. *Cannon*'s on next. I got no interest in watching some fat detective growl at everyone, so I turn off the TV. Henry's hanging by his wrists, his knees almost touching the tub.

I turn off the water. "Henry, Henry, Henry."

Before I even ask, he shakes his head.

I motion for Kevin to untie him. I don't know what to do next. Then a word pops into my head—*buckwheats.*

"Keep him here, Kevin. I'll be right back."

When I return, I have Kevin get Henry down on his knees next to the tub. "Pull his pants down." After he does, I instruct Kevin to push Henry's head down into the tub and hold it there.

"Henry, there's a term you probably haven't heard, but you're gonna learn all about it now. It's called buckwheats." With that, I try to push the barrel of my M-1 up Henry's ass. He's resists and squirms, trying to say something. I stop. "Ready to call some people?"

Nothing. I grab a bar of soap from the sink and rub it against the end of my M-1. "Say goodnight, Henry." I gently slide my M-1 into his ass. He lets out a strange, guttural moan. There's nothing he can do but wait for me to pull the trigger.

I'm in LA County with Jimmy, shaking his head again. "Jesus, Michael. Did you pull the trigger? Wait. No, I don't want to know," Jimmy says.

You're impressed.

His Montblanc pens shakes ever so slightly in his perfectly manicured nails. He flips over to a fresh yellow sheet on his legal pad. I look up into his blue eyes which match the pinstripes in his custom dress shirt and silk tie. "If I pulled the trigger, it would have been a buckwheats."

"And?"

"When I glanced over at Kevin, his eyes told me how ready he was for his first killing, but then looking down at Henry all bent over the tub with the bloody bag over his head and my rifle stuck up his ass, I figured he wasn't worth doing life."

"So, what'd you do?"

"I waited until dark, then dumped him underneath the West Side Highway. The same place we left Tyrone. Remember, the drug lord we shook down for a million dollars?"

Jimmy nods while he scans through my rap sheets until his finger stops on an entry. "Is this the arrest for kidnapping Henry?" He turns the page for me see.

"Yeah."

"And it looks like you didn't do any time for it."

"That's right. I worked out something with Giuliani."

34

Five Years

I like this Giuliani guy, and not just because he was born four days after me in 1944, and we both are working comb-overs. It looks like he's gonna take my 125 years for interstate car theft, and my other outstanding warrants, and shrink it all down to five years' probation. He says we'll meet in a week to make it official. It's too good to be true.

It's mid-April 1973, and all I gotta do is stay clean and serve up one very dirty cop, Angelo Bencivenga. Nothing like a cop on the take to give a gangster like me a free pass.

There's only one thing Giuliani won't fix. New Jersey's warrant for my parole violation seven years ago. They want to bring me back to The Garden State to serve out two-and-a-half years on a beautiful farm.

I remember Sergeant Shannon's last words to me on June 6, 1966, when I walked out the front door of the Bordentown Reformatory. "See you soon, Hardy." That's a face I don't want to see again.

My lawyer, some no-name public defender, delays my New Jersey extradition court date as long as he can. In fact, today is supposed to be the last day Jersey can come get me. For them it's just collecting garbage. Giuliani's worried I won't have Angelo gift-wrapped for him before I go away.

I step into Judge Wexler's New York State Supreme Court, and right away spot two Jersey State Corrections officers standing to the side. They're tall, wear powder blue shirts with black ties and badges, and black hats that look like they're stapled to their heads. They nod at me and smile. One jingles a pair of hand cuffs, the other, leg irons.

You want me bad, don't you?

The assistant DA for Manhattan represents New Jersey. He states how simple the case is. The way he stands with his slicked-backed brown hair and dark suit makes him look invincible. I violated parole, *in more ways than you'll ever know*. I look to my lawyer next to me and he's not doing shit. In fact, he's kinda nodding his head like he agrees with everything.

I whisper to him, "Hey, can't you object or something?"

He mumbles under his breath, "There's nothing to object to, Michael. Everything they're presenting is accurate and in order."

I gotta make a move.

My eyes bounce around the courtroom for something to latch onto. Not the court reporter. Not the bailiff. Not the court clerk. The two Jersey corrections officers inch toward the courtroom doors, my only escape.

Fuck. They caught me looking.

The court clerk holds up a calendar and answers some question from the prosecutor. As he hands it to Judge Wexler, it hits me. I turn to my lawyer and ask, "What's today's date?"

"Why do you want to know?"

"Just tell me."

"April twenty-fifth."

I grin. "Today's my ninety-first day, not the ninetieth."

"Are you sure, Michael?"

"Yeah. They fucked up because they didn't count February right."

My lawyer stands. "If it pleases the court, I have come upon an important fact which should put a halt to these proceedings."

Judge Wexler looks over his glasses and leans back in his chair. "Proceed." I can tell he kinda likes the action.

"Your honor, the arrest period for Mr. Hardy's return to the State of New Jersey is stipulated at ninety days. It expired *yesterday*. Today is the ninety-first day."

The assistant DA stands. "That's not—"

Judge Wexler holds up his hand and stifles a grin. "Hold on, counselor." The judge hands the calendar back to his court clerk. "Can you please count out the days, one by one, from the issuance date of this order?"

My lawyer tugs on my elbow to stand. I shoot a look at the two Jersey officers and they're squinting at the judge, no smiles on their faces now.

The court clerk ends with, "Ninety-one, your honor."

"But we've been waiting—" the prosecutor's plea is cut off.

"Save your breath," the judge says. He turns to me. "Looks like it's your lucky day, Mr. Hardy." The judge eyes the two Jersey corrections officers. "Gentlemen, you won't be needed in my court today. This order is rescinded." Turning back to me, he says, "Mr. Hardy, you're free to go, but don't you go thinking the State of New Jersey has lost interest in you."

"Thank you, your honor," I answer.

I grin as I brush past the two officers on the way out of court. They puff out their chests as if to say, 'We'll get you, Hardy. Your kind always fucks up.'

Not me. Not anymore.

I've got a court date with Giuliani and Judge Gurfein tomorrow to clean up a few more things. For some reason, I'm extra nervous and have trouble sleeping. I can't figure out why, but my little voice keeps telling me something's not right.

My lawyer, David Kaplan, tries to reassure me. "I've been over all the paperwork, Michael. It's as straightforward as anything I've seen. Five years' probation. That's it. Keep your nose clean and you'll never have to do any time. Do you think you can do that?"

I nod when we walk into Inspector Hess' office, located in the World Telegram and Sun Building. We're here to meet with Giuliani to finalize the deal. He's sitting at a desk reviewing some papers and only glances up to see who came in. He looks pissed, a scowl on his face, like he's constipated. Paranoia hits me.

I grab Kaplan's sleeve. "Can I go to the meeting room next door for a minute?"

"What's going on, Michael?"

"I just need a couple minutes. Okay?"

"Wait here."

Kaplan approaches Giuliani. I can't hear what they're saying, but they look over at me a few times. I'm trying to stay cool, but I'm already thinking of ways to escape.

Giuliani gets up and comes over to me. "Five minutes, Hardy?" he asks.

"Yeah."

Kaplan and Giuliani lead me out of Hess's office and into the meeting room.

"Come get me in five," I tell them.

They close the door behind me. I take a deep breath, go to the window, and open it. I stick out my head. Two pigeons nearby on the two-foot ledge give me a nasty look. I lean out farther. From six stories up the city looks different. Yellow Cabs inch through traffic, horns honk, a siren echoes off the tall brick and concrete buildings. The usual odor of exhaust and despair is missing. The sun breaks through the haze. I smell freedom, if freedom has an odor. I look back to the meeting room door one last time.

See you later, guys.

I try not to look down at the busy street when I get out on the ledge. I suck in my belly as I hug the wall and inch my frame toward the next office. No one's inside, but the window's locked. I come to the corner of the building and hug it to make it around to the next office. The window's open and luckily no one's in the office. Once inside, I let out my breath, like I've been holding it for the past few minutes.

I slowly open the door to the hallway and look around. No Giuliani or Kaplan. No cops. There's an exit sign at the end of hall, maybe fifty feet away. That's where I find the stairwell and take the stairs down two at a time.

When I hit the second-floor landing, a voice above me bellows, "Hardy, get back here!"

I freeze until I hear a cop's footsteps coming after me—I'd know that sound anywhere. When I reach the bottom of the stairwell, I burst into the garage, and head toward the street, but instead of going outside, I slip in behind a black '72 Buick near the entrance. I struggle to hold my breath when the staircase door slams open.

"Hardy. Hardy! Come back."

I peek over the trunk of the car and spot Bill Irwin, the most honest cop I ever met. I duck down. At six-foot-two, he's got a tall view of everything. Since he doesn't hear anything, he heads to the garage exit into the street. I watch him look right, then left.

Whichever way you go, I'll go the other, so choose.

Irwin just stands there with his hands on his hips. *You're thinking too much.* He cranes his neck and pauses, turns around, and heads back into the garage. He drops down on all fours to scan under the cars, then stands.

"Come on out, Hardy."

Fuck.

I stand and shuffle over to him.

"Dumb move, Hardy," he says, as he grabs my arm.

"Maybe."

"What were you thinking?"

"Bill, I thought Giuliani was gonna double-cross me."

"Well, we're going up to Inspector Hess' office right now to find out."

The elevator ride up is quiet, like the building's waiting for my verdict to come down and gonna shit me out. I walk in to find Giuliani and Kaplan standing nose-to-nose, their faces beet red.

"I'm going to report you to the bar," Giuliani yells at Kaplan.

"I didn't know he was gonna skip," Kaplan pleads.

Giuliani turns and gets in my face. "I ought to forget our deal and lock you up right now, Hardy."

It takes five minutes of convincing to get him calmed down. I remind him how dirty Angelo Bencivenga is and how I can set him up good.

You gonna get some kind of medal for this, Rudy?

"Tomorrow morning at nine, Hardy. Judge Gurfein's court. We're going to try this again, okay?" Giuliani asks.

"Yes, I'll be here," I answer.

At nine the next morning, Kevin the cock, my protégé, and I check into a cheap motel in Haverstraw, New York.

Sorry, Rudy.

In think of calling my mother, who's doing four years in a California prison for her part in the car theft ring, but there'd be nothing to say.

You put me in the middle of all this shit.

Thoughts of my kids and Sheila stop me for a moment. *I can't go there. That's too dangerous with her dating a married cop.*

There're two things I need—money, and to be able to trust Nancy Jonas with my life. While she's shaking her ass and tits at a local strip club, I'm working out my next move. When *General Hospital* comes on, I turn off the TV. Kevin and I are so bored, even a soap opera can't fill the mindless afternoon. I pull out my Dirk knife from the sheath behind my back and flip it in my hand. I've got it down perfect for both single and double rotations. Kevin tries to mimic me, but with his snub-nose .38. He's sloppy.

"Think you're fast with that thing?" I ask him.

"Sure."

"Faster than me with my knife?"

He lets out a teenage grin, his crooked teeth showing. "Yeah, but how you gonna prove it?"

"Empty your bullets on the bed and stand up."

Kevin complies and I count to make sure there's six bullets on the pink comforter. "You stand over by the wall. We'll hang our arms by our sides, and I'll count to three."

He moves over by the bed, maybe fifteen feet away from me near the wall, faded blue and green butterfly wallpaper framing him. I pick one out a big one above his head.

"Do we throw down on three, or like one-two-three-go?" Kevin asks.

"On three."

He winces. "You're not gonna hit me with that, are you?"

"Jesus, Kevin. You've seen me hit cockroaches with this. You a cockroach?"

"No."

"Good. Ready?"

Kevin nods.

I shake my arm loose and let the end of the hilt of my Dirk dangle by my fingertips. His fingers are white, squeezing the .38. *That's good.* "Okay. One. Two. Three."

My arm comes up and I let my knife fly. Kevin's hand is raised only a few inches when my Dirk sinks into a green butterfly above his head. He ducks down and looks behind him.

"Jesus Christ, Michael!"

I've got just enough money to buy fifty rounds to fill the clip for my Thompson. We're gonna need a lot more money if I'm going on the lam with Nancy and Kevin, plus my blue '68 Ford Fairlane needs a major tune-up. Nancy comes back from the strip club with fifty-three bucks, all singles.

After we finish Chinese take-out, I announce, "We're gonna hit Mike Messi."

"The bookmaker?" Kevin asks.

"Yeah, at his home tonight. He won't say shit, since I know he's fucking Reggie, some young Black dude."

Kevin cringes, like he sucked on a lemon.

"Don't worry. Being homo ain't contagious." I laugh. "Kevin, you're going in, 'cause he knows me. You take the Thompson."

Kevin's eyes light up.

Nancy leans into me, and whispers, "Isn't Messi associated with the Gambinos?"

"Like I said, he won't say a thing."

At nine that night, I park down the street from Messi's home. I go to the trunk and hand Kevin my Thompson. "Make it quick. In and out. Don't worry about jewelry or anything else. Cash. Just cash. Got it?"

Kevin's bouncing he's so amped up. He nods at me and he's gone.

Twenty minutes later, the front door opens, and Kevin comes out. I pull up and he jumps in the back seat.

"Well?" Nancy turns to ask.

I pull out and spot Kevin grin in the rearview mirror.

"Around five grand."

"That's good. Real good. But why'd it take so long?" I ask.

"I had to tie up his family to get him to cooperate."

With the trunk full of guns and clothes, we leave the city and head to Evart, Michigan. That's where Nancy's sister lives at some hippie commune. Four hours later, I let out a deep sigh when we pass the state line, "Welcome to Pennsylvania, Virtue, Liberty, and Independence."

Can't get me now, Rudy.

I take side roads and hop on and off the interstate. The Fairlane's running like shit, but I don't wanna stop for anything but gas. It's mid-afternoon when we pull into the farm. Gretchen, Nancy's sister, is all happy to see her. All I wanna do is sleep, and that's what I do until the next morning.

Sunrise Farms is located almost dead center in the middle of Michigan, a few hours south of the Canadian border. *Maybe I can go there.* The farm is really something with people coming and going all the time. There's a big farmhouse and barn. After my two-and-a-half years at the Bordentown Reformatory, I know how a farm and ranch works, but I'm not saying anything.

They're growing some kinda crops, have chickens and a cow, do candle-making, and leather tanning. One guy travels around selling everything and comes back every few weeks to bring back cash and pick up more goods. I think about ripping him off, but I don't feel right about it once I see how everyone works so hard, and they seem happy.

For two weeks, all we do is lay low. I get lots of practice with my Dirk and impress some of the hippies. I realize though that I got nothing going, and I gotta make a move. Even though the population of Evart is only 1,700, and they have some kind of sheriff who goes to bed at six, I can never get too comfortable. Can't stay anywhere too long when the law's after you.

I phone Lalli Berger, a lawyer I knew from the Tombs, the Manhattan Detention Center, where I spent some time. Lalli got me a tuna fish sandwich and some joints once while I was inside. He's okay. I tell him I need a place to crash for a few days.

"And can you find out if there's any APB's out on me, Lalli?"

"I don't need to ask. There lots of heat on you, Michael. US Marshals, state police, city police. And Giuliani's extra pissed because his whole case against some cop is falling apart because you're gone."

I'm thinking heading to Canada until one of the drug dealers on the farm says that Canadian Mounties are all over the border. "They're looking for draft dodgers and drug dealers."

My best option is to head back to Brooklyn.

It's one long day on the road when we arrive in Brooklyn where I can get something going before I figure out my next move.

We stay with Lalli for a day while I line up a couple of drug rip-offs from two stoned Puerto Rican dealers. It totals around a thousand bucks. We head to Florida, the opposite direction of where I expect the cops will be looking. Somewhere in Virginia, we get a hotel room and I leave the Fairlane at a garage to get tuned up. That costs me $176.

There're six things I care about right now—money, food, sleep, gas, Nancy's ass, and not getting busted. Two days later we're north of Miami Beach. I rent a place in Hollywood for fifty-five bucks a week, and it's even got a pool. Nancy uses a fake birth certificate to register with the police so she can be a dancer. *Even at twenty-nine, with your ass, you can bring in some nice coin.*

I look up Tiny Keene who I used to hang with when I lived here in 1957. I take Kevin when go out for some fun and catch up. He's as nice and as huge as ever.

For a few weeks, my pattern's the same—looking around for some easy stick-ups, but nothing seems right. Twice a day, I drive back and forth from Hollywood to North Miami Beach to drop off and pick up Nancy at the Havana Club. For some reason, it doesn't bother me knowing greasy Cubans stuff money in her G-string.

After tripping over another pile of garbage Kevin left on the living room floor, I yell, "Get a job."

"Whadda ya mean?"

"You're eating all the fucking food and leaving a mess everywhere. I'm giving you a nice place to stay. Nancy's doing her thing to help out. It's your turn."

He gives me a *what are you doing?* look, but only says a droopy, "Okay."

I drop him off at a supermarket to apply for a job, pick up Nancy, and go home. Nancy's getting supper ready, and I'm about to head out to pick up Kevin, when the phone rings.

"Michael, it's Tiny. Kevin just got busted for burglary. I don't know what to tell you, man, but I wouldn't hang around too much if I were you."

"Thanks, Tiny."

I hang up and turn to Nancy. "Shut down everything. We gotta go."

She knows not to question me when I get like this. When one member of your crew fucks up, you go on the lam and leave them behind, otherwise everyone could go down.

On the AAA map of Florida, there's four roads going north, and I pick the one I guess will have the fewest cops. Nancy and I sleep in the car the first night at a rest stop. I have a real fucked-up dream. I get busted. I'm standing in George Ahren's office surrounded by everyone. Giuliani's there and he's in my face, screaming, "I'm throwing the book at you!"

The next morning, we hit the road.

"Where we going, Michael?" Nancy asks.

"I called my aunt. We're headed to High Point, North Carolina. That's where she lives. My Uncle Frank died seven years ago, and she sold his gas station. That's the last time I saw her. It's real quiet there. You'll like it."

We pull up late that morning. I toot the horn and Aunt Treva steps out on the porch and waves. I can't remember when it felt this good to see someone. Her hair's got more gray now and it seems like she shrunk a little. She gives me a big hug and has us come in for some sweet tea.

As conservative as she is, she doesn't object to Nancy sleeping in the same bed with me. But we can't fuck when she's around because the bed squeaks so bad. And besides, it's too fucking hot.

Three days later, she makes a few phone calls and gets me a job at an air conditioning company working new construction. I'm back to using Richard Mandell, my alias, and the same name I used in prison in Mexico. I'll work my ass off for two-fifty an hour. With such a small city, there's no strip clubs around, so Nancy stays home and helps Aunt Treva around the house and garden.

We're in the middle of this routine for several weeks and it feels good. I don't mind a little hard work, especially since I'm getting in shape.

On Sunday, July 15, 1973, at eleven in the morning, while Aunt Treva is off to church with some of her friends, I put a move on Nancy. I've got two fans blasting us to keep us cool while we tangle between thin blue cotton sheets. I'm just about to get down to it when the bedroom door busts open.

I spin around to find two federal agents and three members of the High Point Police with their guns drawn. I glance around for my piece, but remember I left it under the back seat of my car. One of them yells, "Don't move, Hardy."

Another barks, "Show us your hands."

One of the Feds pulls off the sheet to find me and Nancy naked. They give us some time to put on some clothes. They're all checking out Nancy, and she gives them a little show, bending over to let them see her sweet ass.

Jesus, I'm gonna miss that.

"Turn around, Hardy," a Fed barks.

They cuff me, toss me into the back of their unmarked gray sedan, and take me to the High Point police station as their federal prisoner.

"How'd you find me?" I ask, as we pull up.

I watch them exchange glances. They're not giving that up.

It can't be Kevin. He doesn't know about Aunt Treva.

A week later, I find out Giuliani traced a call I made seven months earlier to North Carolina when I used the phone in George Ahren's office. I waive a lawyer and extradition. I could fight it, but it'd only make what's coming worse.

The night before I'm supposed to be transported back to New York City, I try to escape jail by cutting my wrists with a razor blade so they'd take me to the hospital. In theory, that sounded like a good plan, but five marshals positioned themselves throughout the ER, so there's no escape.

Dr. Arnold treated me. We spoke as he cleaned my wounds and patched me up, just a few stitches needed. "What brings you to our lovely little hospital tonight?"

He's got a kind face. I tell him why and a little of how I got here. He seems like he cares, shaking my hand and telling me, "May the Lord be with you."

A shudder of warmth and shame goes through me.

The next week, two standard-issue US Marshals pick me up for the two-day trip back to the West Street jail. When we pull up, the other three times I've been here come back at me. There's a smell to places like this. Each jail or prison carries its own distinctive scent. West Street is garlic and old men, the garlic from all the Guineas cooking their food.

The first time I was in West Street, there was no TV and no windows. The next time, we got to watch TV with earphones, but had to turn it off by eleven at night. The next time, we could watch all night. Now, there's radios on top of the TVs, but no headphones, so everything's blaring.

I've got Murray Mogul as my lawyer. I tell him at our first meeting, before he can even start going on about all his motions, "I gotta take the fucking music, Murray. Fuck, I coulda got five years' probation."

"You know, Michael," Murray says, "Rudy Giuliani's ass is on the line for mishandling you. And I heard he's not too happy about the marijuana seeds you put in his office plants. Don't expect this to go well."

I can't even crack a smile.

Two weeks later, I'm in a holding cell at court. I'm in here over half an hour when the door opens and Giuliani sticks in his head. "Come with me, Hardy."

I try to swallow but my throat's dry. I get up and follow him. *Why no cuffs?*

He leads me into Judge Gurfein's court, right up to the bench. I look around. The court's empty except for the three of us. No court clerk. No reporter. No lawyer.

Gurfein's pissed. "By all rights, I should throw the book at you, Hardy." He glances over at Giuliani, then back at me. "We've given you ample opportunity to help the prosecution, but you seem hell-bent on doing your own thing. Anything you'd like to add, Mr. Giuliani?"

"No, Your Honor."

"Well, Mr. Hardy. I only have one regret. I should give you a maximum sentence, but I can sleep knowing you'll be locked up for the next five years." He raps his gavel.

That night, back in the dorm with ninety-nine other criminals, the smell of garlic still hangs in the air. Someone at the other end of the room erupts in a deep hacking cough. A guy two beds over talks in his sleep. It hits me.

I'll be thirty-four by the time I get out.

35

Back with Jimmy

It's Wednesday May 15, 1991, a week before my forty-seventh birthday. I've been locked up now for over six months, held at Wayside Super Max in Los Angeles awaiting trial. Marsh Goldstein, with his crippled hand, and Marcia Clark, the special domestic abuse prosecutor he brought in, are building their case for "The State of California vs. Michael J. Hardy for murder in the first degree, with the special circumstance of depraved indifference." They don't have proximate cause. They can't prove how my wife died five years ago. So, they need to convict me on my past, and I've given them plenty to work with.

A guard leads me into our usual meeting room, the one where my lawyer, Jimmy Blatt, and I spend countless hours. Nothing's changed. There's the odor of old disinfectant, the dull gray walls, the scratched black table and four chairs, the buzzing fluorescent light. I'm wearing a county-issued blue jump suit that I stuffed my six-one, 260-pound frame into. As always, Jimmy's dressed impeccably. He's brought fresh tapes, batteries, and blank yellow pads with his Montblanc pen. We've been getting to know each other. I can trust him now. I should since I agreed to pay him $75,000 for the privilege.

When we started out, we hit a few rough spots. He talked to the DA without telling me about it. He thought he could suppress my past, but that didn't work out. He keeps telling me time is on our side, that the longer it takes for Marsh and Marcia to put their case together, the better. I don't see it.

I'm getting anxious just sitting in my cell trying to figure out what to do next. I need to make some kind of move, any kind of move. I picture my kids being tossed into one foster home after another and that really pisses me off. That's no way for a kid to grow up, I should know.

At least Jimmy's really getting into our talks. Today as usual, he sets his tape recorder in front of me and pushes the red button. The little black wheels turn.

He leans in, "I want to hear more of what happened to you after you got out of La Mesa. And then, of course, your time in Hollywood, strangling Angelo Buono, your appearances on TV talk shows, the kidnappings, the gunfight at the movie studio—"

I hold up my hand and grin. "Whoa. One at a time, Jimmy. One at a time."

36

Prison Time

Giuliani's had enough. He tosses me into max seg at West Street. That's where I'm housed with the infamous awaiting trial—the French Connection convicts, a few members of the Black Liberation Army, the Dog Day Afternoon bank robbers, E. Howard Hunt from Watergate, and Carmine "Mr. Gribbs" Tramunti, the boss of the Lucchese family, just to name a few. Right away, my situation gets to me.

Jesus, I dodged my New Jersey parole violation, and I was one decision away from five years' probation. How the fuck did this happen?

I look around, expecting someone to come after me because I worked with Giuliani to put away a dirty cop. Everyone in here hates Giuliani, especially since he locked up some of them. They hate rats even more, but give me pass because I was ratting out a cop.

I've got five years ahead of me rotting in a cell and there's nothing I can do about it. It's even worse since my mother put me here. Captain Caballo and the warden don't like me, and I don't give them any reason to change their minds. I bust their balls every chance I get when I don't feel their respect.

Rawls, a half-nut guy, tries to hang himself with a noose he made from sheets, Black Liberation Army soldier Andrew Jackson and I grab his legs and hold him up while guards cut him down. I get nine guards to sign a petition stating I saved Rawls' life. I receive a commendation.

At least there's something good on my record.

That doesn't last long. Since I kept Rawls from killing himself, he takes it upon himself to steal a Clark Bar from my locker, like we're friends now. I know because I catch him in the rec room with his mouth full of the chocolate and peanut crunch, the wrapper still in his hand. Three hard lefts to his face and he's out cold on the floor, my chewed-up candy bar and a few loose teeth dribbling out of his mouth.

Captain Caballo hears the commotion and storms in. "Hardy, what happened here?"

"He fainted while he was watching TV. Something must have scared him."

Caballo glances around the room for a prisoner he can squeeze, but all he finds are smiles. He glares at me before he walks out. I don't need to look around the room, I know I got the respect of everyone. Since they know how far I'll go over a candy bar, they're sure I'll kill for something more, but they don't know how much more.

A few weeks in, I get a big smile. Aunt Treva mails me a few bucks along with a newspaper article from her hometown in North Carolina. The headline reads, "20 High Point Police Officers Arrested in Burglary Ring." These were the same cops who kept my guns when they busted me. I guess she's forgiven me for putting her in a tight spot when the Feds busted me in her home.

Life isn't too bad in West Street. The place constantly smells Italian with all the cooking the mob bosses do in here. Carmine Tramunti and his Mafia friends even arrange a small concert with an orchestra featuring Frank Sinatra, Sammy Davis, Jr., and Dean Martin. I can't attend. The warden invites all his friends. You know who got front row seats.

The pace of life inside is a continual slow motion mind fuck, the only thing entertaining is an occasional fight or lock-down. I get a visit from my sister Nancy and her boyfriend, Ira. It's Tuesday afternoon, November 14, 1972, the first day of a cold snap to hit the city. They huddle around the phone on the other side of the thick scratched plexiglass. I look down the row at the other fourteen seats, guys leaning forward, whispering into their phones, hoping someone on the other side cares.

Right away I gotta ask, "Where's Morty? I've been waiting all week for his visit."

Nancy's eyes moisten, she glances down, then looks to Ira. He takes the phone and leans in. "Morty died this morning, Michael."

"What the fuck?"

"They found him sitting in his cab with the engine running, parked in front of his girlfriend's house."

I can't stop shaking my head.

My uncle. My friend.

"Jesus, he was only forty," I whisper, my voice shaking.

Nancy leans into the phone. She's trying hard to be brave, but tears streak down her face. "He loved you, Michael."

Something about those words stick in my throat and I can't swallow.

Loved me. I loved you too, Morty.

"They're sitting shiva. You know how that goes..." Nancy's voice drifts off into a moan.

I can't go and neither can my mother. She's in prison in California. "At least you and Ira'll be there." I try to sound encouraging but don't feel it.

The rest of our time is spent on small words and avoiding feelings we can't share.

That night I toss and can't sleep. All I see is Morty's face and hear his voice—going to Brooklyn Dodgers' games, moving to Florida with him and Carol, re-selling that fucking monkey, him bailing me out over and over, living on his couch, the Chinese girl he and Ira got me for my twenty-fifth birthday, and all those visits with me in Mexico.

Why'd you have to leave me?

It doesn't help that old man Carmine Ponzio, on the bunk above me, keeps getting up at night to hawk bits of lungs into the sink. I finally bark at him, "Hey, cut that shit out!"

The next day, I'm still in a daze and don't want to socialize, thoughts of Morty so strong. After breakfast, I go back to my cell and crash on my bunk. Ponzio's above me sleeping like always. I'm in the middle of a hard dream when I hear Ponzio deep six off the top bunk and thud onto the concrete floor. He doesn't make a sound. I roll over and drift off.

A while later, Captain Caballo comes by my cell and bangs his stick on the bars. "Hey, Hardy. Look what happened to your friend. Why didn't you do something?"

I look up at Caballo, then down at Ponzio. All I can think of is Morty laying in a cold box somewhere. No better than here.

"I'm a deep sleeper, Captain."

A couple of guards come in and scoop up Ponzio. I never see or hear of him again.

I'm in the break room, keeping my head low, drinking a Coke, and reading over a letter from my nine-year-old daughter for the tenth time. Her crayon signature is below those two words again—*love you*. I gaze at her school picture and soften. Brown bangs framing dark eyes, and a bright—a smile that melts her father's heart.

Armstrong, a skinny Black junkie, catches me reading the letter and looking at the picture. He leans over my shoulder. "Ho, dat. I gonna fuck her good," he grins, a gold front tooth shining.

His comment takes me by surprise. I look him up and down, the picture of him on top of my daughter is too much for me to take in, but I won't show what's going on inside.

Go ahead. Smile for the last time, motherfucker.

I *accidentally* spill my Coke on the floor, stand, and walk over to Captain Caballo. "Mind if I get the mop? I made a mess on the floor."

Caballo nods.

I head over to the wall and roll over the bucket with the wringer and mop inside. I get to the table and junkie Armstrong's still standing there, like he's waiting for my answer. I wring out the mop and swab up the mess. When I go to put the mop in the bucket to squeeze out the liquid, I grab the metal wringer and swing it into Armstrong's face as hard as I can.

His head cracks. He crumples to the ground and clutches his face. "What the....," he groans.

"Ho dat, motherfucker!" I yell. I'm on top of him swinging.

Caballo waits a few seconds before he blows his whistle to bring in other guards. I guess he wants to see Armstrong get what's coming to him too.

A couple months later, my stay in West Street ends because of five Chileans who are inside. They're accused of killing Allende, the Chilean president. They walk around like they own the place and they're always watching old black and white bull fights in the rec room. One of them gets pissed at Tariq, a skinny Jamaican kid who sits next to me listening to rock and roll on his transistor radio. The Chilean on the other side of Tariq, reaches over and changes the station to some kind of spic trash. I reach over and change it back. He changes it again. Tariq leans back and shifts his worried eyes from side to side, the radio on his lap now becoming the center of some kind of coming shit storm.

I glare at the Chilean. *You really want this?*

"You like listening to your spic music, don't you, Paco?" I ask the Chilean with a smile. He doesn't understand me, but nods anyway.

I reach over to change the station again, but instead, in one motion I stand, grab the radio, and smash it into the Chilean's head. When his hands go to his face, I grab a leg of his chair, yank it out from under him, and kick him in the nuts. While he curls up in a ball on the floor and moans, I pick up the chair and spin around, waiting for his four friends to try something.

Everyone else in the rec room eggs them on, yelling, "Kill him," "Don't take his shit," and "Get him. Get him good."

They hope the show will get better, their only amusement for another boring day inside.

Guards hear the ruckus and run in to settle things down. One gives me a smile.

You like that I beat on one of the Chilean assholes, don't you?

I'm taken to Captain Caballo's office. He keeps it simple. "I'm putting you on the chain, Hardy. It's time for you to move on anyway."

"What's that supposed to mean?" I ask, while two guards place waist and ankle chains on me.

"They got room for you at Danbury. Say your goodbyes because tomorrow afternoon you're gone."

The next day, two Feds drive me to the Federal Correctional Institute in Danbury, Connecticut. They don't say a word during the two-hour ride. I watch the scenery pass by and find myself looking for places where I could hide, if I escaped. I step out of the car onto the asphalt outside the main entrance gate, high concrete walls towering above me.

It's Monday, November 26, 1973, just after Thanksgiving, and I didn't get any turkey. It's a cool day and it smells good too, kind of like High Point, North Carolina, but crisp, with lots of tall oak trees in the distance.

My ankle chains rattle as I shuffle toward the door and step inside. There's always an odor to a prison. In La Mesa prison in Mexico, it was sweat, fried tortillas, and fear. West Street, Italian cooking. Here? Here, I'm not sure yet.

After the two Feds sign me over, I get checked in. I strip down and place everything I have, except my Star of David and shoes, in a clear plastic bag. In return, I get prison-issue beige pants, beige shirt, a dark blue peacoat, white jockey shorts, white socks, and my bedding. I barely fit into my new clothes, now up to 280 pounds after a year of doing nothing in West Street.

My life's been reduced to one plastic bag.

I'm escorted to the dormitory where I'll spend the next four years of my life with 100 roommates. On the way, I ask the guard about the private cells we pass, "How do I get one of those?"

"You got to do good and stay out of trouble, Hardy."

I can do that.

I've already been in some serious jails and prisons, so I know how to keep my mouth shut, look around, check things out, play the big dumb white guy for as long as I can. I know my biggest problem will be my intolerance for idiots. That's where my head's at, and it's at an all-time high.

There's lots of firsts waiting for me in Danbury. My first dinner inside is sirloin steak, medium rare. My first color TV. *Kung Fu's* on in the rec room with Caine walking around in brown rags, kicking ass. There's a list for what gets shown on TV, a committee picks them. I hear they had to do that because the blacks would switch channels all the time. It's good there's some order, because most of my fights in prisons and jails have been over the TV, radio, or food.

A week in, I go to my second prison concert ever. When Richie Havens plays his version of a Beatles song, he gets everyone to sing along with "do-do-do-do-do" after he lets out his "Here comes the sun." Even I join in. I've never been in an auditorium with 900 guys singing anything, and it changes everyone's mood—for a couple days.

Since I understand the drill so well, I know I gotta get a job, and there's some real shit details in here. Right off, I get to know Joey, an Italian kid from Huntington, Long Island. He's in for small-time counterfeiting. He says the work in the warehouse is great. That's where he is.

I speak Long Island good, so I ask, "Hey, can you get me in?"

"I think so," he says.

A week later, the captain of the guard okays my work detail, with conditions. He stands there all important-like, tapping his clipboard. "Hardy, we're going to try you out in the warehouse. If you fuck up or cause any problems, you'll find yourself in the laundry, and nobody wants the laundry. I've got you on a thirty-day probation. Think you can handle that?"

Probation here too?

"Sure."

It takes me a week to figure out how everything works in the warehouse, where the holes are in the system for tracking supplies. We've got everything in here too. All the food, arctic jackets, pea coats, jungle boots, leftover Vietnam Army surplus, but no cigarettes. Like most prisons, they're currency for everything you buy or trade for, and the brand doesn't matter.

Within thirty days, I'm made the clerk of the warehouse, 'cause I'm good with numbers. Butchie Angel and Donald LaCost work with me. They both have black belts in Kung Fu—Butchie in Tiger style, Donald in Dragon style. They practice their moves in front of me and bust up a lot of the empty crates and boxes. They look like they could take on the world and not get a scratch.

One afternoon while we're on break, I ask, "Hey, can you guys teach me that shit?"

"I don't know," Butchie jokes to Donald. "Think he might be too fat to train?"

"Fucking fat?" I snap back.

They look at each other and smile.

"Hey, I can lose the weight," I say.

They grin.

I can, assholes.

Donald nods at me and says, "There's this new grapefruit diet."

"Tell me," I demand.

"It's simple. Eat only grapefruit for breakfast, lunch and dinner. Five days a week, nothing else. Weekends, eat anything you want."

"I'll do it."

Danbury's an interesting place. We got a famous writer in here, Clifford Irving. He wrote a fake biography of Howard Hughes. He's tall and skinny, with glasses. We got Mayor Jackson from Atlantic City in for some kind of fraud. Then there's the Berrigan Brothers who burned draft registration files to protest the Vietnam War. One of them's a priest, and they're both homos. Boo Bullet is the shot caller for the DC Blacks, a real pain-in-the-ass group in here. Even Howard Hunt's afraid of them. Since I grew up in Bedford-Stuyvesant, I speak Black real good, so I got no problems doing business with them. Besides, money's got no color.

With a duplicate key I make for the cheese locker, I sneak out two pounds of Velveeta a day and make lots of friends, especially Boo and his DC Blacks. One bad thing about that much cheese though, gallstones. Fuck, they are a pain. It sends me and a couple guys to the infirmary.

I get tight with Tony Maida and hang with him a lot, providing him with extra supplies from the warehouse. Tony's got long sideburns and slicked-back dark hair. Your typical jabroni with great stories about the mob, especially the legends who used to come see him. He owned a couple of Italian restaurants in the city, and he heads up a team who cook Italian every Friday night for the Mafia's made guys. I get invited because I hook him up with some great veal. He's in for tax evasion or stolen property, maybe both. It doesn't matter in here.

After sixty days, I get called into Warden Wagner's office. All 900 federal prisoners in Danbury go through this drill. He was an assistant warden at Alcatraz. I walk into his office and right away spot a piece of the Rock on his desk.

Why kind of trophy you plan to take from this place?

"Hardy, sit down."

He nods for the guard to leave the room. Wagner wears a suit and tie, maybe sixty years old, and has an ash tray on his desk that's full. He's got my file open on his desk.

"I've been reviewing your sheet, Hardy. You know, I was in Alcatraz, and I've known some tough customers. But you, you just might have the worst record of anyone in here."

I nod like I'm all concerned. *That's good, right?*

He continues, "Chief Assistant Federal Attorney Rudy Giuliani called me and told me a few good things about you."

"That's nice. Say hi to him for me."

He leans in. "Hey, don't get smart with me, Hardy."

I sit up straight.

"Now, if you feel you have to talk to someone and need some advice, here's my best tip—don't come to me. If you get into any trouble here, I promise you, you'll wind up in McNeil Island on the other side of the country."

He picks up his letter opener, some Asian design knife with fake gold, and taps it on my file while he looks me over. "If you have any problems, get rid of them now. I'm used to guys like you. It's a shame they shut down Alcatraz, you would have fit in there perfectly. You know, you kind of remind me of Doc Barker back in thirty-nine. He got shot dead trying to escape Alcatraz." He smiles. "Any questions?"

It takes me three months to lose a hundred pounds, and by the time I'm finished, I never want to see another grapefruit. Between pumping iron and Karate training, I'm down to a thirty-four-inch waist and weigh 180 pounds, the best shape of my life, even better than the Army. I've become lethal with my hands and feet, not that you need it in Danbury.

This prison is more like a country club. Between movie nights and concerts, they even got self-improvement classes going on in the evenings. Maybe I'll sign up for a couple.

1973 Danbury Federal Penitentiary, Connecticut
Michael J. Hardy, 29, 6'1", 180 lbs.

37

German & the Bible

My nail-chewed-down-to-the-quick left index finger runs down the list of classes on the clipboard and stops. "Sign me up for German."

Gary, a gray-haired trustee with a limp, raises a bushy eyebrow. "Oh, really?"

"Yeah. I wanna be able to talk to Nazis before I kill them."

Why am I explaining myself to you?

I heard that Mrs. Reich comes to the prison every Tuesday afternoon to teach German in her one-hour class. Her husband, Wilhelm, was the guy who wrote *Origin of the Orgasm*, the real reason I want to meet her. He was Sigmund Freud's protégé back in the twenties and fled Hitler in 1940 to come to New York City. He died in prison in 1957 where he was doing two years for creating some gadget called the Orgone Accumulator for harnessing sexual power.

Fucking censorship.

I can't take more than two weeks of *Frau* Reich. Not only is she boring and refuses to talk about her husband's book and machine, but she looks like she modeled for the Quaker Oats box, less the nice smile, her gray hair in a tight bun, her face all scrunched up.

Funny things happen in prison, like when you run into someone you should know, but don't remember them. That's what happened with Jack Morris and me. We share a cell, with him on the top bunk. He's about my age with long brown hair. It's a late January 1974 night, and I've been in for a few months. We're just lying there talking about shit.

He asks me, "Where you from, Michael?"

"Brooklyn, Brownsville area. What about you?"

"Yorkville. You know, over by seventy-eighth and third."

"Yorkville? Hmm, I ripped off this dealer three times in his fifth-floor studio over there. The last time, me and Tony wore masks."

It gets real quiet in our cell, but I don't notice.

"When we walked in, I used my usual opening line, 'Everyone, on the floor.' Then I told all eight of them not to look at me or Tony. That's how you get crowd control. But right in the middle of our shakedown, it hits me. I'd been snorting some coke to get me amped up. You know how they lace it with baby laxative sometimes? Well, that shit literally hits me in the middle of everything. I tell Tony to hold his .45 on them while I take my ass and my two snub-nose .38s into the bathroom to do my business. I keep the door open so I can hold my guns on them.

"I have Tony go through everyone's wallets. While I'm sitting on the can, I tell him, 'Check the secret compartments. Sometimes there's extra cash in there.' Well, he finds lots of cash. When I finally get out of the bathroom, I count everything. Just over five grand in cash and a couple grand in coke and weed.

"Then this guy decides to lift up his head and look at me. I tell him to put his face on the floor, but he refuses. Now that pisses me off. So, I cock my .38 and press it against one of his eyes and say, 'Check this out, motherfucker. If you don't put your head down, I'll blow your eyeball out of your head and into the floor below. Then you'll get to see what's happening from downstairs. You won't think too good after that either.'"

I chuckle thinking back about that.

Jack Morris' pokes his head down from the upper bunk. "That was you?"

"What?"

"That was you who ripped me off?"

"That was your apartment?"

"Yeah."

Fuck.

"Well, Jack, I guess we got two choices here. We can either settle this right now, where one of us goes to the infirmary and the other to the hole. Or..." I let my thoughts drift, hoping he'll fill in the answer.

"Or what, Michael?"

"Or you can let it go, man. It's nothing but history, a story we can tell our grandkids. That way we can both go to sleep."

We go to sleep.

By many standards, Danbury Federal Penitentiary is considered progressive. We get to watch porno films and read girlie magazines. But they won't let us see the movie *Executive Action.* Apparently, they decided a movie about a conspiracy theory involving the Kennedy assassination wouldn't play too good in here.

We're pretty civilized with an inmate congress involving fifteen convicts and some mess hall guys, completely different than any prison I'd been in. This group's mission is to handle disputes between prisoners and the warden and his guards, to give the 900 members of the population some kind of say. Since I got lots of juice running the warehouse, I know a lot of what's going down inside. I'm approached to join the congress, a current member getting demoted or kicked out. I don't remember, but it opened up a slot.

Doc Boriscano, who's in for performing abortions and income tax evasion—to me, one's illegal and the other a necessity—heads the group that meets twice a month in the education center. Joining him running things are Clifford Irving, the author who's in for writing the fake biography of Howard Hughes. Then there's Joe Carlo, a Gambino made man. Carmine Lombardozzi's brothers, John and Andy are on the committee as well. We don't really do much, but we get a special meal out of the meetings. They always ask my opinion, and it's not because of my mother's connections or because I run the warehouse. It's because of how I think, and how I get things done. That's nice.

One of the other benefits of being in the congress is I get a private cell. I tape the picture of my nine-year-old daughter—no, she's ten now—to the wall.

Fuck, where's the time going?

I go back to the education department to see if there's something else besides German I want to take. I got nothing going on Wednesday nights and spot something interesting. "Always wanted to know what the big deal was. Sign me up for Bible study," I tell Gary.

This time both his eyebrows go up, but he knows better than to say anything.

There's ten guys in the class along with Albert, the instructor. When I walk in, I'm given a brand new Lamsa Bible, some local do-gooders providing them to inmates. I take a seat in a circle of chairs set in the middle of a large meeting room in the education center. We go around the group and introduce ourselves. Just our names, not why we're here. By now, everybody knows anyway.

I touch my Star of David, then finger the gold-embossed lettering on the leather cover, *The Holy Bible from Ancient Eastern Manuscripts.*

Albert opens by clearing his throat. "Today, let's start by going over last week's reading assignment. Hardy, just follow along the best you can. You'll catch up in no time."

A guy next to me opens his Bible and shows me the page number. I thumb through the Old Testament to Job 1 and read to myself. "There was a man in the land of Uz whose name was Job; and that man was innocent and upright, and one who revered God and turned away from evil. And there were born to him seven sons and three daughters. His substance was seven thousand sheep and three thousand camels and five hundred yoke of oxen and five hundred she-asses and a very great household; so that this man was the greatest of all the men of the East."

This Job, he was doing good.

Well, he was doing good until a few verses later. What happens next to Job blows me away. How he doesn't blame God, that gives me something to think about. The discussion is intense. The men are smart and really get into it. I look around the room and listen to them speak. Memories of my 108-year-old Granny telling me stories of the Civil War and all that followed tug at me and my eight-year-old mind. I can feel my Southern Baptist roots spread out to seek water, my branches reaching for the sun.

After class, everyone grabs coffee. Judd Tanner, a distinguished, happy man with a thin gray mustache, comes up to me. "So, whadda ya think, Hardy?"

"Coffee's not that good," I answer.

"Yeah, we ought to do something about that. You know anyone in the warehouse who can get their hands on some good stuff?"

I grin. "Maybe."

"How 'bout we take in the yard before hitting the rack?"

I nod, and just like that, we begin a ritual of how we cap off each day, strolling around the yard, talking about life, our families, the world. Judd was big in the Maritime Union. He was convicted of sabotaging a ship where three people got killed. The way he talks, or stands, or sits, it's like he knows something no one else does. There's a calmness and a peace about him too, something I've never had. It's not like he's resigned himself to his three years' time, but that he's good with everything going on around him.

A couple weeks later, after Bible study, Judd asks, "What do you think of the inmate congress?"

I shrug. "Got me a private cell." I lean in and whisper, "But it's really nothing more than a bitch session. Hey, you ought to get involved."

He grins at me. "Not really. I don't bitch."

"Yeah, I noticed. Nothing seems to get to you."

His eyes brighten. "Want to know why?"

"Sure."

"I believe in a higher power and give my worries to him."

I can't help but roll my eyes. "Judd, you've been reading too much of the Bible, man."

Judd places his hand on my shoulder, like a caring father would. "Michael, if you really want to know what it's all about, let's talk. I mean, really talk. Just let me know when you're ready."

I thought that's what we've been doing. Talking.

We head off to our private cells.

Lying back on my bed that night, I can't quite shake the feeling Judd knows something I'll never get.

Life in Danbury falls into a nice routine, daily walks around the yard with Judd, Wednesday night Bible study, every other week with the inmate congress, working deals with everyone, even the guards, for supplies from my warehouse.

Judd surprises me in my cell on my thirtieth birthday, Friday, May 24, 1974, with a small gift. Something that didn't come through the warehouse. I would have known.

"Thought you might like this."

"How'd you know it was my birthday?"

Judd grins a little extra. He always does when he bests me at something. "Michael, you've put in thirty years on this planet. A milestone in a many men's lives. Time to take measure of who you are as a man, and who you want to be. Go ahead, open it."

Who am I as a man?

It's a silver Omega Constellation watch. Beautiful white face with a red omega at the twelve position, polished, gleaming. The day and date already set.

"Put it on," he urges.

I wrap it around my right wrist, the cool steel bringing my hand to life. I snap it in place and flex my hand. It looks good but feels better.

"Thanks, Judd."

"You're less than halfway through your life, Michael. With all you've been through, you should realize by now there's a reason you're still here. Do you?"

I stare at the second hand of my new watch as it ticks by, then glance at him. "Not yet."

He reaches over and taps on my Lamsa Bible, his manicured nails making small indents in the soft leather. "You might find the answers in here."

Yeah, sure.

I'm surrounded by what they call white-collar criminals. Most of these guys are out of shape and much older than me. I just turned thirty, am staying at 180 pounds, pumping iron, working hard on my Kung Fu moves, but I want to do something else. I take up paddleball and I'm a quick learner. Seems that's the game the Mafia guys like most. It takes me several weeks to move up the ladder to play Bernie Stein, the biggest bookmaker in New York City.

"I'm glad your mom moved to California, Michael," he tells me, after our first game. "She ran things so tight; I couldn't get any action."

"Yeah. That was her all right."

Bernie's got a wicked backhand, but I'm ten years younger and faster. We get to the point where we're playing four times a week. Too bad about Bernie. Nice guy. After he gets out, The Westies, a gang out of Hell's Kitchen, put a few bullets in him, took his book, and buried him in three different states. Seems the Irish didn't want to earn their way into that game.

In June 1973, seven months into my stay, two important things happen to me. First, I get called into my counselor's office in the education department. He's the typical bureaucrat—fifty, overweight, balding, and with a boring voice. He confirms my release date, December 20, 1974. *I guess I've been behaving.* It's been just over two years, May 2, 1972, since three Feds grabbed me at Nancy Jonas' Spring Valley home, because my mother fingered me.

I'll be out before you, Mother.

"Unless you fuck up, Hardy, you'll be home for Christmas," my counselor says.

I reach under my shirt, dangle my Star of David in front of him, and smile.

"Oh, yeah, right," he says, staring down at my file. "Uh, how are things in Bible study?"

"I'm learning about your Jesus. Seems he was a nice enough guy, until the Romans killed him. Most people blame us Jews."

The second good thing that happens is I sign up for acting classes. For some reason, the poster on the bulletin board catches my eye, something about "Learn to Act from a Broadway Pro." In no time, Tuesday nights become my favorite part of the week. I'm having more fun than anything

THE LAST JEWISH GANGSTER | 293

I've ever done, doing improvisation and scenes from famous plays.

Daniel, the instructor, says I'm a natural. After class one night, he asks me to stay. "Hardy, where'd you'd learn to act?"

"Nowhere."

"Oh, come on. You must have been in school plays?"

"Nope."

"Well, you picked it up somewhere. You do anything I ask you. You're fearless."

Popping into my head is the Brando line I used to say when I was fifteen and hanging out with my gang. "I'm afraid of you? Are you cracked?"

He wrinkles his forehead. "What's that from?"

"Brando. The Wild Ones."

"Yeah, Brando. He's really something. You should have seen him on Broadway in Streetcar."

You saw Brando?

"Hey, can we do that here?"

"Sure, we'll do some scene work."

Fucking Brando, man.

On one of our daily walks around the yard, out of nowhere, Judd asks, "You know the passage in the Bible, 'I stand at the door and knock'?"

"I heard it."

Judd smiles like a kind father would if I had one. "The Lord's waiting for you, Michael. You're going home soon and need to make a decision about what you're going to do with your life."

"Judd, you were born with Jesus. You're Catholic. I've broken every commandment."

"I understand, Michael. But Christ forgives all sins." He rests a hand on my shoulder. "I tell you what I'm going to do. I'm going to pray to the Lord, ask Him to guide me as to what I should say to you."

I grin and nod. "You do that, Judd. Go on and do that."

Maybe this'll work.

In my cell that night, I make a prayer. "God, I don't want to do the things I've done before. I don't want to rob and kill. But I need a good job, something to do. If you can show me that Christ is who he says he is, I'll pray to him."

There's no response. No answer. I'd usually get pissed, but a calmness fills me.

38

Dignitaries & Getting Out

It's October 1974, two months before I get out of Danbury and we're doing our every other week inmate congress. Doc Boriscano pounds the table to bring all eighteen of us to order. He's in his late fifties, got a well-fed Italian gut, and slicked back dark hair he dyes. He says he's got the perfect plan to fuck with the warden because he ignored the last proposal we sent him, something about conjugal visits—again.

Doc stands and paces in front of us, a Cheshire cat grin on his face. "This is what I want to do. Invite Congressman Lowell Weicker, Father Drinan, senators, supreme court justices, even the mayor of Atlantic City. About two hundred altogether. We'll give them all something like humanitarian awards." He can hardly control his excitement, bouncing on his feet, like a kid who's standing over the school bully he just beat up.

One of the mess hall guys asks, "When's this supposed to happen?"

"A month from now. We'll hold it here. Right here. We'll feed 'em. There'll be speeches. We'll do it up right."

I shake my head and smile. "The warden ain't gonna like this."

"He doesn't have a choice." He glowers at everyone in the room. We're sitting up and paying extra attention. "I had Wally in the print shop make up the invitations all nice and official. The mail room sent 'em out yesterday as official prison correspondence."

I'm proud of what Doc did, but we look at each other with concern, worried about what the warden's gonna do.

We didn't have to wait long. Three days later, Warden Wagner calls the inmate congress together for a special meeting. He's so pissed, he throws a chair against the wall to get our attention.

The guards step forward.

The Warden growls when he says, "I won't have a bunch of highfaluting freeloaders coming in here to feed off my dime. By God, I will not." He glares at all of us, his eyes settling on Doc. "Fix it!"

Doc does nothing, and the calls from congressmen and senators to the warden's office don't stop. It takes four more days, but the warden's in front of the inmate congress again for a special meeting. His face a shade of red somewhere between rage and embarrassment.

"You think you're so smart? Well, you'll have your goddamn meal and speeches. But first, you're going to scrub and paint this place until everything shines like a new nickel. And when we're done with your little party, ours'll just be getting started."

The Italians put together the menu. Antipasto salad, minestrone soup, a choice of chicken parmigiana or baked cod with scallions and olives, a pasta side, string beans almondine, gelato for dessert. We got to sample it a few weeks before the event. One hundred dignitaries are set to show up and it's the most nervous I've been in my life. There'll be three speakers for the event—Warden Wagner, Doc Boriscano, and me, Michael J. Hardy.

A week before the event, guards come to take Doc and me to the warden's office. Warden Wagner's got his serious don't-fuck-with-me look, sitting behind his big desk with bookcases filling the wall behind him, books I'll never read. He shakes his head. "This shindig you put together will become your ruin or a triumph. It's up to you." His eyes are more on Doc than me as he blabs on some more, warning us to play it cool with what we're going to say. He ends with, "You guys want to say something stupid and hang yourselves, go ahead."

Walking the yard with Judd the day before the event, he asks, "You putting the final touches on your speech, Michael?"

"Almost. I've been working on this for almost a month. I typed and retyped it so many times it's not making any sense. There's so much I want to say. And I want to say it right. This is some hard shit, brother."

We pause. Judd tilts his head. "You know, every time I had to get up in front of a big crowd, even the House of Representative, I got nervous as hell."

"You, Judd?"

Judd nods.

"What'd you do?" I ask.

"Kept it simple. Focused on the message. You know, two or three major points. I made sure everyone in the room walked out knowing, and remembering, exactly what I said."

"Could you look over what I got so far?"

"Sure, Michael."

I don't sleep well that night. I keep remembering the tips Judd gave me, waking up, jotting down notes, erasing others. I finally doze off just before morning roll call. When I wake up, I see the mess I made, scribbles all over my papers.

The prison's on edge all day. Everyone's hair is cut and trimmed, uniforms are clean and crisp, the guards wear either their dark blue or bright yellow blazers. I head to the education department and sit in front of a typewriter, my chubby index fingers smashing down one letter at a time. The clock's never moved so fast.

At six o'clock the dignitaries arrive. Warden Wagner brought in a five-piece prison band to play during the reception. Even though it looks and smell tasty, I don't touch my food. When I look out at the crowd of senators, congressmen, and judges, possibly a few I've stood in front of, it's overwhelming. I lower my head.

How the fuck can I speak here? What can I say that will make any difference to them?

Then I remember the hundreds of times I robbed people. How I controlled the situation just by saying, "Everybody, get the fuck down!" And they did. The words from my drama teacher come back to me too, "You can really act, Michael."

That's what I'll do. I'll play the part of a gangster who's about to be released from prison.

Warden Wagner gives his speech and goes on about the wonderful things he's done and how we're all model prisoners in his model prison. There's lots of applause.

Doc Boriscano's next. I don't know what got into him, but everything coming out of him is sour grapes, like he's not responsible for the shit his life's become. There's some polite claps for him.

I look over at Judd and he gives me a thumbs up. I walk to the podium, my page of notes shaking in my hand.

You can do this, Mike.

There's a spotlight in my eyes so I can only see a few people at the tables close to me. I take a deep breath.

"My name is Michael Hardy and I'm here to talk about reform. I'm doing time for some bad things I've done. I'm scheduled to get out of Danbury next month. December twentieth to be exact."

A few chuckles ripple through the room.

"That's something we do in prison. We get good at counting. The minutes, the hours, days, weeks, and months. You look forward to the simple things. A letter from someone who cares. A visit from a family member or a friend. But then you start to look inward, inside the prison walls—to the library. Maybe take an acting class, or Bible study, paddleball with some Italians, even giving your two cents at the inmate congress."

I don't remember much of anything else I say, except for how I end my speech. "Listen, people wind up in here because of what they've done. They created their own situations, but there's a social reason why. It doesn't take much of a brain to figure it out. I remember reading a quote once. 'You can either feed a man a fish each day, or you can teach him to fish for a lifetime.' That's all I gotta say. Thank you."

The applause is unlike anything I've ever experienced, my chest swelling with pride. I spot Judd with his thumbs up and a huge grin.

Warden Wagner comes up to the microphone, shakes my hand, turns for a few pictures with me, and thanks everyone for coming. Then all these dignitaries come up to me and give their congratulations. I spot Doc and there's no one around him.

When I returned to my cell, a group of guys comes up to me. They already heard, but they want to know more. I'm in the middle of giving a play-by-play when a guard approaches.

"Hey, break it up here," he barks.

The group shuffles off, but not so far that they can't hear the guard say, "Hardy, I'm putting you on report for having an unsanctioned meeting."

"Hey, these guys just wanted to talk about the big dinner. You can't put me on report. I'm getting out a month from now."

"Yeah. We'll see about that."

The warden doesn't take the guard's report to heart and my get-out-of-prison date is still solid. My last week in Danbury is filled with hope—hope I can build a new life outside of these walls, hope for a good job, and new life without crime. I know a lot of things will be different. No Morty to bail me out, no Aunt Florence to come to my rescue. They died from broken hearts caused by my mother's and my arrests.

After the last Tuesday night in drama class, my instructor asks me to stay. He tells me I should think about a career in the theater.

Really?

"You've got something to say, Hardy. I've never met an actor like you before. Definitely not in here, and not many on Broadway. I'm giving you the names of a few people I want you to look up in the city and in Hollywood, should you land there." He hands me a slip of paper.

My eyes blur and my voice cracks. I lower my head. "Thanks."

The day before my release, Judd and I walk the yard wrapped in our dark blue wool peacoats. We're not saying much until the cold finally gets to us. We stomp our feet when we enter his cell and unbundle. He says he has something special for me. I expect him to reach into his locker and pull out a gift, something he smuggled in.

Instead, he takes me by the shoulders and stares directly into my eyes. "You're leaving tomorrow, Michael. Stay the road. It's set for you. Understand?"

I bob my head.

I got no idea how to do that.

"If you ever need me, call. I'll send my Lear jet for you. If you need money, or anything, call me. Stay the road!"

"I will, Judd." I nod. I mean it.

"No one else in here knows, but I'm set for a two-week furlough over the holidays. I'll be leaving here in three days. Going down to Florida to be with my family."

"That's great, Judd. I know how much that means to you."

"You seeing your family over the holidays?"

"I don't know, man. There's hardly any of them left."

He bobs his head. "Let's stay in touch, okay?"

We come as close as two men can in prison to giving a hug, grasping each other's arms, not wanting to let go.

After leaving Judd's cell, I bump into Mikey Coco Cifelli, a goombah and Genovese associate from the Italian Harlem in the Bronx. You don't bump into Mikey, he finds you.

"Hey, Michael," he says, reaching up to pat me on the shoulder.

"Mikey, how you doin'?"

"Good. Hey, I know you're getting out tomorrow. I got a couple of guys on the outside. They already lined up some work for you."

I chew on his words. He knows I did fourteen hits for the Mob four years earlier. I'm curious. "Really? Whatcha got in mind, Mikey?"

"Some heavy lifting. Taking out some trash. Pay's real good. Better than whatcha got before." He grins like there's only one answer I can give him.

Judd's words "Stay the road" ring in my ears.

I shake Mikey's hand and look him square in the eyes. "I'm good, Mikey, really. Thanks anyway, but I'm good."

I sign the receipt and take my clothes out of the plastic bag where I put them thirteen months ago. Something about their odor reminds me of a different person. A different life. They don't even fit me anymore, hanging on me loose like they belong on the body of another man—a gangster and a killer. Not me.

I've got a bus voucher to take me back to the city, to a halfway house where I'm supposed to live for the next six months, and a parole officer I'm supposed to report to.

Halfway. That's how I feel.

It's one o'clock Friday afternoon, December 20, 1974, when a guard checks my paperwork for one final time and swings open the last gate. I step outside, in front of Danbury Federal Penitentiary, and take a deep breath. I look back at the concrete and wire, and flip up the collar of my peacoat, the cold wind already trying to find a way to get at me.

Riding in the back of the Greyhound bus, I reach into the grocery bag that holds my personal items—a comb, wallet, a pinkie ring with a tiger eye stone, keys to a car that's no longer mine, a dirty shirt a couple sizes too big. I'm starting over.

I pull out my Bible and open it to where I left the red satin ribbon marker. Revelations 3:20, the verse Judd gave me. "Behold, *I stand at the door, and knock:* if any man hears my voice, and open the door, I will come in to him, and will sup with him, and he with me."

Where's my door?

39

Halfway

After a few bus transfers, I end up at the St. George Hotel at 6:30 in the evening. It's nothing more than a thirty-story, eight-dollar-a-day flop house in Brooklyn Heights. Everyone gets processed through St. George before they're sent to one of three hotels where a floor or two are set aside for parolees. I look up at the stained concrete and old brick knowing what waits for me.

Processed is how I feel when I walk into the lobby. Derelicts lounge on tore-up sofas and chairs. It reeks of stale cigarettes and dirt. An old clerk with a bad eye nods at me to come over to registration. He knows why I'm here and pulls out a sheet of paper. I spot my name, reading upside down a specialty of mine.

"Hardy. Michael Hardy," I say, pointing to the line.

He scratches off my name with a pencil, grabs a key from a wall of small cubbies behind him, and hands it to me, bored from saying these words hundreds of times. "Anything missing in the morning, we'll bill your parole officer."

Room 812. Nothing special about the number or the room, but I've seen worse. I drop my grocery bag with the remnants of my prison time onto the bed, go to the window, and open it. A blast of cold Brooklyn slaps me in the face. Car horns blare below in the street, traffic not moving an inch. It's five days to Christmas and I don't feel a thing, except alone. Uncle Morty and Aunt Florence died while I was away, my kids are with their mother who's seeing a married Puerto Rican cop, and my mother's doing time in California.

I go out, grab some Chinese from around the corner, and bring it back to my room. I watch Caine in *Kung Fu* on a small black and white, then fall asleep to the *Six Million Dollar Man*. I wake in the middle of the night to static from the TV and hold my breath while I try to get my bearings. When I remember I'm in a hotel and not in prison, it doesn't help get me back to sleep, so staring at the dirty popcorn ceiling is how I spend the next hours until I get up and take a shower.

The check-out clerk hands me a bus pass with a slip of paper informing me of my six-month halfway house location.

"Where the hell's the Bryant?" I ask.

"On the Eastside," he says without looking up, back to flipping dirty magazine pages.

It's late morning when I arrive. The Bryant Hotel is a big step up from the St. George, no bums in the lobby. They've got a Japanese restaurant inside the hotel with an attached bar. When I check-in, I'm handed a weekend pass and room key 262 by another expressionless clerk.

"Curfew's at eight. And we check, sometimes call your room."

"Got it."

First thing I do is call Theresa Gonzalez and tell her I'm coming over 'cause she's got lots of my clothes, I hope. I don't have much money, saving it for food, so I hitch rides. When I get there, she's got my clothes in a duffle bag.

She grins. "Michael, wow." She checks me out, up and down.

I don't get it. "What?"

"You—you musta lost fifty pounds."

"Oh, that. Eighty's more like it. Grapefruit diet and some martial arts." I strike a few poses and slash my hands in the air, doing a sideways leg kick.

She laughs, then offers me a drink. We talk some about what's been going on since I went away. I tried to fuck the lesbo out of her once, but that didn't work. As horny as I am, she's not what I want.

I head back to the Bryant, change my clothes, and call Heddy Halpert. "Heddy, it's Michael."

"Michael? Is it really you?"

"Yeah. I got a weekend pass."

"Where are you? I'll be right over."

I wait in the lobby of the Bryant in my maroon silk Italian suit that's two sizes too big for me, when half an hour later, she honks by the entrance. She looks better than I remember, and I remember everything. Dark brown hair, dark eyes, slim waist, looks like Natalie Wood, who looks like my wife, Sheila.

After pulling her body into mine for a long kiss, she breaks away. "God, you look great, Michael. So fit, so strong." She strokes my arms. I like it. "Let go to Max's to celebrate, okay?"

"Sure."

I drive our way through traffic to Park Avenue South. Billy Swan's singing I Can Help on the radio and everything's feeling right. I pull over a half block before the nightclub. We sit in the car and do some catching up. Every time she asks to get out to go to the nightclub, I make up an excuse. I don't want to go in there. Nothing but loud music and loudmouths who'll probably say something about Heddy I don't like, and I don't want to be tempted to shut them up. I'm on parole.

"I've been naughty lately, Michael," she says with a grin, tilting her head to the side and flipping her hair back, like she's trying to get me all hot.

It's working. "Like what?"

"You know." She arches her eyebrows, slides over to me, gives me a deep kiss, and rubs my crotch.

She wants me bad, and I'm more than ready after being locked up so long.

"I want to make love to you, Michael," she breaths in my ear.

"So do I. Let's get in the back."

"No, not in the car." She gasps as I slip my hand under her skirt.

"We can't in my hotel, and I got no money for a room."

"That's okay, I'll pay."

As I drive us over to the National American Hotel in Long Island, near the Kennedy Airport, she snuggles into me, kissing my neck and rubbing my chest.

Room 329 sees more action in one night than ever before. I fuck Heddy in ways I never thought possible, getting only two hours' sleep.

She shakes me awake just as the sun comes up.

"You wanna go again?" I tease, grabbing a handful of her ass.

"I can't. I'm too sore." A sadness crosses her face, her lower lip pouting like she used to do. "Is that all you want from me?"

I take my hands off her and hold them up, like someone's got a gun on me. "Hey, I been locked up for two and a half years. I gotta let off some steam."

She doesn't say a word on the way back to the Bryant. She drops me off and pulls away. I know her well enough to know I'll be seeing her again.

I guess you wanted some romance. Sorry, it ain't in me right now.

I meet with Edward-something on Monday, December 23. He's my parole officer in Brooklyn He looks just like Dustin Hoffman. *Papillion* came out the year before and he should have been nominated for an Oscar—at least his character escaped from prison but died after. Edward adds two more butts to his overflowing ashtray while we talk. Files are stacked all over his desk. He drones on like a Chatty Cathy Doll who only knows a few phrases.

He talks about all the things I can't do, not much about what I can. No guns. No association with known felons. Curfew at the Bryant. No leaving the city, state, the country, the planet.

"So, then *unknown* felons are okay?" I ask, just to see if he's listening or got a sense of humor. He is, and he doesn't.

I'm to report to him weekly. He hands me a little pamphlet with the smiling face of an old Black man on the front. It's got information about where to go for social services I might need, like I'm some charity case. He gives me an index card with the dates and times of our scheduled get-togethers for the next six months.

He leans forward, all intense. "My recidivism rate is the lowest in this office, and I intend to keep it that way."

All I can do is nod since I don't know what *recidivism* means, maybe how often he jacks off?

"If you're going to miss an appointment, and there'd better be a good reason, call me before you're late, Hardy. My number's on the literature, meeting card, and my business card."

Two days later, on Christmas morning, I wake up to someone in the room next to me getting laid. The girl's screaming and the man's yelling, "Yes. Yes. Yes," over and over. I cover my ears with my pillow, but it doesn't help much. After they stop, and maybe because I'm so fucking lonely, I make a few calls.

Judd's doing fine with his family in Florida but a little distracted. His grandkids squeal in the background.

"Sounds like you're busy," I say.

"Yeah, but it's so good to hear from you, Michael. How you doing on your road?"

"Fine, Judd. Five days so far. Strange is all, with no one around anymore."

"Psalms, twenty-seven ten. 'Though my father and mother forsake me, the Lord will receive me.' Remember that, Michael. You reading your Bible?"

I look over at the brown shopping bag on the nightstand. I haven't touched my Bible since I got out five days ago. "You always know the right things to say, don't you, Judd?"

"It's all there waiting for you in the good book."

There's that awkward pause before someone on the phone says either "well" or "so." I plop on the bed and let out a sigh. "Well, I'll talk to you later."

"New Years' Eve. Call me if you're not too busy celebrating in the Big Apple."

"Sure, Judd."

I stare at the phone after I hang up, the sound of his grandkids' laughter still echoing in my ears. I pick up the phone to call a good friend who never disappoints.

"Mrs. Dee, Merry Christmas. It's Michael, Michael Hardy."

"Oh, you don't have to say that. I'd know your voice anywhere, Michael."

Her voice sounds like warm bread. The mother I never had.

"How's your Christmas been?" I ask.

"Wonderful, now that you called. Where are you?"

"Staying at the Bryant Hotel for the next six months." I pick at the frayed edge of the yellowed lampshade next to my bed, wondering what to say next.

"Is it nice?"

"It's okay."

We're not talking about what we should—her daughter, Dorothy, and my son, Mark.

"I'd like to see you, Michael. You're one of my favorite people."

Her words stick in my throat, but all I manage to get out is, "That'd be nice."

"Penn Station, this Friday at six o'clock, after I get off work? How's that?"

"Under the big clock?"

"Perfect. See you then, Michael. Oh, and Merry Christmas to you and your family."

Me and my family—what a joke.

I hang up, go to the window, and look out, leaning on the sill. Frost creeps in from the edges. I let out a full breath, fogging up glass, the colored holiday lights all blurry, maybe from my eyes.

40

Jimmy's Deal

It's July 1991. I'm in LA County Jail with Jimmy for our weekly meeting. He's looking good in tailored Armani and I feel like an overstuffed sausage in a blue jumpsuit at 280 pounds.

"Twenty years? Twenty fucking years, Jimmy? What kinda deal is that?" I can't sit down, gripping the back of my chair, my knuckles white, wanting to throw it against a wall.

Jimmy waves his hand to calm me like he's trying to slow traffic in a construction zone. "It's what they put on the table. Marcia Clark's one hell of a bulldog. Marsh Goldstein's more reasonable if that's any consolation."

I snarl. "I don't give a shit about her. Besides, you said you could handle her. Can you?"

"They still believe they've got a strong enough case, mostly based on your past." He clears his throat, a little smile tugging at the corner of his mouth.

"What?"

"I told them how you got MacLaren Hall closed down for abuse and saved all those foster kids. They didn't like that."

I take a seat and relax a little. "I got lots more good stuff, if you want it."

Jimmy sits up, his black Montblanc pen hovering over his yellow pad. "Really? Like what?"

I stare at chewed fingernails and dig deep. "Well, I kept that American kid, Bob what's-his name, from getting killed in Mexico when I was in prison, but the DA doesn't know anything about me being locked up there. Then there was Raleigh Studios in '78 where I took six bullets trying to protect my family. I didn't kill Sammy the Bull or Ally, and I shoulda." I look up at Jimmy.

He's not writing anything down, his mouth open. He shakes his head. "Every one of your examples is tied to some kind of violence, something the DA is trying to prove. You're not helping."

"Well, I'll think of some." I read the huge number he wrote on his pad—twenty. I'll be sixty-six by the time I get out. "What do I have to do to get that number down to five? I can live with five."

"*Live* with five. That's an interesting way of putting it, Michael."

I lay on my cot and listen to the night sounds of LA County Jail. I'd know Roscoe's cough anywhere, down a level and to the right. Rumor is, he's got TB. Jerry, I forget his last name, six cells away, always hums *You are My Sunshine* to himself just before he falls asleep.

I can't get the number twenty out of my head.

That's almost half my life. My life.

When I was fifteen, I rumbled with my gang in Brooklyn, shooting anyone who came at me. At nineteen, I got shot by the Gotti brothers twice in the same day. At twenty-four, I worked for a gay drug lord in a Mexican prison where I killed three men. At twenty-six, I did fourteen hits for the mob. At thirty, I got out of Danbury prison, weighed 180 pounds, felt like I could make it, reading the Bible, working to stay on the path. Now at forty-six, my mother is dead from diabetes, and my son turned me in for murder. I got $150 grand to get my movie made, not the way I wanted with Patrick Swayze and Halle Berry, but they won't release the film because I got arrested for murdering my wife.

In twenty years, my kids will all be grown, I'll probably be a grandfather many times over, and I won't even know what they look like.

I won't sleep good tonight.

41

Death & Shakedowns

It's Friday, December 27, 1974, at six o'clock. Right as the minute hand hits the twelve, Mrs. Dee arrives. She's the same as always—warm, gives me a long hug. I know there's the announcements blaring about trains coming and going from Penn Station, and people rushing by, but I hear none of it.

She wears a long dark wool coat, a matching hat, and a big smile. She pulls away and takes me in, looking at me without judgment. She never does. "Michael, the last time I saw you in this kind of shape was when you got out of the Army. When was that, anyway?"

I tilt my head and squint my eyes, doing the math in my head. "May, nineteen sixty-two. Almost twelve years ago."

She sighs. "That's when you met my Dorothy." She reaches out and pats my shoulder.

"Yeah." I change the subject because there's a lump in my throat. "Wanna get a cup of coffee?"

"Sure, Michael." As we walk up the stairs, she takes my arm and nuzzles into me.

"I ran the warehouse in Danbury with a couple of guys who did karate, you know, that kung fu shi—, uh, I mean fighting stuff. Then I went on a one-hundred-day grapefruit diet. Lost eighty pounds."

"Feels like it." She squeezes my bicep and gives off a little laugh.

We step outside into the chilly city air and spot a diner half a block away. We sit and I order us two coffees and slices of apple pie like we used to.

I know she's waiting for me to ask, so I do. "How's Mark and Dorothy?"

"They're doing fine. She still lives with me, but I think she's got a beau who's very interested in her." She searches my eyes for something.

I got nothing to give her but misery.

Not knowing what to say, I dump lots of cream and sugar in my cup and watch it blend together in a tan swirl.

"You know, Michael, she loved you a lot. It's taken her twelve years to get over you."

I look up at her. My cheeks burn in a combination of shame and hard memory. I bow my head.

She whispers, "I don't think it's best for you to see her or Mark, Michael." She reaches over and takes my hand, slipping some paper into it.

My eyes sting because the words hurt, but I feel their truth. I stare at a twenty-dollar bill in my hand. "Mrs. Dee, you don't have—"

"Yes, I do," she cuts me off. "Maybe this time you'll…" her voice falls away, like to say the words out loud will forfeit their hope. She takes a bite of her pie. "This will be our little thing, every Friday at six o'clock, here at Penn Station."

Just like that, we're back to being good friends—me, the son she never had—her, the loving mother I never knew, and the grandmother of my baby no one in my family knows about.

That night, as I lay on my bed in the Bryant and stare at the cracking yellow ceiling, I pick up my Bible for the first time since I got there. Like I did in prison, I flip through the pages and jab my finger to see what I might find, maybe see what fate has in store for me. This time it's Proverbs

14:29. "A patient man has great understanding, but a quick-tempered man displays folly. *"*

I'm not the first kind of man. I gotta change that.

The next four days are the same drill. Curfew at eight. I see my parole officer Monday. It's hard for me not to call Stevie, Duke, Kevin, Sammy the Bull, or any of the other guys I used to roll with to get some action going, but Judd's *stay the road* sticks with me.

New Years' Eve rolls around. At ten o'clock, I call Mrs. Dee to wish her a happy one. She's as warm as ever, her words like a caring mother.

Next is Judd. A woman answers. "Hey. Is the big guy around?"

"Who is this?" a trembling female voice asks.

"Michael, Michael Hardy."

She sniffles. "Michael, he told me about you. This is his wife, Helen. He, he—Judd's gone," she gasps out the final words.

Gone?

"What happened?" I slump onto my bed.

"I woke up this morning and reached over to him. Cold, Michael. He was cold. Have you ever touched a dead person?" She breaks into deep sobs.

Yes.

I mumble something to try to console her, but I don't think she's listening. I hear her in the distance like she dropped the phone, followed by a low wail. I hang up.

I bend over and hold my gut, like someone hit me with a baseball bat, all the wind knocked out of me. I rock back and forth, fighting to understand what happened. My friend. My mentor. My guide to a new faith and a new life. I feel like I'm in a boat in the middle of the raging ocean, without a sail or rudder.

He's gone.

Things don't get any better after that. The two US Marshals, Douglas and Austin who run the Bryant Hotel's halfway house program leave a note under my door. I meet them at four p.m. on January second for a "get-together." Of all law enforcement branches, I like US Marshals best. I should, after spending nearly two months on the road with them during cross-country treks in 1972, staying in jails along the way, bouncing between federal courthouses in San Diego and New York.

"Have a seat, Hardy," Douglas says, trying to act all nice, his dark brown moustache dancing on his broad face when he speaks. They look like Wyatt Earp wannabes. We sit in their Bryant hotel suite at a round table. I spot an unmade bed in the next room and can't help but wonder what kind of action they got going.

Austin's got my file open, tapping the thick stack of papers with the pink eraser on his pencil. "Your record's not very promising, Hardy. One of the worst we've seen, and I'm sure it doesn't come close to what you never got busted for."

I size them up, not that I plan to take 'em down or anything, just to see what they're made of. "That's the shit I used to do. I'm rehabilitated now."

First Douglas, then Austin, throw their heads back and howl. They can't see, but my fists are clenched under the table.

Motherfuckers.

Douglas claps his hands. "That's a good one, Hardy." He waves his arms around like he's about to sing some opera. "Everyone at the Bryant's been rehabilitated."

Austin leans in, all intense. A vein on his forehead throbs. "This is how it's gonna go down, Hardy. You're gonna give us five bucks a night not to stay here."

"What the fuck?" I almost laugh but realize they're not joking by the greedy eyes.

"You heard us," Douglas barks.

You shaking me down?

"My parole officer will wanna know about this."

Douglas shows all his teeth when he grins, like a hungry shark. "No, he won't. He gets a piece of this, so no use crying to him."

"Hey, man, I don't cry to no one."

"We'll give you tonight off, free rent, but tomorrow it starts. Got it?" Austin's scrawny sideburns look like dog shit's been smeared on his face.

"Where am I supposed to get five bucks?" I ask.

"That's your problem," they say in unison.

You do this to everyone here, don't you?

Almost like he knows what I'm thinking, Douglas adds, "If you don't work with us, we can make your time here miserable, maybe even write you up. You'll be back in the slammer before you can say 'five bucks.'"

I don't give them their five bucks the next day, so they turn off the heat. On January 12, I watch Super Bowl IX by myself in my room, teeth chattering, spooning lukewarm minestrone in my mouth. It looks almost as cold on the field at Tulane Stadium as it is in room 262. Pittsburgh steps all over Minnesota, beating them by ten points. I don't really follow sports since the Brooklyn Dodgers moved to LA in 1958, but it's something to do.

By late January, it's worse, a cold snap hitting the northeast. I sneak out after midnight as often as I can and go over to Heddy's when her father's out of town. At least it's warm there, I get a good kosher meal, play time with Heddy, and some conversation, but no real comfort. Nothing seems to be able to fill the hole when Judd left.

I head back to the Bryant, wrap myself in some blankets, and throw myself a pity party. If I was a drinker, I'd have polished off a bottle, so there's nothing to dull my pain. I count up who's gone from my life—Daddy Roy, Grandma Edith, Uncle Morty, Aunt Florence. If I want to go back further, there's my great grandfather from Ukraine, Abraham

Blaustein, and all the others. Then there's Judd. Depression hits me like an avalanche, my only solution is to end it all.

Before I go too far down that road, I force myself to think of something good, like the first smile coming out of my baby Robert's toothless mouth when I was nineteen and in Bordentown Reformatory in New Jersey doing graves detail. Then there's Uncle Morty and how we kept selling that crazy monkey over and over and going to the World Series. My eyes tear up and I give a weak smile.

My family may be gone, Judd too, but I feel parts of them that want to live in me. I just don't know how to bring out their goodness.

I gotta get something else going, so I reach out to George Ahrens, a Fed I worked with a few years before to help Giuliani nab a dirty cop before I screwed things up and Giuliani sent me away. I tell George that I got more bad cops for him to bring down. He bites. We set up a weekly meeting at his place. They'll have me wear wires, get dirty cops to say stupid shit, and a few Mob guys they think I might deliver. At seventy-eight bucks a week, the price is right. I won't spend a nickel of that on the US Marshal's five-dollar-a-night shakedown. Combined with the twenty bucks I get every Friday from Mrs. Dee, I'm living. Not great, but okay.

It's late April, only two months more to go at the Bryant—at least the weather's warmed up.

I'm forty-five minutes late to a meeting with Ahrens and he's pissed. "It's ten blocks from the Bryant to this office. What's with you, Hardy?"

He's got two new Feds in the office with him, papers scattered around a table. Some big plans for me. I motion

Ahrens over to the corner of the room and whisper, "I don't stay at the Bryant but one, maybe two nights a week."

"Hardy, that'll violate your parole. What the hell are you thinking?"

Should I tell you? What the fuck.

"I won't cough up the five bucks a night the marshals want from me."

"For what?"

"They shake down everyone at the Bryant. We're supposed to pay them five bucks a night *not* to stay there."

Ahrens glances at the other two Feds, then back to me, his eyebrows all scrunched in disbelief. "You're not bullshitting me, are you, Hardy?"

"You know me better than that, George."

He places a kind hand on my shoulder, like an older brother might, one who cares. I like that. He's six-foot-one, so we're eye-to-eye. "Maybe we'll have you work on that first."

It takes a month of the same routine until I get some good tape on Douglas and Austin, but I gotta pay them five bucks a night to make it happen, and that doesn't feel right, even though Ahrens gives me the money. I sit in the US Marshals' office with Ahrens waiting to tell my story to someone higher up, flipping through magazines on their veneer walnut coffee table. Everything about the place is cheap.

Someone walks in and stops right in front of me, blocking my light. I look up at a fat Black woman. She's got her hands on her hips and looks like she could be a professional wrestler.

She wags a finger in my face, her chubby underarm jiggling like a waterbed. "It's a damn shame you got a good man like Alan Douglas in trouble, Hardy. I'm gonna remember your name."

Ahrens doesn't like her comments. He calls Giuliani, who calls Federal Judge Joe Jaffe, who calls the US Marshal of the Southern District to tell him that a woman in his office disclosed witness information and messed things up.

The Bryant Hotel scam gets shut down. That's all I cared about anyway, and saving five bucks a day.

A week later, Ahrens picks up a wiretap communication about me with US Marshal John Farrell. Tasty but not enough. Farrell's working hard to get me to break parole and send me back to prison. Ahrens sets up a meeting with Farrell and me at Aldo's Bar. It's supposed to clear the air and put everything back to normal.

We sit in one of the dark booths in the back, no patrons around. At three-thirty, it's just the musty stench of cigarettes, bourbon, and old men. Ahrens is on my right, Farrell to my left. He looks like a fat old man in a cheap suit, combs his gray hair over his balding head, just like Giuliani and me. They order bourbon. I get a Coke.

I snack on a bowl of salty peanuts. It's all normal chit-chat until I turn to Farrell. "Hey, I heard you might be retiring soon."

He juts his chin out at me. "Yeah. So, what's it to you, Hardy?"

"I don't know, Man. Maybe one day you're gonna turn around and I'll be there."

He goes red in the face. "Ahrens, did you hear what Hardy just said? He threatened me."

"I didn't hear anything. I was stirring my drink."

Farrell slides out of the booth and tries to come off all menacing with his fat hands on the edge of the table, his face almost purple now. "Goddammit, I put in my thirty years, good years. Someone like you's not gonna jeopardize my pension because of my loyalty. Fuck you!"

Farrell storms out the door and I crack a big smile.

"Why do you hate cops, Mike?" Ahrens asks.

"Not you, George. You're cool. But most of my life, I saw dirty cops, politicians, and judges take payoffs from the mob."

Ahrens turns gray. "What?"

"For fifteen years, my mother, Shirley, took care of them. She was the go-between for payoffs from the mob. Meyer Lansky set it all up. Cars would double-park in front of her place, they'd run inside, take an envelope, and leave. You know, cops got the worst shoeshines?"

Ahrens takes a quick peek under the table at his shoes. "Your mother? She's still locked up out in California, right?"

I nod, sit up, and stick out my chest, a strange sense of pride coming over me—*my mother*.

"No wonder…," Ahrens words trail off as he shakes his head and studies me.

Yeah, no wonder.

42

Brooklyn to Hollywood

It's Friday, May 23, 1975, at six o'clock, the night before my thirty-first birthday. So different this year with everyone gone. There'll be no cards or phone calls from relatives who care or feel obligated. I do get a cup of coffee, a slice of pie, and some good conversation with Mrs. Dee at our favorite diner outside Penn Station. We don't talk about her daughter and my son. Besides the usual twenty she gives me every Friday, she hands me a gift, wrapped real pretty in a silver bow. A bottle of Brut Cologne. Classy, just like her.

You remembered.

"You didn't have to, Mrs. Dee." I blush, feeling unworthy. With her I always blush.

"It's nothing, Michael. You know, I'd do anything for my grandson's daddy." She pats my hand and means every word. The only woman I've ever been able to trust.

I slough around the Bryant Hotel lobby Saturday night. Not exactly a party place, the second and third floors filled with felons. I got my hands in my pockets, shifting from foot to foot, feeling the need to do some celebrating on my birthday, anything, but I can't. There's two new marshals running things tight at the Bryant now with curfews, sign-ins and sign-outs, destinations listed with names and phone numbers. Douglas and Austin are long gone. I hear they cut a deal. They'll get no pension, but no prison time. Too bad. I got some friends inside who'd love to *talk* to them.

I grab a stool at the lobby bar. A lone black and white TV, mounted high on the wall above rows of cheap booze bottles, blares the six o'clock news. The few bar flies either got their faces buried in a drink, or their heads tilted back like Pez dispensers watching. The TV anchor with the serious eyes tells how NBC canceled the Smother Brothers Show, and New Jersey started a lotto called Pick It.

I wonder how the Mob's going to like that, another piece of their business going to the government.

Thirty-one years ago, I was born to two first cousins. I glance at the other convicts. They're like me, halfway. I sip on a Coke and add up what I got going. No money, no job, no car, no guns, no crew, living on seventy-eight bucks a week ratting out dirty cops.

My daughter, Cheryl, will be eight years old in a week, and my son Robert will turn ten in August. They wouldn't recognize me, not really father of the year material. Robert was three when I shot Tommy Fomero in the chest because he wouldn't let me take Robert out of his apartment. I've maybe seen Cheryl and Robert half a dozen times since their mother shacked up with that married Puerto Rican cop.

What would you think of your old man now, kids?

I'll leave the Bryant next month, but for what? My mother gets out of federal prison in California in July and will go to some halfway home as well. Knowing her, right away she'll find some man with money and turn him into her slave. She used up all her Mob connections to get a good lawyer for her trial, and I don't think they liked that she ratted me out. Good news is she won't be asking me for anything, but I'll always listen.

I leave the bar and take the stairs up one flight to my room. This isn't how my thirty-first birthday is supposed to be. I slump on the edge of my bed and look around the dump that's been my home for five months. The lone window is painted shut with thick yellow paint and my view is a dirty brick wall twenty feet away. There's some kind of faded brown wallpaper pattern on the walls, might have been fall leaves at one time. Everything smells old and worn, like me.

A horn blares outside. It gets me wondering what kind of car it is. Then all the wheels I've had over fifteen years pop into my head. The things I've done with cars, and in cars. Making out with Sheila. The drive-by shooting on July fourth after those Blacks yelled at her. Taking brand new Caddies across the country, thirty times for my mother to sell in La Costa. Okey-dokeying drug lords and cop bag men into a trunk. Their muffled voices pleading through the back seat.

God, I miss the action.

I pulled lots of those jobs with Sammy and Allie. Sammy.

I phone Sammy. I always called him Sally, short for Salvatore. Most people know him as Sammy the Bull Gravano. He's not a felon—yet, so I can talk to him. He and the other four fingers of the Mob's car theft ring didn't lift a finger to help me when I was trying to get a good lawyer or cut a deal. I did get a letter from them when I was in jail in San Diego awaiting trial. A classic. I didn't need a decoder ring to figure out they'd whack me if I turned state's evidence.

"Hey, Sally. It's Michael." The phone's quiet. "Michael Hardy."

"Big Mike?"

"Yeah, but I ain't so big right now."

"What's that mean?" He laughs.

"I lost a load of weight while I was inside. I got nothing going, Sally."

"So, why you calling this goombah?"

He's careful with his words, not like before. Maybe he knows I wore a wire to deliver dirty cop Angelo Bencivenga to Giuliani. "I could use a couple bucks, Sally. Help me get on my feet." Begging sucks, but I've got to try.

My request hangs in the air until Sammy clears his throat. "You know, Mike, ever since we shut down the car business, things have slowed down—a lot."

"I can dig it, man." I wait. It's his turn now. He owes me and he knows it. He worked in my crew when we pulled twenty-three jobs together, taking down a couple million dollars.

"Hey, maybe we can grab coffee sometime."

"Sure, Sally."

He hangs up and I stare at the receiver. I know what *grab coffee sometime* means.

Motherfucker.

"I said, Sammy the Bull Gravano, Allie Boy Cuomo, Louis Milito, and Mimi Scialo took out the Dunn brothers in nineteen sixty-nine. But it was Sammy who pulled the trigger."

There's no statute of limitations on murder.

George Ahrens, the Fed I worked with to get rid of the dirty Marshals and dirtier cop, Angelo, leans forward in his office chair and pushes aside some files on his desk to get a better look at me. He lights another Winston and cocks his head trying to get a read, knowing I got some angle working. I do, but he'll never know.

"So, Hardy, how do you know he did it?"

"He told me."

"What?"

"After we pulled a big job, uh, I mean, we did some work over in Bensonhurst, we grabbed some Italian. He had a few glasses of wine. We were comparing dick sizes and he just had to one-up me."

He grabs a pen. "What kind of details did he give you?"

"You know, the usual. 'I whacked 'em both, Michael, and they never saw it coming.' He pointed his finger like he was pulling a trigger. You don't ask a made man how he does his business."

"I'll need the date you met with Sammy, and the restaurant. You'll sign a statement. Oh, and I'll want to put this in front of Giuliani."

Giuliani again? Nice.

"You know I can deliver."

"Yes, I do, Hardy."

"Okay then. What can I get outta this, George, besides protection?"

"That's something Giuliani will address."

"I'm thinking something more than seventy-eight bucks a week from you guys."

"Oh, yeah. I'm sure we can work something out."

Just like that, I'm back in business, but it could be dangerous business.

Two weeks later in George Ahren's office, I attest to Sammy telling me he whacked Arthur and Joseph Dunn who owned a Coney Island car shop. And that Louis, Mimi, and Ally Boy were a part of it. Mimi's dead now, so he doesn't matter, but putting Sammy, Ally, and Louis in hot water is all I care about.

Ahrens tells me I'm going into some kind of witness protection. He stubs out his Winston into a full ashtray, blowing his last lungful of smoke toward the ceiling. He hands me an open plane ticket to LA.

"We need to make up a new ID for you, Hardy. Any ideas?"

I've used over ten aliases in my life, but I get to pick this one with the Fed's blessing. I think of all the gangsters I admire. Bugsy, Dillinger, Capone, Joey Gallo. I go farther back and remember one from the wild west, John Wesley Hardin. He once shot a man for snoring too loud.

"Hardin. Let's use Michael Hardin."

"Hardin it is."

He calls someone in the building, gives them my new name, and tells them, "Yeah, he's here right." He turns back to me. "It'll be ready in half an hour. Want to wait in the reception area?"

"Nah, I'm good here."

George busies himself with paperwork while I flip through a worn *Saturday Evening Post*, Gerald Ford's picture on the cover with some kind of horoscope crap. I'm trying to keep from bouncing in my chair, I'm so amped. Twenty-five minutes later, I sign my New York State drivers' license, and stare at it, wishing somehow I'm a distant relative of famous gunfighter John Wesley Hardin. I'd like that. I grin.

"We'll fly you back for the preliminary trial, maybe even for some depositions," Ahrens says.

"Gotcha." I stuff my new license into a pocket of my black leather car coat.

His squints at me with intensity. "This is some serious shit, Hardy. We're counting on you."

"I'll be okay, George. Now, what about my parole officer here?"

"We've taken care of that."

"And what'll I do for expenses in LA?"

"You'll check in with our office out there. They'll take care of that, too. Here's your contact information."

He hands me a single sheet of paper. I glance it over. Some dos and don'ts, a name, address, and phone number. I look up at George, his face all crinkled with concern.

You like me.

"George, I'll be fine. I know how to take care of myself."

"Yeah, but you don't do too good at flying under the radar."

We share a knowing smile when we stand, then he walks me to the door. He gives me a firm handshake and a pat on the shoulder. "You take care, Michael. Any problems, give me a call."

"Will do, George." I step across the hallway to the elevator and punch the down button. He waits by his office door, like he's leaving his kid on the first day of kindergarten. The elevator opens and I step inside. I give him a little wave and grin as the doors close.

Hollywood, here I come.

As my American Airlines 747 lifts off from JFK, I let out a deep breath. I can't help but smile when I think of all the shit that's going down for Sammy and his "friends" at the moment, and if he guesses I fingered him. He'll know soon enough when the DA goes through discovery with his lawyer. I wish I was there to see his face and him wondering why we didn't *grab coffee sometime.* It'll be more fun after the DA figures out Sammy didn't whack the Dunn brothers, but that'll take a while, maybe a couple of years, and meanwhile I get a free trip to Hollywood and don't have to report to my parole officer.

This flight to LA is different than every time before. I came out when I was nineteen to meet my father, Joe Hardy, for the first time. That was my first time on a plane. I was so nervous, clutching the arm rests for six hours. That trip was really about me killing time and staying out of trouble while my Mob lawyer waited for the "right" judge to dismiss my assault and battery case against an ice cream truck driver.

I learned my father was nothing more than a street hustler, pretending he was a merchant marine who'd fallen on hard times, selling a dollar-fifty fake watches to tourists for thirty-five bucks.

My next trip to LA was in early 1968 following my escape from prison. Actually, I escaped from the state mental hospital where I was getting tested after going crazy in court. I drummed my fingers the whole trip, expecting US Marshals to be waiting for me when I landed. Instead, one of my mother's slaves picked me up. A month later, I was in a Mexican prison for counterfeiting. My mother's crime, with twelve years ahead of me.

I flew to LA another dozen times in 1970 when Duke, Stevie, and I were doing our airline ticket scam, cashing in round-trip, first-class tickets to Hawaii for $2,400 each after we landed in LA. My mother drove up from San Diego a few times to get a taste, one time with a baby she bought in TJ to work some angle to get welfare money.

Always something.

This time it's the best. Summer in LA in 1975. Got to love it. I get a couple cans of Coke to go along with the beef stroganoff the cute stewardess serves, and I get to spread out across three empty seats to nap. I got headphones on and listening to *Cat's in the Cradle*. I think about my father and wonder if I'm doing the same shit with my kids. I let the thought go because it wants to give me guilt which is too much right now.

There'll be no cops waiting for me when we land. No need to scam, or shove a gun in someone's face, or pass bad money, or use fake babies for welfare checks. No, this time it's just me. Actually, it's Michael Hardin, and all of Hollywood is out there waiting for me. Maybe I'll look up a few people I know. Maybe take some acting classes. Who knows?

Right now, though, *Benji* is on the in-flight movie, and I think I'll watch that for a while.

43

WITSEC & Movies

I jerk awake when the 747 bounces off the LAX runway on
Saturday, June 7, 1975, at one in the afternoon. I had fun
chatting up Sherry, the tall sexy stewardess, for half the trip.
I tell her I'm headed to Hollywood and plan to get into the
movie business. She says I look a lot like Robert Redford. I
still got my Fu Manchu and long blond hair, and only gained
twenty pounds since I left Danbury, so I can dig it. I get her
number, but don't think I'll call. As good as she looks, and
probably tastes, I got more pressing issues coming at me
besides getting laid.

I grab my two duffel bags off the carousel and lug
them outside the terminal—entire life in these bags. Smog.
Besides stinging my eyes, I forgot it had a smell, kind of
like moth balls in your dead grandma's closet. I spot the
Fed in his sunglasses, slacks, and Hawaiian shirt. I'm sure
it's covering a standard-issue .38 and cuffs. He leans against
an unmarked gray Dodge Monaco. Everything about him
tells me he doesn't want to be here babysitting some ex-con
witness from New York, and on a Saturday.

"Hardin?" he asks.

"Yeah."

"I'm Special Agent Robinson."

"Okay."

There's no handshake or chit chat on our half-hour drive
to the Relax Inn Motel on La Brea. He handles my check-in

and puts it on some kind of Fed account, then follows me to my room. I toss my bags on the bed and it sags, the dull floral bedspread already wrinkled.

Won't be sleeping good tonight.

He closes the door and starts in. "This is how things are going to work, Hardin."

I'm polite and nod, but don't really listen after he says, "We've got your file, so we know what…"

Eventually, he hands me an envelope. "Your per diem for two days."

What the fuck's per diem?

I open the envelope and find five ten-dollar bills. My time in LA in '68 comes back at me, like a sour burp, when we got caught passing my mother's fake tens in Mexico, and all the shit that followed. I take one out and snap it, holding it up to the light, making sure it's not one of hers still floating around.

"You expect me to live on twenty-five bucks a day?"

"There's a McDonald's two blocks north and a Burger King three blocks south. You want more, you figure it out." He hands me his card and mumbles that he'll see me at Denny's Monday morning at nine for breakfast. Then he's gone.

I empty my bags, hang some clothes, and stuff everything else in a cheap four-drawer pine dresser. At the bottom of the last bag, I pull out my Lamsa Bible. The promise I made to Judd before leaving Danbury six months before comes at me. "Stay the road," he told me. But Judd's dead and this Bible feels like a dead weight, not light or salvation. Still, the red satin ribbon asks me to open it up. I do.

I read aloud the first verse my finger touches, just like Judd and I did in Bible study in Danbury. "Psalm 141:4— Let not my heart be drawn to what is evil, to take part in wicked deeds with men who are evildoers; let me not eat of their delicacies."

I slap the book closed and drop it into the nightstand drawer, shutting it with a finality. I don't realize it at the time, but I'll never read a passage from that Bible again.

I need a woman and a gun.

The next day and a half, I wander around the neighborhood checking things out, find the fast-food restaurants, the bars, watch some TV, and stare at the pink rotary phone in my room, wanting to call someone. My sisters, Nancy and Cindy, are somewhere in the LA area, but if I go down that road, that means my mother gets involved—and her reach, even from prison, is long and hard. I heard my father is now in San Diego running more of his short cons. I got nothing in common with him, but if I had to get in touch, well...I don't know.

Nick Avenetti could be my ticket into Hollywood. I met him when I was out here in '63 visiting my father, but he's probably still tight with the Mob, and that's a place I can't go now after ratting out Sammy. I met a character actor at a Denny's on Sunset Boulevard during a trip out in early '68. His name was...I scrunch my eyes, working to grab the memory. Michael, Michael Pataki.

The weekend's over for me at eleven o'clock Sunday night. The TV weathermen are boring, talking about the LA forecast for ten seconds, then spending the rest of their time telling everyone how fucked up the rest of the country is. I should be doing something big, getting into some action, not lying on a sagging bed in a cheap motel.

I feel like a weed stuck in a sidewalk crack, with barely enough dirt, water, or sunlight to keep me alive. At any moment someone could step on me and end it all.

I meet Agent Robinson the next morning at the Denny's four blocks away. He's in full uniform, a Fed-issued gray suit and thin black tie. I order a full breakfast—eggs, bacon, pancakes, hash browns, smothering it all in Tabasco. He gets coffee. After we get through the how'd-you-get-settled-in crap, he slides an envelope over to me.

"There's a week's worth in there," he says, grinning at me, like I just hit the lotto.

I can do a lot with a hundred seventy-five bucks.

"Hardin, it looks like we won't know anything more about your case for several weeks, or longer, so this'll be your situation for a while."

Sammy must have lawyered up, and he's stalling for the right judge.

I take in Agent Robinson again. Nice enough guy. Gold wedding band. Six-feet tall. Crew cut. I'm guessing early forties. I give a grin. "Got any kids?" I ask, trying to get a little personal with him, hoping he'll slip me some extra cash.

He tilts his head, a smirk wanting to come out.

You've been played before.

That's his signal to leave. Robinson stands and grabs the check. "See you next Monday, Hardin. Stay clean. And don't be surprised if I call or drop by every now and then to see what you're up to."

It takes a day to get in touch with Michael Pataki. We meet at the same Denny's near me, the one that'll become my office for the next month. I forgot he was so small, his face pock-marked from teen acne, his dark hair curly.

You're an actor?

He's all smiles and goes on and on about how busy he is. I don't like people who are only into themselves, but I'm patient. I got nothing else to do.

That's good for you, motherfucker, but what about me?

I interrupt his drone. "So, Pataki, what's some of the movies and TV shows you've been in? You know, stuff I mighta heard of?"

"How much time you got?" He laughs big, enough to make all the people in the restaurant look at him, just what he wants.

"Well?" I clench my jaw and lean forward. His eyes go to the eagle tattoo on my left forearm, the one I got after leaving the Army when I was seventeen. I flex, and the wings flap ever so slightly.

He smirks. "That movie I asked you to get into, remember, the last time you were here?"

I nod, realizing how much I fucked up then. No excuses because I was hiding from the cops.

"*Easy Rider* did pretty good, didn't it, Michael?"

I stare at him with a you-wanna-tell-me-something-I-don't-know expression.

He talks so fast, I can hardly pick out any of the seventy-four movies and TV shows he's been in—but *The Flying Nun, Star Trek,* and *Kung Fu* jump out at me.

"Kung-fucking Fu?" I ask, my mouth open. "You worked with Caine?"

"Well, yeah. I worked with David Carradine."

"God, he kicks butt."

He stifles a smile. "Michael, it's TV. He's an actor playing a part. They choreograph everything."

"But what about all the martial arts shit?"

"It's dancing mostly, in slow motion, and using fancy camerawork."

"What the fuck?" I slide out of the booth and strike a few poses, kicking out my legs, slashing my arms through the air, just a few of the moves I learned from the guys in the Danbury warehouse.

Pataki's mouth drops open a little.

You're impressed.

I put my hands on the edge of the table and lean into him. "That can't be right. There's guys flying through windows, falling off roofs, and bleeding all over the place."

"It's Hollywood, Michael. Stunt men, make up, and special effects."

I shake my head in disbelief, plop down in the booth, and stare at my plate, my bubble burst about Caine and *Kung Fu*. "No shit."

"Yeah, no shit. There's a lot to learn about Hollywood." He leans back in the booth, his curly hair jiggling as he bobs his head and smiles.

I shovel cold pancakes in my mouth and wash them down with some orange juice. "Hey, I did some acting inside and know two kinds of martial arts. Think I could maybe get some work, you know, even as a stunt man?"

Pataki cocks his head and squints his eyes. He looks at me different than he did seven years before, not like I'm the same outlaw he met in '68 with cops after me. He doesn't know I killed eighteen men since then. "Yeah. Let me look into it and see if I can find you something."

I heard that line before.

I'm surprised I get a call from Pataki the next day. "Why don't you come with me to the set tomorrow? I'm working on a TV series called *Paul Sand in Friends and Lovers*."

"What the fuck is that, some hippy shit?" I laugh.

"Yeah, yeah. But it pays good. I'll pick you up at six tomorrow morning, okay?"

"I'll be ready."

It's Friday, the 13th, and I'm waiting for some kind of bad shit to happen. Yeah, I'm superstitious. It's boring on the TV set, except they got great food. Pataki calls it craft services. When I see how long it takes to shoot a few scenes, I begin to understand why movies cost so much, and this is TV. I hang out in the trailer he shares with a couple other guest stars on the show. I can feel it.

This is something I could do.

Afterward, Pataki takes me out to dinner, nothing too fancy, some steaks at a place he likes. I get a porterhouse. He has the filet mignon.

"So, Michael, what'd you think of being on a TV soundstage today?"

"Slow. But it's cool." I slather butter on a piece of sourdough bread and sop up the juice on my plate.

He drops me off at my motel and says he'll get back in touch. It's not like he gave me Sammy's line of "let's do coffee sometime." I believe him.

I head to my room and the light's blinking on my phone. I call the front desk. It's a message from Robinson. He dropped off next week's per diem a few days early and we won't be meeting for breakfast Monday morning. I rush down to registration to pick up the envelope. I'd ask the night clerk where to go to get laid, but he might be tight with the Feds, and I don't want anyone knowing my business.

I take a shower, shave, but before I put on my maroon Italian suit, I iron out the wrinkles, something I learned to do years ago. I'm filling into it more now, probably up to 210 pounds. I only take a hundred bucks with me, not wanting to tempt myself into more trouble.

It's Friday night in LA. I step outside and close the door. The air's cool, the smog gone. The hum and rhythm of the traffic on La Brea tells me there's something waiting for me out there.

I just gotta find it.

44

Making Moves

Nothing happens Friday night except striking out with a few good-looking women at a bar. I leave the drunk tramps alone—I still got standards. Maybe it's because I'm in the wrong part of town, or my Brooklyn accent. Maybe because it's Friday the thirteenth, or my suit's too much, not enough Hollywood about me.

A call Saturday morning from Pataki changes all that. "There's a studio I know that could use someone like you. I shot a pilot there."

"You killed a pilot?"

Pataki laughs. "No. No. We filmed a TV pilot. The first show in a TV series to see if it's any good."

"Sounds cool. When you wanna go?"

"Today. We'll do lunch today."

"Do lunch?"

"Oh, yeah, that's what they say out here."

I dress up for our meeting, wear my maroon silk suit from last night, but with a black T-shirt underneath. On the drive over, Pataki yaks my ear off about all his shit again. I just nod and pretend to care, taking in the city that's my latest temporary home.

I'm impressed with the Raleigh Studios setup, and not because of the gourmet sandwiches with carved turkey and avocado. Their operation takes up an entire city block, eleven acres, as Bill Trumble, the president tells me on his tour. I want to go inside one of the big soundstages but can't because they're filming something.

We end up in his office where Vicki, his cute blonde secretary with a short skirt, pours us drinks, mine a Coke. He settles in behind his polished mahogany desk and lights a thin brown cigarette, probably French.

"Michael Pataki tells me you've got experience handling *touchy* situations."

I glance over at Pataki, and he grins, raising his hands like I pointed a gun at him.

What the fuck did you tell him, Pataki?

"You could say that."

"Like what? Can you give me some examples if you don't mind?"

My mind races across the past twelve years, starting when I was nineteen. I could tell him about the fourteen guys I whacked for the Mob, or when I worked for a gay drug lord in a Mexican prison. That's probably too much. The wires I wore for Giuliani to rat out some dirty cops might make him take notice.

I study him and sip on my Coke to give me a moment. Late fifties, colors his hair, well groomed, wears a wedding ring. Vicki probably fucks him because he promised to make her a star. I'm in no hurry. Would he like that I shot it out with the Gottis and took two bullets from them within twenty-four hours? Maybe. What if I told him I went crazy in court, was sent to Bellevue, and escaped after being transferred into a New York State mental hospital? Now, that was acting.

I got it. Bugsy.

"My godfather was Benny Siegel. You'd call him Bugsy."

He puts his drink down and sits up. Out of the corner of my eyes, I spot Pataki take a hard swallow.

I continue. "I shared a cell in West Street jail with E. Howard Hunt, you know, from Watergate. Been inside with

Johnny Dio, a capo in the Lucchese crime family, Big Paulie Vario and his brother Peter, both members of the Lucchese family, and Carmine "Mr. Gribbs" Tramunti who ran the Lucchese family."

I let the names float in the air in front of them like a tasty dessert, Trumble's mouthwatering. "I wasn't just inside with them; I broke bread with them. Those boys sure know how to make some fucking grade-A gravy."

"You—you've been in prison?"

You're impressed.

"I did some time." I rub my finger around the edge of my glass, a soft hum coming off the lip.

"Are you, or should I ask, wanted by the law right now?"

"Well...not exactly."

It's time for me to say as little as possible. The more I say, the less I get. I wait.

"I'd ask you for references, but..." He pauses and gives me an uncertain smile, knowing what my answer will probably be.

Pataki jumps in. "Hey, Bill, tell him what you told me, you know, about the finance guys you're having trouble with."

Now it's Trumble's turn to check me out. I give him my dead eyes, but a friendly grin. I'm not staring him down, but he has to look away.

He fumbles with some papers on his desk, stubs out his cigarette and looks up. "I have investors from time to time who, well, who want to get more involved in the day-to-day business of my projects. You know, to watch over their investments."

"And you don't want them involved so much."

He sighs and nods, relieved I understand.

I keep my voice emotionless. "You want 'em hurt?"

He almost jumps out of his seat, quickly shakes his head, and holds up his hands. "No. No, nothing like that."

"So, you need them persuaded to leave you alone?"

"Exactly."

Pataki adds, "I'm sure Michael knows how to do that, don't you?"

I glance at Pataki with a back-the-fuck-off look, then turn to Trumble. "Tell me when and where, and I'll be there."

Just like that, a week into witness protection, and I'm in the movie business.

Security. That's my title, and it covers lots of activities. I wear a laminated ID badge around my neck with "Michael Hardin," my picture, and the Raleigh Studios stamp on it. I wear my long black leather car coat all the time, and sunglasses, even at night. Got to be in character, as the muscle.

The coolest part is they send a white studio Lincoln Continental to pick me up, so I don't have to worry about getting rides. It's nice having a driver, my usual is Jaime. I sit in front with him. Earth Wind & Fire's "Shining Star" seems to always be playing on the radio every time he takes me to work. That's exactly how I'm beginning to feel.

Jaime tells me how he crossed the border from Mexico years ago and has a wife and two kids. I share some of my jailhouse Mexican slang with him, trying to practice what I picked up in La Mesa del Diablo. He doesn't understand much of it but laughs and rattles off a string of words that contain *gringo*.

Bill Trumble and I never talk money. He just slips a couple hundred in my palm every time I show up. I like this guy and he likes me, and the stories I tell as I shadow him around the lot. I let him know I can't make Monday mornings before eleven because I meet with the Feds. He's dying to know what that's about, and I leave it that way.

Three days later, Trumble calls me to do my first persuasion happens. As we're walking around the lot, Trumble tells me what's up, so I know how hard to persuade.

"A year ago, this guy Sal puts up half a million for us to make a movie." He takes a final drag on his cigarette, drops it, and crushes out the butt with his green alligator shoes. "He's starting to threaten me with all kinds of legal problems. Tell him it's still in development."

I got to ask. "What happened to the money?"

"You know, expenses." He's a little embarrassed, like his dick's caught in his zipper.

Probably spent most of it on Vicki. I can use that.

"What's development mean?"

"It's like we're still attaching talent, finding the right director, polishing the script, you know, and location scouting. I usually drop a big name or two, people I know he can't check out."

"You say that to him before?"

"Yeah."

"That gonna be a strong enough answer this time?"

"With you here, yes." He grins at me like we're best friends. "Tell him we're in discussions with Jack Nicholson or Coppola. I don't think I used them before."

"Coppola. Nice Italian name. I'll take care of it."

I spot them coming toward Trumble after lunch. One's got a briefcase, most likely the lawyer, the other must be Sal. Lots of gold dangles around his neck, and it looks like his toupee's melting.

I turn to Trumble. "Get lost. I got this."

He ducks into a soundstage side door, and I take up residence in front of the doorknob. At six-one and two-twenty, these guys aren't moving me.

"Gentlemen, how can I help you?" I ask with my best Brooklyn accent from behind aviator sunglasses.

"We're here to see Mr. Trumble," the lawyer puffs up his chest for Sal's benefit.

Gotta earn your fee, don't you?

"And you are…?"

He pulls out a card from his suit pocket and holds it out. I don't take it. "Lawrence, uh, Lawrence Feldman, attorney at law. This is my client, Sal Hornsby, Mr. Trumble's investor." He puts his card away.

I only look to the lawyer, but behind my sunglasses I catch Sal sweating a little. "And?" I ask.

"Well, we'd like to speak with Mr. Trumble about a private matter."

"It's not that private. He told me all about it." With my middle finger, I poke my sunglasses back to the bridge of my nose.

Sal dances a little, like he's about to pee his pants. He can't control his frustration any longer, and blurts out, "That son of a bitch has half a million dollars of my dry-cleaning money. When the fuck's he gonna make my movie?"

I shift my weight, clench my jaw, and lean forward. They both step back.

Pussies.

"Check this out, Man. Mr. Trumble's a very busy guy. He's script polishing, doing talent, scouting locations. He's got lots on his plate."

"But what about my money?" Sal whines.

"You seen what it takes to make a movie?" The lawyer's useless now. It's just me and Sal.

"But—but he said we'd be shooting by now…" his voice trails off, his eyes pleading.

"Look, just yesterday, I heard him talking to Nicholson and Coppola about your project."

"Really?" the stupid dry cleaner asks.

"Yeah, really. Mr. Trumble's got big plans for your project. Oscar-type plans." It's time for them to leave.

Sal sticks out his hand. I squeeze it hard enough to let him know I mean business. His knees buckle a little. He tries to catch the name on my badge.

I help him. "Hardin. Michael Hardin."

"That's all I wanted, Mr. Hardin. You know, to know how things are going with my movie."

I give a crisp nod. "They're going."

As they shuffle off to his Mercedes, I watch Sal lean into his lawyer and say, "Coppola. Oh, my god."

Later that afternoon I'm having drinks in Trumble's office. I tell him how it went down with the dry cleaner. He gets a big kick out of it and slips me five hundred bucks as a bonus. I don't smile too much. I got to let him think it's hard work.

I love making movies.

45

Hollywood to NYC & Back

When I'm not hanging with Trumble, I go anywhere I want on the Raleigh Studios lot, and there's lots to see. Commercials and TV shows are filming all the time, a few movies, mostly with what they call B-actors, but I don't care. There's wardrobe people, makeup artists, camera guys, people called grips, dozens of people needed on every set.

I figure out where the best craft services tables are and always got some food in my hands. I catch people staring at me. I can tell they wonder what I'm doing here, but they know I'm not the kind of guy you ask questions like that.

Trumble and I get in a groove. He even invites me along for big dinner meetings with potential investors, knowing they'll dig he's got a bodyguard. I wish I had a gun, tucked in my back belt or shoulder harness. I miss the weight of it, not just in ounces, but how that hunk of metal can change conversations. The meetings end up being nothing special, but I get a good meal out of it.

Special Agent Robinson is happy I'm keeping busy and not hustling the streets. His job is to make sure I stay out of trouble, and I don't give him any reason to worry. A buck-seventy-five a week from the Feds, three to five hundred a week for a couple days at the studio, that's keeping me clean. I'm anxious though. I feel like a shark, knowing I'm a predator and there's plenty to hunt in Hollywood—and if I don't keep moving, I'll die.

Monday morning, June 30 at our weekly breakfast meeting, Robinson tells me, "Looks like we'll fly you out next week for a deposition." He dumps some cream in his coffee and takes a sip, then looks at me all serious. "You haven't talked to anyone about your case, have you?"

I drown my hash browns with Tabasco. "Why would I do that?"

He sighs. "I need a yes or no from you, Hardin."

"No."

"Good. Now, we'll get—"

I interrupt. "I wanna drive back."

Robinson's forehead wrinkles. "What are you talking about?"

"I don't like to fly, and love driving. So, why not?"

He tilts his head; I'm sure wondering what kind of scam I'm trying to work. "I don't know about that, Hardin. I'll check."

"I can make it out in three days. It'll be cheaper than flying and I'll have some wheels when I'm back in the city. You know, so no cab fares."

"Like I said, I'll let you know."

Hertz lets me choose between an Olds Cutlass or Chrysler Cordoba with its "soft Corinthian leather." I pick the blue Cutlass with only 5,000 miles on it. I'll more than double that on my trip. I stop by the studio on my way out Monday morning, July 7, to snatch some food and get Donna in wardrobe to give me some new threads. She shows me how to hook a clothes rod across the back seat of my car and I'm all set. She's five-foot nine, thin, red hair, late twenties, just what I like. I ask her if she'd like to go out when I get back. She's down with it.

Trumble's not too happy with me being gone a couple weeks. "Michael, what's with the sudden trip? Can't it wait until September, after sweeps?"

What the fuck's sweeps?

I jut my jaw out a little and clench it, gotta keep him in his place. "I told you I got something going with the Feds."

"Oh." He raises his eyebrows, all curious, but embarrassed to ask.

There's several ways to go coast to coast in 1975, and I know them all. The I-80 to the north and I-40 to the south are the most direct routes. I'm in a rental so I don't care if the car overheats. I choose the southern direction. For two years, I drove twenty-seven new Cadillacs out for my mother to sell to rich people in La Costa who thought they were getting a deal. They were. Had she not got so sloppy, and an old lady next door not complained to the cops about cars parking near her driveway, we'd still be clearing $4,800 a car.

I'm glad I'll be in New York during the middle of July. I'll miss Mother's release from prison in California. That's a reunion I don't know if I can handle.

I'll drive fifteen hours the first day, the same the second, and cruise into Brooklyn on Wednesday afternoon with my deposition scheduled for Friday. George Ahrens has a room waiting for me at a safe house, one of his "on ice" places no one's supposed to know about, just in case Sammy and his friends get ideas about getting rid of the star witness. I like that, being a star.

The radio keeps me company on the drive. "Gold, sister, Gold" seems to play every hour. Linda Ronstadt belts out, "You're No Good," reminding me of my past, and I sing along to Elton John's "Lucy in the Sky with Diamonds," with no idea what it means. To cover gas, food, and lodging, my per diem is $300 a day, so I stay at cheap motels and eat fast food so I can pocket the rest.

I meet with Ahrens, Giuliani, and his assistant in my hotel room Thursday afternoon to go over things. Giuliani remembers me. He should. I gave him Angelo Bencivenga, one of the dirtiest cops in Manhattan, before I took off. As it turned out, Rudy got lots of points for that. His combover has thinned since I saw him two years ago after he got tired of my shit and threw me in Danbury prison. I'd tease him, but he's not one to laugh. All business. We go over my testimony for the next morning. We've worked together before. He knows what to expect.

"Don't deviate, Hardy. Keep it simple. Yes and no answers. Got it?"

"Yeah."

After he and his lackey leave, Ahrens and I do some catching up.

"What you been doing, Michael, you know, to stay out of trouble?"

"Got a gig doing security for a movie studio."

"What the hell?" He snubs out one Winston and lights another.

I hand him my card.

His eyes widen. "Producer? Meet any stars?"

"All the time." I poke at my room service steak and eggs, not really hungry. Giuliani does that to me.

"Like who?"

"Chuck Connors."

"The Rifleman?"

"Yeah. They've been shooting pickups for the TV show *Police Story*—something you probably watch."

"Yes, I do." He nods, a big grin on his face.

I'm a little nervous going in for my deposition because everything's so formal. Big conference table, a court reporter with her little machine in the corner. Stale coffee and dry sweat hang in the air. Giuliani's mouthpiece sits next to me. He's maybe thirty, tight suit, hungry to impress his boss.

Sammy's lawyer tries to bust my chops a couple times, but I won't let him. The deposition ends up being a piece of cake. After I'm done, I meet with Giuliani and Ahrens.

"I hear you did well, Hardy," Giuliani says.

"Yeah. How much more of this I gotta do before the trial?"

"That depends on if you can tell us something more about Gravano and the rest of his associates' activities." He stares at me all intense. I know what he wants.

I crack my knuckles, interlock my fingers, and stretch my arms out in front of me. I give him a smile. "Can I get immunity?"

"Yes, for anything but murder." He and Ahrens exchange a glance.

You want Sammy that bad?

"A lotta what we pulled when Sammy and Allie worked in my crew was never, uh, reported. Ya know, like holding drug lords for ransom, hitting dealers for their stash and cash. Your dicks won't have files on that."

"No, we won't," Giuliani says.

There's never any handshakes with Giuliani, like he doesn't want any of my criminal to rub off on him, and then have to spend an hour scrubbing his hands.

The next day, Ahrens hands me $1200 cash for my four-day trip back. "Trial won't happen for some time. We'll contact you when and if we need you."

I decide to make it to Vegas in two days and spend some time there. I leave Giuliani and New York City in my rearview mirror on Sunday afternoon, July 13. It didn't hit me until I was a hundred miles east, but I'd been holding my breath while I was in the city, wondering if Sammy, Ally, or Louis, or one of their associates, would try to whack me. I decide then and there, I'll have a piece on me when I come back. To hell with me carrying as a felon.

My Cutlass handles the trip just fine, but there's bugs caked all over my windshield and grill when I pull up to the Stardust Hotel under the bright lights. I got a two-day beard and I'm dying for a soft bed. That my godfather was Bugsy Siegel doesn't pull any weight here since he's been dead nearly thirty years. They got a mid-week special for $125. A room for two nights and a show. Just what I need.

After a great night's sleep, shave, shower, and room service, I wander around the casino. I don't like gambling. Never have. There's no excitement in it for me. The house always wins. It's for suckers.

I drink a Coke at one of the bars off the casino floor where up-and-coming or on-their-way-out entertainers play cover songs and act all happy. A five-piece combo tries to sing "Kung Fu Fighting," but they suck. I look around. All eyes search green felt or spinning wheels for numbers that'll make them rich, for a minute or two.

That night I dress up real nice and share a table with two ladies from LA whose husbands would rather gamble than watch the *Lido de Paris* show. I hand them my card. They dig it that I'm in the movie business. It doesn't say "security" or "bodyguard" like I'm doing. It says "producer." They're impressed, the reaction Trumble said I'd get. Ninety minutes of tall women with three-foot headdresses gets my head spinning, and my balls aching.

After the show, I find a young bellman in front of the hotel who looks like a hustler.

"Tall. Redhead, if you got one." I slip him a hundred bucks. "Room eleven twenty-three."

He smiles and nods.

An hour later, there's a knock on my door. I don't care that she wears a wig. At that moment, a redhead is everything I ever wanted.

I roll into Raleigh Studios late Thursday afternoon all relaxed and head for Trumble's office. He's not happy. Two days before, a couple guys tried to put a move on him, shake him down for some hard cash, maybe take over one of his production offices.

"Why weren't you here, Michael?" He's pacing around his office like wild animal in a cage.

"Hey, I told you I was back east doing some work for the Feds. Now, what did they want?"

"They got some shit on me, Michael."

"Vicki?" I ask, knowing his secretary crawls under his desk at least once a day.

"Yeah, and, well, some other stuff." He stops pacing and leans on his desk chair, letting out a deep sigh, but his arms shake.

I roll my eyes. "Bill, who are they?"

"Skaggs is one guy's name. I don't know the other."

"How'd they leave it?"

"Michael, I don't know." Trumble plops down in his chair and buries his head in his hands. "They said they're coming back next week."

I've never seen him this way before. Now I'm pacing the floor on the other side of his desk, ready to throw down on anyone who walks through the door. I stop. "They connected?" I wonder if the Mob's got an angle on him and want to squeeze me.

"I don't think so." His hands tremble while he lights one of his brown cigarettes. "My wife can't find out, Michael. She just can't."

"Listen, man. This is how it's gonna go down. You be all nice to them and set up an appointment that me, your producer, will attend. I'll take it from there."

I gotta get a piece.

46

A Kinda Girlfriend

I got a good thing going—getting cash from Raleigh Studios
every week, depending on how many people I keep off
Trumble's ass, $125 a week from the Feds, free rent, and a
limo driver. I knew it couldn't last. Nothing good ever does.

A name I didn't think I'd ever hear from again gives me
a call. Lester Auerbach, my mother's ugly gnome of a slave.
He only did ninety days at Terminal Island for his part in the
car theft ring, turning state's evidence to nab Ed Mann, the
California DMV employee who got two years.

"Hey, Michael. It's Lester."

How the fuck did you find me?

I let his raspy voice hang in the air.

"Michael?"

What the fuck do you want?

"Lester." It's more disappointed than hello.

"How ya doing?"

I grunt and let out, "Okay."

"Hey, uh, I gotta little problem, and could use your
help."

"What'd you fuck up this time, Lester?"

"You know, Michael, Queenie gets out in ten days."

I don't want to see her.

"And why do you think I'd be interested in what my
mother's doing?"

"Well, I've been watching over her place her in La Costa."

"Nice to know you got such a cool place to stay. So…?"

"Someone robbed her."

I straighten and clench my fists.

Motherfucker! You let someone rob my mother?

"What the fuck did they take, Lester?"

"All her Lalique crystal."

I laugh. "Oh, man, are you in some deep shit."

"I know. I know."

I wait. I can hear him shriveling up on the other end of the phone.

"Michael. Please," he snivels.

"What am I supposed to do, Lester? I want nothing to do with my mother after she—"

He interrupts. "It was a hooker."

"What was?"

"The girl who took her crystal."

"What's a hooker doing…? Never mind. So, have her give it back."

"She said she already sold it."

"Oh, you are a royal fuck-up, aren't you?"

"Come on, Michael. Can you just come down here and help me figure something out? Please?"

Yeah, right.

I borrow a black studio Lincoln and show up at Lester's two days later on Saturday morning. Lester greets me at the door. He's smaller now, bent over further, bald, gray mutton chops, and plaid green bellbottoms. He can't hide how disgusting he is.

He looks down almost like he's gonna kiss my shoes. "Thank you, Michael. Thank you."

I take in my mother's place. She'd call it "well-appointed." Tan Naugahyde couches and crushed red velvet trim, gold throw pillows everywhere. I step into her formal dining room and spot the empty buffet shelves. I shake my head. "You were sleeping, weren't you?"

Lester shuffles his feet and looks down. "Yeah."

"Get your hooker on the phone and have her come over."

"What?"

"You heard me."

Deborah Lynn rings the doorbell just before eight that night. Long blonde hair, hot, wild eyes, early twenties. She steps in the front door wearing a white miniskirt, pink tube top, and chunky platform heels. Her clothes are so tight, I can tell she's got no underwear on.

Since she expected to bang Lester, her eyes widen when she sees me. "Well now, who are you?"

"I'm Michael, and it's my birthday. Lester thought I could use a present."

She takes my hand and leads me toward the stairs. "Well, come on then."

The legs and ass in front of me know what they're doing. I look back to Lester and grin. "See you in a couple hours."

It's after ten when I finish with her, or she finishes with me, I can't tell. I see why Lester fell asleep. She does anything and everything to get me off three times. I'm resting in a chair wearing black Levis and a black T-shirt when she comes out of the bathroom tossing her blonde hair to the side, and strutting around, all put together, her clothes back on. She picks up her purse, grins, and holds out her hand.

"Two hours. I drove here. That'd usually be two hundred, but since it's your birthday, I can do one-fifty."

I give her my dead eyes. "You got that wrong."

Her forehead wrinkles. "What?"

"You owe me. Or should I say, you owe my mother."

"Who's she?"

"She owns this place. You took her Lalique crystal."

Her mouth drops open. I stand and move to her, grabbing her wrist. She flinches but doesn't pull away. I sense she likes it rough.

"You either return the crystal, or you're gonna work it off. Five thousand dollars' worth."

"I—I can't."

"You can't what?"

"Like I told Lester, I already sold it."

"So, buy it back."

A little tear runs down her face and she wipes it away with the palm of her hand, smearing her mascara.

You playing me?

That night, I drive her over to her apartment. We clear out all her clothes and toss them in her car. She pleads a little, but nothing she says is working on me. It's around one o'clock when I leave her faded yellow VW Bug with Lester, kind of like a down payment for the crystal.

"See you later, Lester." I toss him Deborah's keys.

He doesn't get what's going on, his face all scrunched up like a dried-up prune. "What'll I tell Queenie?"

"You'll think of something."

On the drive to LA, I lay it all out for Deborah, what she's going to do for me, which is basically anything I want. She seems okay with it, even sliding over and getting all affectionate. I tell her how Bugsy Siegel was my godfather and that I've got connections and add how I'm producer at a movie studio. She rubs my inner thigh and asks about the tattoo on my left forearm. I tell it's from my time as a paratrooper. It's not the whole truth, but it gets her hot.

You must be patriotic.

She puts her head in my lap and goes to work. I got a smile on my face that stretches from San Diego to Hollywood.

Deborah's lots of work. Right away she starts asking when we'll eat, she wants to go shopping, and meet the stars at Raleigh Studios. I tell her how I'm kind of in witness protection because I fingered a killer in the Mob, and that I've done hard time. That I've killed. That gets her hot again, the sex incredible.

After I bust my nuts, I'm back to reality. Now I got to feed her. She complains about the room the Feds got me with its saggy bed, she wants me to dress nicer, go to good restaurants. She doesn't say it exactly like that because she knows I'll get pissed. She plays me some, but I don't mind. I tell her I know how to get all the money we need, but as a felon, I can't carry. I need a gun moll.

Her eyes sparkle with excitement. "I can do that."

Through a prop man at the studio, I get my hands on a .45. I like them because they're big and get the reaction I need without pulling the trigger. My plan is to go after drug dealers like I did in New York. They got lots of cash and plenty of drugs I can turn into cash.

Deborah likes everything there is about my idea. "I can hook, too," she offers, her chit in the game. She looks to me for my reaction, like she wants to know if she's my girlfriend or maybe that I'm her pimp.

"We'll see."

It's not about repaying the crystal she stole from my mother anymore. It's about the action. I know she's going to love it.

I use her to find drug dealers, not the stand-on-the-corner-near-a-pay-phone kind of small-time hustlers, but their bosses. She tells them she's headed to a Hollywood party and "wants to make a big splash." They're the ones holding a couple grand and got a big stash of drugs.

Our first score is located at a nice ranch home in the San Fernando Valley. Ivy covers most of the front yard with neatly trimmed shrubs perfectly spaced across the front of a cream-colored stucco house. There's a late model black Corvette in the driveway. This is nothing like the tenements and cheap hotel rooms I robbed in New York.

"What's our play?" Deborah asks before we get out of the car.

"You mean what's *my* play?"

Her eyes drop. "Uh, yeah."

"I don't know what I'm gonna do, but I know what I'm doing. Just follow my lead."

We move to the front door. I nod to Deborah, and she rings the doorbell. It's around two in the afternoon. A long-haired hippie-type, maybe forty, with one gold loop earring, opens the door.

The barrel of my piece is tucked under my belt in the back, nudging the crack in my ass. I give him the warmest smile I got. "I'm Michael. This is Deborah. Antonio sent us."

His eyes are all over Deborah.

Must not had a piece in a while, right, pirate?

"I'm Ray. Come in. Come on," he waves us in, a greedy smile taking over his face.

We plop down on a brown corduroy sofa in his living room that overlooks a pool. The water's green and there's leaves floating in it. The windows are open, and a neighbor's dog whines. It doesn't look it, but it smells like there's money in the walls.

"Nice place you got here, Ray," I say.

Ray sits in an easy chair, a wagon wheel coffee table between us. "Yeah. Me and my old lady, we got lucky."

He's talking to me but checking out Deborah the whole time. She's wearing tight white short shorts with another tube top, her smooth legs crossed, one bouncing back and forth a little.

You sure know what you're doing.

He shakes his head clear. "So, what you need?"

"What you got?" Deborah asks in her sexiest voice.

He's melting under the heat of such a hot piece of ass. "Let me show you." He reaches behind his chair and grabs a small case, almost like a tackle box, then takes a seat next to Deborah on the sofa—she's in between us. She places a hand on his thigh, pretending to steady herself. He sucks in a short breath.

He goes into his spiel about the kinds of weed and coke he's got, how much each costs. The kind of high we'd expect. "You say you're going to a Hollywood party?"

Deborah nods.

"Well, this coke'll blow their socks off and everything else, but it's a little pricey."

"How much?" Deborah asks, all breathy.

"Five hundred a gram."

He notices Deborah's raised eyebrows.

"But I could cut you a better deal depending on how much you want, or…"

"Or?" Deborah asks.

"You know, maybe we can work out something—in trade." He rests a tentative hand on her knee.

Now it's my turn to turn up the heat. "Hey, you hitting on my girl?" I lean toward him and stick out my jaw.

He takes his hand away and leans back, his hands up. "No, uh, I didn't mean nothing by it." His voice is weak, and I smell fear on him—like stale bread.

I lean across Deborah and poke Ray in the chest. "Let's just stick to a cash deal. Now, what can we get for three grand?"

"Three grand?" He's all smiles again. "For that, I'll give you seven grams."

"Kinda like buy six, get one free?"

He lets out a nervous laugh and stands. "You got it. I'll be right back."

He disappears into a wing of the house where the bedrooms probably are. I turn to Deborah. "Find him, check out the score, and get friendly if you want."

She gives me a questioning look, then bounds off the sofa and down that hall. I take out my piece, slip it behind a cushion and wait. Deborah's giggles echo down the hall. I can't make out what she's saying, but I know she's working it. After ten minutes, they walk back into the living room. She's got a hold of his arm and he's swinging some bags of coke from his free hand. A small nod and wide eyes from her, tells me there's more.

"Can we sample the goods?" I ask.

"Sure, sure," Ray says and opens a baggie. He pours some out on the glass-top of the coffee table, removes his divers' license and taps out three lines. He pulls a $100 from a wad and rolls one up. I catch Deborah's eyes sparkle.

"Your home. You go first, Ray," I say.

He grins, lowers his head, puts the Benjamin to his nose, and snorts up the line. When he raises his head, my piece is in his face. The high in his eyes is confused by the muzzle of my gun.

He mumbles, "What the fuck?"

Five minutes later, I've got him duct-taped to a dining room chair, a dirty sock from the laundry stuffed in his mouth, his pants around his ankles. He's not happy, squirming around like a fish on a hook. After we go through his place, I grab his car keys. We stuff thirty-six grams of coke, a kilo of weed, and just under seven grand in cash in a pillowcase. I have a little chat with him, the barrel of my piece stuck in his left ear, the one with the earring.

"You're gonna forget all about us, like we were never here." I take my gun out of his ear and lean down to whisper. "From one pirate to another, consider this the cost of doing business on the high seas, Ray."

He grunts something I don't understand.

At the front door, I turn back. "You're welcome."

We laugh on the way out to his Corvette, the southern California sun hitting me in the face, the breeze full of freedom. I'm right back where I belong, and all Hollywood is my playground.

47

Jimmy's Questions

It's late July 1991 in LA County Jail. "Jesus, Michael. You're telling me you went back to robbing drug dealers?" Jimmy switches off the tape recorder and shakes his head. The little black wheels stop spinning just like our conversation. He's not amused.

"I know, I know." I shrug. "I needed quick cash. And part of me was trying to keep Deborah from tricking. You know, going straight."

He shakes his head. "You think that's going straight, her being an accomplice to armed robbery?"

"Hey, he was just a fucking drug dealer."

We stare at each other a few seconds, then he gathers up his stuff.

"You leaving, Jimmy?"

"Yeah. Got to prepare for another case...," his voice trails off.

He's disappointed. I can tell. "I was never charged with any of those scores. And I did hundreds."

He stands and puts his yellow pads, recorder, and Montblanc pen in his leather attaché case, not looking at me. He makes eye contact with the guard on the other side of the window and gives him a nod.

I stand. "When we gonna talk again?"

The door opens and Jimmy heads for it but stops before leaving to look over his shoulder. "In a couple days. I expect to have a deal from the prosecution for you by then." His head bobs like he wants to say something or maybe he's rethinking why he's representing me.

There's something about being alone in a cell at night in LA County's millionaires' row with lights out. The strange noises. It gets spooky. Someone mumbles with a bad dream, someone takes a leak, heavy breath from an asthmatic two doors down.

Me? I'm thinking about the look Jimmy gave me, like I was stupid or something worse. That's not like him.

Being locked up so long, I begin to question everything.

Did I really have to rob all those drug dealers?

Did I have to kill my wife?

Did I hire the right lawyer?

Am I going to the electric chair?

PHOTOS

1973 Danbury Federal Penitentiary, Connecticut
After a grapefruit diet that got Hardy down to 180 lbs.
Courtesy Ira and Nancy Kutner

*1974 Danbury Federal Penitentiary, Connecticut.
Before walking the yard in the winter with Judd Tanner.
Courtesy Ira and Nancy Kutner*

For More News About David Larson,
Signup For Our Newsletter:

http://wbp.bz/newsletter

Word-of-mouth is critical to an author's long-term success. If you appreciated this book please leave a review on the Amazon sales page:

http://wbp.bz/jewishgangster2a